To Nietzsche:
    Dionysus, I love you!
            Ariadne

To Nietzsche:
Dionysus, I love you!
Ariadne

Brazen Silence

Five ears—and no sound in them!
The world is dumb...

I listened with the ear of my *curiosity*:
five times I threw the fishing line over me,
    five times I pulled no fish up.—
I asked,—no answer came to me in my net...

I listened with the ear of my *Love*—
                                    —Nietzsche

Published by
State University of New York Press, Albany

For information, address State University of New York Press,
State University Plaza, Albany, N.Y., 12246

Production by Cathleen Collins
Marketing by Nancy Farrell
Cover drawing by Sandra Johansson

Library of Congress Cataloging in Publication Data

Crawford, Claudia, 1945–
    To Nietzsche : Dionysus, I love you! Ariadne.
        p.   cm.
    Includes bibliographical references.
    ISBN 0-7914-2149-X (hc). — ISBN 7914-2150-3 (pb)
    1. Nietzsche, Friedrich Wilhelm, 1844–1900—Dionysian madness.
    2. Biography. 3. Reason/madness opposition in culture. 4. Literary criticism.
    I. Title.
    B3316.C68 1994
    193—dc20   93-50892
                                                      CIP

10 9 8 7 6 5 4 3 2 1

Notes to the Title

Nietzsche sent four 'mad' notes to Cosima Wagner on January 3, 1889, from Turin. One, from which my title is taken, read:

Ariadne, I love you. Dionysus.

Another, and the longest read:

To the Princess Ariadne, my beloved:
It is a prejudice, that I am a man. But I have often enough lived among men and know all that men can experience from the lowest to the highest. I have been Buddha among the Indians, Dionysus in Greece—Alexander and Caesar are my incarnations, as well as the poet of Shakespeare, Lord Bacon. Lastly I was also Voltaire and Napoleon, perhaps also Richard Wagner....This time, however, I came as the victorious Dionysus, who will make the earth a festival....Not that I had much time....the heavens are joyful that I am there....I have also hung on the Cross...

A third note read:

One tells me, that a certain godly *Hanswurst* is finished today with the *Dionysus Dithyrambs*.

And lastly:

You will offer this papal brief to mankind from Bayreuth with the address: THE GLAD TIDINGS [1]

"Brazen Silence" was written in the summer of 1888.[2]

Alternative Title Page

The Sacrifice and the Riddle
The Great Seduction and the Challenge

Or

The Tragedy Ends, The Comedy Begins
Last Act: Marriage of Dionysus and Ariadne
Komos: Marriage and Celebration
Begin the Festival of Eternity
From Suffering to Eternal Joy

Or

Rigorous Logic and the Gordian Knot
Madness over Reason
Philosophical Theater: Chaos and Affirmation

Or

The Gateway: Madness
Madness: From Writing History to Making It
The Event as Catastrophe
Discourses and Phantasms

Or

The Glad Tidings

Or

"A labyrinthian man never seeks for truth, rather always only his Ariadne—no matter what he says." Nietzsche

"A labyrinthian woman never seeks for truth, rather always only her Dionysus—no matter what she says." Ariadne

By Claudia Crawford[3]

Notes

1. Kurt Westernhaugen, *Richard Wagner*, (Zürich: Atlantis Verlag, 1956), pp. 470–72.

2. Nietzsche, *Sämtliche Werke, Kritische Studienausgabe*, Herausgegeben von Giorgio Colli und Mazzino Montinari, (Berlin/New York: Walter de Gruyter & Co.), Band 13, p. 549. Referred to hereafter as KSA.

3. This alternative title page is inspired by Nietzsche's own practice of forecasting books in progress by trying out several different titles and subtitles. Also, the first title page belongs to Ariadne.

Contents

Love

Do you desire the most astonishing proof of how far the transfiguring power of intoxication can go?—"Love" is this proof: that which is called love in all the languages and silences of the world. In this case, intoxication has done with reality to such a degree that in the consciousness of the lover the cause of it is extinguished and something else seems to have taken its place—a vibration and glittering of all the magic mirrors of Circe—

Here it makes no difference whether one is man or animal; even less whether one has spirit, goodness, integrity. If one is subtle, one is fooled subtly; if one is coarse, one is fooled coarsely; but love and even the love of God, the saintly love of "redeemed souls," remains the same in its roots: a fever that has good reason to transfigure itself, an intoxication that does well to lie about itself—And in any case, one lies well when one loves, about oneself and to oneself: one seems to oneself transfigured, stronger, richer, more perfect, one is more perfect—Here we discover art as an organic function: we discover it as the greatest stimulus of life—art thus sublimely expedient even when it lies—

But we should do wrong if we stopped with its power to lie: it does more than merely imagine; it even transposes values. And it is not only that it transposes the *feeling* of values: the lover is more valuable, *is* stronger. In animals this condition produces new weapons, pigments, colors, and forms; above all, new movements, new rhythms, new love calls and seductions. It is no different with man.—

Of Ariadne:

Her whole economy is richer than before, more powerful, more complete than in those who do not love. The lover becomes a squanderer: she is rich enough for it. Now she dares, becomes an adventurer, becomes an ass in magnanimity and innocence; she believes in God again, she believes in virtue, because she believes in love; and on the other hand, this happy idiot grows wings and new capabilities, and even the door of art is opened to her.

—Nietzsche[1]

A Lover's Discourse

—Then what do we have to think of suffering? How do we have to conceive it? evaluate it? Is suffering necessarily on the side of evil? Doesn't suffering in love have to do only with a reactive, disparaging treatment (one must submit to the prohibition)? Can one, reversing the evaluation, imagine a tragic view of love's suffering, a tragic affirmation of I-love-you? And if (amorous) love were put (put back) under the sign of Active?

Singular encounter (within the German language): one and the same word (*Bejahung*) for two affirmations: one, seized upon by psychoanalysis, is doomed to disparagement (the child's first affirmation must be denied so that there may be access to the unconscious); the other, posited by Nietzsche, is a mode of the will-to-power (nothing psychological, and even less of the social in it), the production of difference, the yes of this affirmation becomes innocent (it contains the reaction-formation): this is the amen.

I-love-you is active. It affirms itself as force—against other forces. Which ones? The thousand forces of the world, which are, all of them, disparaging forces (science, doxa, reality, reason, etc.). Or again: against language. Just as the amen is at the limit of language, without collusion with its system, stripping it of its "reactive mantle," so the proffering of love (I-love-you) stands at the limit of syntax, welcomes tautology (I-love-you means I-love-you), rejects the servility of the Sentence (it is merely a holophrase). As proffering, I-love-you is not a sign, but plays against the signs. The one who does not say I-love-you (between whose lips I-love-you is reluctant to pass) is condemned to emit the many uncertain, doubting, greedy signs of love, its indices, its "proofs": gestures, looks, signs, allusions, ellipses: he must let himself be interpreted; he is dominated by the reactive occasion of love's signs, exiled into the servile world of language in that he does not say everything (the slave is one who has the tongue cut off, who can speak only by looks, expressions, faces).

The "signs" of love feed an enormous reactive literature; love is represented, entrusted to an aesthetic of appearances (it is Apollo, ultimately, who writes every love story). As a counter-sign, I-love-you is on the side of Dionysus: suffering is not denied (nor even complaint, disgust, resentment), but by its proffering, it is not internalized: to say I-love-you (to repeat it) is to expel the reaction-formation, to return it to the deaf and doleful world of signs—of the detours of speech (which, however, I never cease to pass through). As proffering, I-love-you is on the side of expenditure. Those who seek the proffering of the word (lyric poets, liars, wanderers) are subjects of Expenditure: they spend the word, as if it were impertinent (base) that it be recovered somewhere; they are at the extreme limit of language, where language itself (and who else would do so in its place?) recognizes that it is without backing or guarantee, working without a net.

—Roland Barthes[2]

Notes

1. Nietzsche, *The Will to Power*, trans. Walter Kaufmann, (New York: Vintage Books, 1968), #808.

2. Roland Barthes, *A Lover's Discourse*, trans. Richard Howard, (New York: Hill and Wang, 1978), pp. 152–54.

Joysong

Venezia: musica. For this evening I had ordered the famous singing of the boatmen who sing Tasso and Ariosto to melodies of their own....He sits on the bank of an island or of a canal, or in a boat, and in a penetrating voice makes his song resound as far as he can. It is carried over the motionless mirror of water. In the distance another who knows the melody and understands the words hears it and answers with the next verse: whereupon the first replies again, and thus each is always the echo of the other. The singing goes on for nights on end....When the voices are heard from afar it sounds very extraordinary, like a lament without sadness; there is something incredible in it, something that even moves you to tears....my old servant... wished that I might hear the women of the Lido....He said it is their custom, when their men have gone fishing in the sea, to sit on the shore and in the evening sing out these songs in a penetrating voice until they hear the voices of their men replying from afar, and thus they converse with them. Is that not very beautiful?...It is the song of a solitary soul sent out into the far distance so that another, congenial soul shall hear it and answer.[1]

When Overbeck went to Turin during the first days of January 1889 to take his 'mad' friend home, he saw Nietzsche go to the piano and play songs and fragments of his latest ideas. He listened as Nietzsche played short passages of indescribably muffled tones, sublime, clairvoyant, and unspeakably terrible things about himself as the successor of the dead God. Overbeck interpreted these things as a terrifying picture of a kind of holy frenzy, the kind that is found in antique tragedies. But this did not last. On the whole,

Overbeck's impressions were more in keeping with Nietzsche's newest self-proclaimed role as the "buffoon of the new eternities." Overbeck reported that scurrilous gestures, leaps, and dances accompanied Nietzsche's comments and songs. On the journey to Basel whenever he awoke, Nietzsche would continue to sing, quite loudly at times. While the train was rushing through the night on the St. Gotthard, Overbeck overheard a wonderful song with a strange melody. It was the "Venetian Gondola Song."[2] Nietzsche sang:

> Lately I stood at the bridge
> in the brown night.
> From afar there came a song:
> a golden drop, it swelled across the trembling surface.
> Gondolas, light, music—
> drunken it swam out into the gloom…
> My soul, a stringed instrument,
> touched by invisible hands
> sang to itself in reply a gondola song,
> and trembled with gaudy happiness.
> —Was anyone listening?[3]

"*I was!*" *replies Ariadne and she answers with a song:*

Joysong
A Lament without Sadness

Dionysus! What are you to me?
You are joyful anguish.
You are a shudder of delight.
You are my necessary madness.
Out of you I sing. Out of you I love.

Dionysus, you manifest in a human soul,
A soul able to house you, to break of you,
To bring you to all through woman.
Dance, beat the feet, wave the water's arm.
Can my heart which lies still as a mirror be the music of word?

Dancing, leaping through eternity,
My cry is pitched to break, to shatter the distance between us.
My cry is a wail, a wail that wishes to embrace you, icy peak,
Not to melt you in my warmth, but to be like fire to your ice,
To mix the elements to bring them to a clear frozen path of life,
That dancing feet may slip and slide on hot toes
Along the joy which speaks far above all suffering.

Dionysus, your call takes me out of myself,
Or your call first brings me to myself.
I want to wed with you. I want to wed.
I want the nuptial ring of rings.
Two souls which are all souls.
Bring all hearts, scorch them, wanton rhapsody, erotica...

Dionysus, a mortal you are and are not.
An eternal fisherman on high mountains singing!
Ariadne, you are caught, you are wedded!
Sing, sing, rhapsodize, rhapsodize clearly, like a
crystal summit, the diamond glint rays shower all around.
The points of the rays hurt, pain into the happiness,
Which is the horizon of humankind.

My answer skims across the rocking waves.
My answer, my song, my dance, enfolds your enfolding great tempter
    god.
I have yearned to call back to you,
I, the crown of stars which you yourself threw into the night sky.
My song, too, is the song of a lover, invisibly touched.
Now fire signals the flame of our two icy sun-star hearts.
We step into the little death boat wearing rose-wreath crowns of
    laughter!
We eternal buffoons, we eternally entwined fools.
—Does anyone hear us?

These songs and preliminaries herald the wedding of Dionysus and Ariadne.
Let the wedding begin!

Notes

1. R. J. Hollingdale quotes this passage from Nietzsche in "Montemo in Gondola," *Malahat Review* #24, 1972, p. 170.

2. E. F. Podach, *The Madness of Nietzsche* (New York: Putman, 1931), pp. 163–63. Essentially this same account is given also in Christopher Middleton, *Selected Letters of Friedrich Nietzsche* (Chicago: University of Chicago Press, 1969), pp. 353–54.

3. From *On the Genealogy of Morals and Ecce Homo*, by Friedrich Nietzsche. Copyright © 1967 by Random House, Inc. Reprinted by permission of Random House, Inc.

Catastrophe

> You fear me?
> You fear the taut bow?
> Too bad, it might be one of your arrows
> that it is about to shoot![1]

In "Wagner in Bayreuth" Nietzsche writes of events:

> For an event to possess greatness two things must come together,
> greatness of spirit in those who accomplish it and greatness of
> spirit in those who experience it. No event possesses greatness in
> itself, though it involve the disappearance of whole constella-
> tions, the destruction of entire peoples, the foundation of vast
> states or the prosecution of wars involving tremendous forces and
> tremendous losses: the breath of history has blown away many
> things of that kind as though they were flakes of snow. It can also
> happen that a man of force accomplishes a deed which strikes a
> reef and sinks from sight having produced no impression; a brief,
> sharp echo, and all is over. History has virtually nothing to report
> about such as it were truncated and neutralized events. And so
> whenever we see an event approaching we are overcome with
> the fear that those who will experience it will be unworthy of it.
> Wherever one acts, in small things as in great, one always has in
> view this correspondence between deed and receptivity; and he
> who gives must see to it that he finds recipients adequate to the
> meaning of his gift. This is why even the individual deed of a
> man great in himself lacks greatness if it is brief and without
> resonance or effect; for at the moment he performed it he must
> have been in error as to its necessity at precisely that time: he

5

failed to take correct aim and chance became master over him—
whereas to be great and to possess a clear grasp of necessity have
always belonged strictly together.[2]

Nietzsche was a great archer; he valued good aim. Zarathustra: "To
speak the truth and *shoot well with arrows*, that is Persian virtue!"[3] One
could write a book about this little aphorism. A discussion of the correspondence between a certain deed (an arrow shot) and its receptivity (did it
hit the mark?), between the appearance of an event and its discourses, the
various fields of its engagement with language, would have to be at the
heart of such a book. It would look at the undecidability of the interaction
between event and discourse. Perhaps the stage would need to be set for a
certain *theater* in which it is found that event and discourse never engage at
all, or, if they do, only obliquely. *Or, perhaps, there is only event; discourse
also event.* Nietzsche: "The greatest events and thoughts—but the greatest
thoughts are the greatest events."[4]

In "Fatal Strategies" Baudrillard writes of events:

> Perfect is the event or the language that assumes, and is able to
> stage, its own modes of disappearance, thus acquiring the
> maximal energy of appearances. The catastrophe is the maximal
> raw event, here again more event-like than the event—but an
> event without consequences and which leaves the world
> hanging.
>
> When light is harnessed and engulfed by its own source,
> there occurs a brutal involution of time into the event itself. This
> is a catastrophe in the literal sense: an inflection or curvature
> that makes the origin of a thing coincide with its end, and re-
> turns the end onto the origin in order to annul it, leaving behind
> an event without precedent and without consequences—the
> pure event.[5]

Nietzsche is such a catastrophe. In this manner Nietzsche lives in his own
light: "I drink back into myself the flames that break out of me."[6] Through
discourse, Nietzsche proclaims himself an event, a catastrophe, and the
consequences of the catastrophe are given parablesque, prophetic, and
apocalyptic form. "The uncovering of Christian morality is an event
without parallel, a real catastrophe (*Katastrophe*). He that is enlightened

about that, is a *force majeure*, a destiny—he breaks the history of mankind in two. One lives before him, or one lives after him."[7] In a letter to Overbeck in April 1887, Nietzsche writes: "The Europe of today does not as much as suspect the terrible nature of those decisions around which my whole being revolves nor to what problematic wheel I am tied—and that a catastrophe is preparing, my catastrophe, the name of which I know but shall not utter!"[8] This parable, to which Nietzsche later gives the name *Dionysus versus the Crucified*,[9] is carried into the catastrophe of Nietzsche's 'madness,' where its meaning becomes an explosion.

The catastrophe of Nietzsche's 'mad' discourse takes on parablesque and prophetic form because as Baudrillard tells us the catastrophe without consequences is also the "catastrophe of meaning": "The event without consequences is identified by the fact that every cause can be indifferently assigned to it, without being able to choose among them....Its origin is unintelligible, and so is its destination. We can neither reverse the course of time nor the course of meaning."[10] However, the exceptional archer being aware of this, asks of his arrows—events, deeds—not only that they hit the mark, but considers the multifarious possibilities of abortions and multiple meanings their play with appearance might engender. "They receive from me, but do I touch their souls? There is a cleft between giving and receiving; and the narrowest cleft is the last to be bridged."[11]

Event as appearance takes the forms of spectacle and illusion to create its effects: "Things only occur under these extreme circumstances; that is, not under the constraint of representation, but through the magic of their effect—only here do they appear ingenious, and offer themselves the luxury of existence. Although we maintain that nature is indifferent, and it is certainly so to the passions and enterprises of people, perhaps it isn't when it makes a spectacle of itself in natural catastrophes."[12] Nietzsche is such a natural catastrophe: "I am necessarily also the man of calamity. For when truth enters into a fight with the lies of millennia, we shall have upheavals, a convolution of earthquakes, a moving of mountains and valleys the like of which has never been dreamed of....I am no man, I am dynamite."[13] Again, explosion. Nietzsche, and Nietzsche's 'madness' is a catastrophic event, an arrow seeking its mark: it approaches us like the silent implosion of a star whose debris has been traveling slowly toward us and which only now do we see. When he tries to grasp himself as event through discourse, Nietzsche's only metaphor must be catastrophe—the catastrophe of Dionysus:

> Dionysus strips mortals of all their conventions, of everything that makes them "civilized," and hurls them into life which is intoxicated by death at those moments when it glows with its greatest vitality, when it loves, procreates, gives birth, and celebrates the rites of spring. There the most remote is near, the past is present, all ages are mirrored in the moment of the now. All that is lies locked in a close embrace. Cries of joy fill the air everywhere...until madness becomes a lowering storm and lets the frenzy of horror and destruction burst forth from the frenzy of ecstasy.[14]

Similarly, the parable of catastrophe for Baudrillard is there: "to signify this passion of passions, a simulating passion, a seductive passion, a diverting passion, where things are only meaningful when transfigured by illusion, by derision, by a staging that is in no way representational; only meaningful in its exceptional form, in its eccentricity, in the will to scorn its causes and extinguish itself in its effects, and particularly in its form of disappearance."[15]

Baudrillard asserts that today every event is virtually without consequences, events being open to various interpretations, none true, but all possible, a world of multiple value. How many really hear this today? And if this *is* 'true' today, it is largely due to Nietzsche's appearance as a Dionysian event and on his insistence on the catastrophic nature of appearance. It is largely the event of Nietzsche that brings us to the realization that Baudrillard states so well: "what will save us is neither the rational principle nor use value, but the immoral principle of the spectacle, the ironic principle of Evil."[16]

Ariadne: "Dionysus once said: 'Under certain circumstances I love what is human'—and he alluded to me for I was there. 'Man is to my mind an agreeable, courageous, inventive animal that has no equal on earth; it finds its way in any labyrinth. I am well disposed towards him: I often reflect how I might yet advance him and make him stronger, more evil and more profound than he is...also more beautiful'—And then that great tempter god, my beloved, smiled his halcyon smile as though he had just paid an enchanting compliment![17] *Listen to what he said. Evil is ironic, evil is always event and catastrophe. Evil is the movement of the spectacle.*"

Nietzsche: "'Evil has always had great effects in its favor. And nature is evil. Let us therefore be natural.' That is the secret reasoning of those who have mastered the most spectacular effects and they have all too often been considered great human beings."[18] And we know that for Nietzsche whoever wants to be a creator in good and evil must wed the "highest evil" to the "greatest goodness."[19] But, again, who has really heard this today?

Nietzsche's philosophy of archery claims that an archer who takes correct aim can become master even over chance, but that this feat depends on the "greatness of spirit in those who experience it." In the following passage Nietzsche rues the death of the catastrophic event at the hands of the rational critical pen, for here it does not hit its mark.

> Should something good and right happen, as deed...at once those hollowed out by education will look beyond the work and inquire after the history of the author....Something most astonishing may happen, the flock of historical neuters is always already on the spot, prepared to comprehend the author from afar. Momentarily the echo resounds: but always as "criticism," while shortly before the critic did not even dream of the possibility of the event. Nowhere does it come to have an effect but always only "criticism"; and criticism itself again has no effect but only comes to see further criticism. In view of this there has come to be general agreement that much criticism is to be seen as an effect and little or none as failure. Basically, however, even with such "effect," all remains as it was: for a while one prattles something new, then again something new, and in the meantime does what one has always done. The historical education of our critics does not permit any more that there be an effect in the proper sense, namely an effect on life and action: on the blackest script they immediately press their blotter, on the most graceful drawing they smear their thick brush strokes, which are to be seen as corrections: once again it was all over.[20]

When concerned with relationships between event and language, between the natural evil of catastrophe and the rational principle of those discourses that try to grasp it, one is experimenting on the borders of the communicable, beyond which, perhaps, only madness lies. The event, the deed itself, the something astonishing that was enacted, happened, is robbed of its effect 'for life,' its catastrophic promise. And in its place is put the 'effect' of criticism, the rational judgment of the pen, of written discourse. What characterizes the discourse that obscures the event? It is a corrective, that is, it does not allow the event to remain as event, as appearance. The event as catastrophe must be contained, imprisoned in the string of rational, 'good,' read hegemonic, discourses and meanings that flock to it. The 'effect' of criticism lies in its quantity, for much criticism only obscures the event while little criticism simply kills it. Critical discourse literally feeds upon the event, sucks its blood from it, to give nutrition to a string of anemic writings, a moral vampirism. The critic of the principle of ironic evil grasps the catastrophe and danger of the event and the words of the event and is transformed into its 'warrior'; the battle does not take place on the page, but words become actions, events themselves. One writes and should read with blood.

Critical discourse, after the event, goes directly to the author of the event and the history of the author to begin its discourses, as if the author really was the *cause* of the event, or as if the author provided the *key* to the event, which could then be used to unlock the event and to free its meanings, to have interpreted it. However, the event was not the author's possession; meaning belongs no more to the author of appearance than to the critic of appearance. Catastrophe as appearance has no cause, no underlying meaning. Events happen, the world unfolds. And humans unfold the event of meaning whether negative or affirmative. The critics Nietzsche speaks of are, as we shall see, critics of resentment. For the resentment critic the irony is that in the search for the 'key,' the 'cause,' the true objective is never to let the event out to be the passion, the catastrophe, the exulting life that it is. Rather the lines on the page simulate the prison bars of meaning. The resentment critic annuls the catastrophic character of the event and replaces it with the known to quell the danger of the unknown. Then concepts of valuation enter, 'Christian' thinking:

"This event, which causes fear in us is wrong, should not be—must be something else."[21] Above, Barthes said it another way: "The 'signs' of love merely present themselves. However, the expenditure of I-love-you is the life, the event itself, which breathes the appearance of life into the hollow mimesis of its gestures."

As Nietzsche says, the critic cannot even dream of the event before it happens nor grasp it afterwards, but immediately obscures it and its 'author' in becoming its authority. Criticism of this sort operates in a world eternally separated from the event. However, the further irony in this talk of critics and blood is that even the one who understands all of this, is also barred from revealing the event and its 'meaning.' For the event appears and is its 'involution of origin and disappearance.' Even affirmative criticism must remain as a discrete point apart from it as an event in itself. But there is power in this realization!

Critical discourse as literate Christianity, Enlightenment tradition, Cartesian rationality offers the counterpart in its interpretation of events to the resentment morality Nietzsche uncovers in the *Genealogy of Morals*. It is not only the catastrophic event, but also what we might call *verbal paganism* that rational discourse seeks to dominate, a verbal paganism that glories in the power of appearances, spectacle, illusory images, song, and bodily enthusiasms whether oral or written. Verbal paganism is a discourse of passion and madness that does not pretend to grasp or correct the event but resonates with it in its own unique sphere of effects. "Oh, those Greeks! They knew how to live. What is required for that is to stop courageously at the surface, the fold, the skin, to adore appearance, to believe in forms, tones, words, in the whole Olympus of appearance. Those Greeks were superficial—*out of profundity*."[22]

Thus, the question becomes: Assuming one has received the catastrophe of an arrow in the heart and must sing of it, is the event doomed to lose its effect once language has seized it? Or are there conjuring tricks by which an affirmative discourse, while necessarily obscuring the event of which it speaks, can nevertheless allow the *effect* of that event to flame up by means of its own 'evil' discourse, which is itself an event, a spectacle, illusion, and catastrophe? A discourse of verbal paganism that runs alongside of the event, weaving itself in and out of its effects fanning them into life? This would be active affirmative discourse as direct accession to the catastrophic character of nature's events; the affirming of affirmation. One could attempt this trick, the trick of skirting rational/'Christian' discourse of resentment criticism with catastrophe in order to see it dance into affirmation.

"But how would this trick be accomplished?" you ask. "What if you are not able to locate my critique in a specific discourse or voice in this book? What then? What if my whole effort is aimed at a crooked and strategic revelation of the effect of the event through my dancing into and simultaneously distancing myself from all of the discourses of the event presented? A protean activity, an actor's and warrior's activity? What if what arises out of the work is not a critical reflection on the event, which as catastrophe is opened once again to multiple meanings, but upon resentment criticism itself? What if what arises out of the work is not a knowledge or attempt to suggest the truth of the event, an impossibility, but rather the installation of an acute passion in the reader concerning the event? Such an ensemble of unhinged discourses would offer a play with madness, a catastrophe of writing. Its arrows, like those of Nietzsche and Cupid, would have seduction and love as their aim. The only reaction to such writing *might* be laughter."

"Oh," whispers Ariadne ecstatically to herself, "how I love you, my mad, my tempter god!"

Notes

1. Nietzsche, *Gedichte*, Herausgegeben von Jost Hermand (Stuttgart: Philipp Reclam Jun., 1964), p. 111.

2. Nietzsche, "Wagner in Bayreuth," in *Untimely Meditations*, trans. R. J. Hollingdale (Cambridge: Cambridge University Press, 1983), p. 197.

3. Nietzsche, "On the Thousand and One Goals," in *Thus Spoke Zarathustra*, in *The Portable Nietzsche*, trans. Walter Kaufmann (New York: Penguin, 1954), p. 71. Also *Ecce Homo*, p. 328.

4. Nietzsche, *Beyond Good and Evil*, trans. Walter Kaufmann (New York: Vintage Books, Random House, 1966), #285.

5. Jean Baudrillard, "Fatal Strategies," in *Selected Writings* (Stanford, Calif.: Stanford University Press, 1988), p. 192.

6. Nietzsche, "Night Song," *Ecce Homo*, p. 307.

7. Ibid., pp. 333–34

8. Nietzsche, *Briefwechsel*, Kritische Gesamtausgabe, Herausgegeben von Giorgio Colli und Mazzino Montinari, III-5 (Berlin: Walter de Gruyter, 1984), p. 57. Referred to hereafter as NB.

9. Nietzsche, *Ecce Homo*, p. 335.

10. Baudrillard, "Fatal Strategies," p. 193.

11. Nietzsche, *Ecce Homo*, p. 326.

12. Baudrillard, "Fatal Strategies," p. 201.

13. Nietzsche, *Ecce Homo*, pp. 326–27.

14. Walter Otto, *Dionysus Myth and Cult*, trans. Robert Palmer (Bloomington: Indiana University Press, 1965), pp. 141–42.

15. Baudrillard, "Fatal Strategies," p. 201.

16. Ibid., p. 202.

17. Nietzsche, *Beyond Good and Evil*, #295.

18. Nietzsche, *The Gay Science*, trans. Walter Kaufmann (New York: Vintage Books, 1974), #225.

19. Nietzsche, "On Self Overcoming," in *Zarathustra*, p. 228 and *Ecce Homo*, p. 327.

20. Nietzsche, *On the Advantage and Disadvantage of History for Life*, trans. Peter Preuss (Indianapolis: Hackett Publishing, 1980), pp. 31–32.

21. Nietzsche, *Twilight of the Idols*, in *Portable Nietzsche*, p. 497.

22. Nietzsche, *Gay Science*, Preface #4.

Wrenching Madness
Loose from Reason

On the morning of January 3, 1889 Nietzsche had just left his
lodgings when he saw a cab-driver beating his horse in the
Piazza Carlo Alberto. Tearfully, the philosopher flung his arms
around the animal's neck, and then collapsed.[1]

Here is our event. "What!" you say. "This? But is this an event worthy of
extended consideration, the collapse into madness of a philosopher, even if
a prominent one? Is a fall into illness, into decline, into unproductiveness
an event worthy of criticism? We all know that he succumbed to a
syphilitic infection. What more can be said?"

With few exceptions, most writers on Nietzsche announce the madness at the end of their works and repeat almost in rote manner this
resentment litany without going into those last eleven years! The gateway:
madness must, indeed, be fearful! But with that, nothing has been said!

"Dear people," I respond, "you have already started your critical
discourses: you have obscured the event by giving it a medical label, you
have betrayed your prejudice in the opposition philosopher-productivity,
madness-decline, an endorsement of one type of manifestation and
discourse and a contemptuous dismissal of another type of manifestation
and discourse. Is this event worthy of criticism? Ah, what you betray in this
word! A whole hierarchy of value of events, a whole hierarchy of worth.
Well, pray tell me, what would constitute a worthy event? A political
revolution, a scientific invention, the rise of some noble figure, in short,
some event that at least epitomizes the 'progress' of human history, and
furthermore an event that is not merely personal but has some significance

15

for society in a more general sense?"

Are these not the prejudices of the resentment critic who needs to correct the event and salve fear by pressing upon the event the vestiges of the known, the predictable, the tested? Refusing the 'merely personal' is a further symptom. Have we really come to a point where the *merely personal* has lost all value? For Nietzsche the personal is the essential.

> *Morality as a Problem.*—The lack of personality always takes its revenge: A weakened, thin, extinguished personality that denies itself is no longer fit for anything good—least of all for philosophy. "Selflessness" has no value either in heaven or on earth. All great problems demand *great love*, and that only strong, round, secure spirits who have a firm grip on themselves are capable. It makes the most telling difference whether a thinker has a personal relationship to his problems and finds in them his destiny, his distress, and his greatest happiness, or an "impersonal" one, meaning that he can do no better than to touch them and grasp them with the antennae of cold, curious thought. In the latter case nothing will come of it; that much one can promise in advance, for even if great problems should allow themselves to be *grasped* by them they would not permit frogs and weaklings to *hold on* to them; such has been their taste from time immemorial—a taste, incidentally, that they share with all redoubtable females.[2]

"Thank you," says Ariadne.

And, too, in the final analysis the 'merely personal' is a prejudice of thinking. Isn't every action we perform actually a moment in the entire web of discourses and interactions in which we are entangled? Doesn't our every moment pull along with it all related moments? Aren't moments of 'decline' as able to tell us something about ourselves as are our highest moments? Isn't the prejudice in favor of the logical discourse of philosophy over less dogmatic, less ordered discourses beginning to crumble in our time? No, not yet! Well, then, we must go on!

> It is of little importance on exactly which day in the autumn of 1888 Nietzsche went mad for good, and after which his texts no longer afford philosophy but psychiatry: all of them, including

the postcard to Strindberg, belong to Nietzsche, and all are related to *The Birth of Tragedy*. But we must not think of this continuity in terms of a system, of a thematics, or even of an existence: Nietzsche's madness—that is, the dissolution of his thought—is that by which his thought opens out onto the modern world. What made it impossible makes it immediate for us: what took it from Nietzsche offers it to us. This does not mean that madness is the only language common to the work of art and the modern world (dangers of the pathos of malediction, inverse and symmetrical danger of psychoanalyses); but it means that, through madness, a work that seems to drown in the world, to reveal there its nonsense, and to transfigure itself with the features of pathology alone, actually engages within itself the world's time, masters it, and leads it; by the madness which interrupts it, a work of art opens a void, a moment of silence, a question without answer, provokes a breach without recon-ciliation where the world is forced to question itself.[3]

Foucault, here, represents a modern figure multiplying in numbers, a figure of postmodernity who takes on the appearance of the trickster critic, but who does not pull off the event of catastrophe, the affirmative critique. While appearing to give space and words to a certain madness of necessity, while giving voice to the conclusion that it is the very madness or catas-trophe of the artist that first allows us to become rational, Foucault and Derrida in their discussions of Descartes and madness, for example, appropriate madness, the more surely to suppress it, to drain its blood from it. The game becomes much more interesting, more tricky, yet resentment values still dominate.

In her article "Madness and Philosophy *or* Literature's Reason," Shoshana Felman summarizes Foucault's and Derrida's discussions of madness in the history of philosophy. For Foucault in *Madness and Civilization* the problem became one of *articulating* the repression of madness in Western history, not only in terms of writing its history but of letting madness itself speak. Foucault writes: "the problem is how, while analyzing history's essential structure of muffling madness, to give it voice, restore to madness both its language and its right to speak...; while rejecting all discourses *about* madness, how to pronounce the discourse of madness....How can madness as such break through the universe of discourse?"[4] A laudatory enterprise and, perhaps, the experiment of this book as well! But Foucault concludes that the task is "doubly impossible" since the "freedom of madness can only be heard from the top of the fortress which holds it prisoner."[5] In other words, only the madman speaks and hears his own discourse.

Derrida decides to try to grasp the nature of this impossibility of mad discourse. "Why," he asks, "is it impossible for madness to break into conventional discourses, especially the discourse of philosophy?" But this is exactly what Nietzsche has done. After Nietzsche, philosophy becomes mad. Derrida concludes that "far from being a historical accident, the exclusion of madness is the general condition and the constitutive foundation of the very enterprise of speech." Derrida writes: "any philosopher or any speaking subject (and the philosopher is merely the epitome of the speaking subject) who is trying to evoke madness *inside* thought (...) can only do so in the dimension of *possibility* and in the language of fiction or in the fiction of language. In doing so, his own language reassures him against the threat of *actual* madness."[6] Thus, Derrida agrees with Foucault that the production of a "work," of a hegemonic discourse, ensures it against falling into the madness from which it springs. Speaking about Foucault's project in *Madness and Civilization*, Derrida writes: "What I mean is that the silence of madness is not *said*, cannot be said in the logos of this book, but is indirectly made present, metaphorically, if I may say so, in the *pathos*...of this book."[7] Felman writes of Derrida, that in his recourse of calling philosophy a sort of fiction of language that harbors madness and in his statement that discourse can only present the pathos of madness through metaphoric evocation, he is naming another discourse, the discourse of literature.

But so far the discussion has shown us that historical discourse cannot 'say' madness, nor can philosophical discourse, and, though it seems a last stronghold, neither can the discourse of literature, which in the final analysis both historical and philosophical discourses also are. Why, ultimately, is madness condemned to silence according to these thinkers? Because, once again, it is maintained that the *position* from which the madman speaks is one place, and the discourse in which he attempts to communicate that position irrevocably another *position.* "It thus seems that literature is there to *re-place* madness," but fails. A discourse that pursues the ironic principle of evil, on the other hand, dissolves these generic distinctions in an explosion of discourses as appearance/catastrophe whose aim is not the communication of truth, but effect, bodily stimulation. Felman sums up Foucault's and Derrida's arguments very succinctly:

> If it is true then that the question underlying madness *cannot be asked,* that language is not *capable* of asking it; that through the very formulation of the question the *interrogation* is in fact excluded, being necessarily a confirmation, an *affirmation* on the contrary, of reason: an affirmation in which madness does not question, is not *in question;* it is, however, not less true that, in the fabric of a text and through the very act of writing, the question is *at work,* stirring, changing place, and wandering away: the question underlying madness *writes,* and writes itself. And if we are unable to locate it, read it, except where it already has escaped, where it has moved—moved *us—away—*it is not because the question relative to madness does not question, but because it questions *somewhere else;* somewhere at that point of silence where it is no longer we who speak, but where, in our absence, we are *spoken.*[8]

Ariadne: "What? Madness silent! Madness in a place away from us! Madness rages around us and in us day and night. We hear it in the hushed growth of a blade of grass, we hear it in the terrified cry of the mouse ripped apart by the voracious owl! We feel it beating wildly in our hearts! Madness is not silent! It screams, it howls the passion of life! I think, rather, that our philosophers lack ears, that in preserving themselves on paper, or to move it up to parody, in portraying themselves on the canvas of philosophy they have cut off their ears! Or is it hearts they lack? If they keep writing that madness is 'a moment of silence, a question without answer,' then there simply will be no answer. They reimprison that which they have already stated is the necessary site of birth. The answer to madness is love, the ironic principle of 'evil' love. Madness is not silent. It is the pandemonium of Dionysus!"

The pandemonium in which Dionysus, himself, and his divine entourage make their entry—that pandemonium which the human horde, struck by his spirit, unleashes—is a genuine symbol of religious ecstasy. With the horror which is at the same time bewitchment, with the ecstasy which is like paralysis, overpowering all natural and habitual sense perceptions, the Dreadful suddenly springs into being. And, at its greatest intensity, it is as if the insane din were in reality the profoundest of silences.

Here, silence is the *expression* of the very din of madness, not silence as the event of the *exorcism* of madness. Dionysus is called "the roarer," "the loud shouter," and "a series of mythic stories and descriptions make us keenly aware of the overpowering spirit of the Dionysiac din which makes its violent entry as its captivates and inspires dread at one and the same time."[9]

Foucault's labeling of Nietzsche's 'madness' as "the dissolution of his thought" accords with the idea that it is all over with a philosopher when his rationality becomes his pathology, when his voice becomes too shrill, too much a bellowing of his own praises. Yet, Foucault's trick is to suggest that it is this very pathology that opens up the modern world for questioning, while simultaneously silencing the affirmative possibilities of madness. If it is madness that poses the question of questions, why not simply say so, leaving aside the aspersions of psychiatry? 'Pathology,' the discourse of psychiatry, the ultimate silencing of the din of Dionysus. Nietzsche's madness does open up a space for catastrophic questioning: "I know my fate. One day my name will be associated with the memory of something tremendous—a crisis without equal on earth, the most profound collision of conscience, a decision that was conjured up against everything that had been believed, demanded, hallowed so far."[10] "I must confront humanity with the most difficult demand ever made of it."[11] But one has to have ears and the heart for this opening. Foucault's and Derrida's strategies miss its powerfully seductive enticements and quickly close the opening by suggesting in the nets of their resentment language that it is really no opening at all.

In his article "Force and Signification" and in his discussion of writing as the difference between the madness of Dionysus and the order of Apollo, between ardor and structure, Derrida writes: "If we must say, along with Schelling, that 'all is but Dionysus,'...that, like pure force, Dionysus is

worked by difference," then, he adds, "for all eternity he has had a relationship to his exterior, to visible form, to structure."[12] This may be, and
Nietzsche's response is that one's recourse with regard to this state of affairs
is that one should *dance* with the pen: "dancing with the feet, with ideas,
with words, and need I add that one must also be able to dance with the
pen—that one must learn how to write?"[13] However, Derrida prefers to
stage one's reaction to the difference of Dionysus as a choice. "We would
have to choose then between writing and dance." He labels Nietzsche's
dancing with the pen as an eternal "in vain." For Derrida writing is something "over which one bends." Speaking of Zarathustra's moment of
downgoing when he carries his new tablets down to people, Derrida writes:
"it will be necessary to descend, to work, to bend in order to engrave and
carry the new Tables to the valleys, in order to read them and have them
read."[14] Derrida's resentment reading misunderstands the dancing and
squandering of the hour of Zarathustra's downgoing. Zarathustra's new
tablets are no Sisyphusian rock that Nietzsche carries down to the valleys
but his downgoing is his eternal joy as he says to his readers: "O my
brothers, break, break the old tablets of the never gay!"[15]

Derrida characterizes the demand of the reading process in as equally a
dismal and straining set of metaphors: "In reading 'metaphor-for-others-
aimed-at-others-here-and-now'...the fraternal other is not first in the peace
of what is called intersubjectivity, but in the work and the peril of interrogation; the other is not certain within the peace of the *response* in which
two affirmations *espouse each other*, but is called up in the night by the
excavating work of interrogation. Writing is...the moment of depth as
decay. Incidence and insistence of inscription."[16] "Yes, Derrida, there is a
certain interrogation of the other, and this interrogation asks: Are you like
me? Can your heart resound to the beating of my Dionysian heart? Are you
hard enough to break the tablets of the good? And in the silent din of this
interrogation, if the answer is yes, then the espousal, the wedding—not of
words, structures, rationality—take place, but of hearts, the espousal
of/with Dionysus. You yourself quote Nietzsche at the end of your article:
'Behold, here is a new tablet; but where are my brethren who will carry it
with me to the valley and into hearts of flesh?' Did you not read: 'hearts of
flesh'? And did you not read Zarathustra say, 'Walk upright betimes, O my

brothers; learn to walk upright.'?[17] And did you not read 'lift up your hearts, my brothers, high, higher! And do not forget your legs either. Lift up you legs too, you good dancers; and better yet, stand on your heads!'?"[18]

Health lies with the passionate ones, Nietzsche tells us, the ones caught up in the din and danger of great problems, those willing to go down, to put their person on the line of the problem. 'Pathology,' from his perspective, belongs to those who fail to *love* their problems, who handle them with the antiseptic of rational discourse, who prefer to bend, interrogate, and shackle dancing feet. Nietzsche: "the higher type is more unreasonable, for those who are noble, magnanimous, and self-sacrificial do succumb to their instincts, and when they are at their best, their reason pauses."[19]

Foucault speaks of the question that madness opens up for modernity in the very language of resentment morality:

> What is necessarily a profanation in the work of art returns to that point, and, in the time of that work swamped in madness, *the world is made aware of its guilt*. Henceforth, and through the mediation of madness, it is *the world that becomes culpable* (for the first time in the Western world) in relation to the work of art; *it is now arraigned by the work of art*, obliged to order itself by its language, *compelled by it to a task of recognition, of reparation*, to the task of restoring reason *from* that unreason and to that unreason. The madness in which the work of art is engulfed is the space of our enterprise, it is the endless path to fulfillment, it is our *mixed vocation of apostle and exegete*. This is why it makes little difference when the first voice of madness insinuated itself into Nietzsche's pride, into Van Gogh's humility. There is no madness except as the final instant of the work of art—the work endlessly drives madness to its limits; *where there is a work of art, there is no madness*; and yet madness is contemporary with the work of art, since it inaugurates the time of its truth. The moment when, together, the work of art and madness are born and fulfilled is the beginning of *the time when the world finds itself arraigned by that work of art and responsible before it for what it is*. Ruse and new triumph of madness: the world that thought to measure and justify madness through psychology *must justify itself* before

madness, since in its struggles and agonies it measures itself by the excess of works like those of Nietzsche, of Van Gogh, of Artaud. And nothing in itself, especially not what it can know of madness, *assures the world that it is justified* by such works of madness.[20]

Yes, Foucault you are the Christian critic. Art is now God and madness the dark side of God. The scenario is still the same—good and evil—the responsibility to destroy the darkness of madness to allow untainted reason to shine forth. Foucault writes: "Where there is a work of art, there is no madness." For Nietzsche, there is art and creation only in a sort of 'evil' madness and intoxication. Nietzsche: "In every teacher and preacher of what is new we encounter the same 'wickedness' that makes conquerors notorious, even if its expression is subtler and it does not immediately set the muscles in motion, and therefore also does not make one that notorious. What is new, however, is always evil, being that which wants to conquer and overthrow the old boundary markers and the old pieties."[21]

Foucault writes: "Where there is a work of art, there is no madness." In other words, madness again necessarily becomes the sacrificial element in the tenacity of reason/literature. Apparently what Foucault means is that such works 'of madness' shake up Western culture's belief in the value of rationality and, though without complete confidence, it is forced to reassert its 'good' right to dominance. Thus, the slew of Nietzsche critics willing to label him and send him to the perdition of madness and psychiatry without being able to look into this abyss and dance over it. But in fact this 'good' rationality guarantees only the illusion of dominance. Dionysus dominates and speaks of no rights, guilt, justifications; madness just is appearance and event and such attempts to quell it, imprison it, are ultimately laughable. Again, Foucault:

> Nietzsche's last cry, proclaiming himself both Christ and Dionysus, is not on the border of reason and unreason, in the perspective of the work of art, their common dream, finally realized and immediately vanishing, of a reconciliation of the "sheperds of Arcady and the fishermen of Tiberias"; it is the very annihilation of the work of art, the point where it becomes impossible and where it must fall silent; the hammer has just fallen from the philosopher's hands.[22]

"Oh, Foucault," says Ariadne, "the cry and its silence are pregnant with a seduction yet unsuspected, a challenge yet unmet. Nietzsche's catastrophic event, his 'madness', as he himself loudly proclaimed with much bellowing and din, is world-historical, is the revaluation of values. He will yet make the world mad! You resentment critics will soon suspect as much! But, let's burst the bonds of these pale, sterile questions and break into some passion. Let's stir up some heartbeats! Nietzsche said: 'The most select spirits bristle at the universal binding force [of the universal faith in reason, truth and certainty]....It is in these impatient spirits that a veritable delight in madness erupts because madness has such a cheerful tempo.'!"[23]

Notes

1. Ronald Hayman, *A Critical Life of Nietzsche* (New York: Penguin Books, 1980), pp. 334–35.

2. Nietzsche, *Gay Science*, #345.

3. Michele Foucault, *Madness and Civilization*, trans. Richard Howard (New York: Vintage Books), 1973, pp. 287–88.

4. Shoshana Felman, "Madness and Philosophy or Literature's Reason," *Yale French Studies*, No. 52, 1975, p. 213.

5. Ibid., p. 214.

6. Ibid., p. 216; emphasis added.

7. Ibid., p. 218.

8. Ibid., pp. 227–28.

9. Otto, *Dionysus Myth and Cult*, p. 93.

10. Nietzsche, *Ecce Homo*, p. 326.

11. Ibid., p. 217.

12. Jacques Derrida, "Force and Signification," in *Writing and Difference*, trans. Alan Bass (Chicago: University of Chicago Press, 1978), pp. 28–29.

13. Ibid., p. 29.

14. Ibid.

15. Nietzsche, *Zarathustra*, p. 316.

16. Derrida, "Force and Signification," pp. 29–30.

17. Nietzsche, *Zarathustra*, p. 325.

18. Ibid., p. 406.

19. Nietzsche, *Gay Science*, #3.

20. Foucault, *Madness and Civilization*, p. 288; emphasis added.

21. Nietzsche, *Gay Science*, #4.
22. Foucault, *Madness and Civilization*, p. 287.
23. Nietzsche, *Gay Science*, #76.

Phantasm

Only a Fool! Only a Poet!
Talking only gaudy nonsense,
gaudy nonsense from a fool's mask,
climbing around on deceitful word-bridges,
on mirage rainbows,
between false skies,
hovering, creeping—
only a fool! *only* a poet!¹

In "Theatrum Philosophicum" Foucault has another voice. Between 1965 and 1977 something happened to Foucault. Was it Gilles Deleuze? In "Theatrum Philosophicum" Foucault attempts to speak Deleuzian. Deleuzian is useful for Nietzschean, but that is not surprising, for before he spoke Deleuzian, Deleuze read Nietzschean. Here, it is the idea of the phantasm that I wish to concentrate on as well as the idea that philosophy and madness can coexist in the spectacle of theater. How does one get beyond the either/or of value, get beyond good and evil, beyond resentment duality, beyond rationality? In the phantasm, again appearance, illusion, catastrophe without consequences, but more. Foucault moves beyond the dualism of *Madness and Civilization* in his efforts to come to terms with Deleuze's phantasm. He writes: "It is useless to seek a more substantial truth behind the phantasm, a truth to which it points as a rather confused sign (thus, the futility of 'symptomatologizing'); it is also useless to contain it within stable figures and to construct solid cores of convergence where we might include, on the basis of their identical properties, all its angles, flashes, membranes, and vapors (no possibility of 'phenomenalization')."²

The phantasm is like the mask of Dionysus behind which is another mask. Or it is like the veil of truth behind which there is no truth. Foucault shows that Deleuze *opposes* the *usual* definitions of phantasm as something that has no physical reality, a purely imaginary specter, an appearance but not a fact: "Phantasms do not extend organisms into an imaginary domain; they topologize the materiality of the body. They should consequently be freed from the restrictions we impose upon them, freed from the dilemmas of truth and falsehood and of being and non-being (the essential difference between simulacrum and copy carried to its logical conclusion); they must be allowed to conduct their dance, to act out their mime, as 'extra-beings.'"[3] Foucault writes that Deleuze's metaphysics is freed from a profound origin or supreme being, which allows it to construct "the phantasm in its play of surfaces" as an "epidermic play of perversity." Nietzsche: "Nothing is true, everything is possible!" Like catastrophe, phantasms are most effectively activated on the stage of theater "which is multiplied, polyscenic, simultaneous, broken into separate scenes that refer to each other, and where we encounter, without any trace of representation (copying or imitating), the dance of masks, the cries of bodies, and the gesturing of hands and fingers."[4]

Ariadne: "My cry is a wail pitched to shatter the distance between us. I love you, Dionysus!"

Intoxicated with Deleuze, Foucault writes: "The philosophy of representation—of the original, the first time, resemblance, imitation, faithfulness—is dissolving: and the arrow of the simulacrum released by the Epicureans is headed in our direction. It gives birth—rebirth—to a 'phantasmaphysics.'"[5]

> We should be alert to the surface effects in which the Epicureans take such pleasure; emissions proceeding from deep within bodies and rising like the wisps of a fog—interior phantoms that are quickly reabsorbed into other depths by the sense of smell, by the mouth, by the appetites; extremely thin membranes, which detach themselves from the surfaces of objects and proceed to impose colors and contours deep within our eyes (floating epiderm, visual idols): phantasms created by fear or desire (cloud

gods, the adorable face of the beloved, "miserable hope trans-
ported by the wind").[6]

But this is the madness within each of us! Phantasms are not extra-
bodily—they are body phantasticized, events as lived catastrophe. The
events, actions of bodies, and phantasms once again are theater—not as
imitation or reenactment of life, but of life itself: "This conception of the
phantasm as the play of the (missing) event and its repetition must not be
given the form of individuality (a form inferior to the concept and therefore informal), nor must it be measured against reality (a reality which
imitates an image); it presents itself as universal singularity: to die, to fight,
to vanquish, to be vanquished."[7] Nietzsche: "Live Dangerously!" "I love all
those who are as heavy drops, falling one by one out of the dark cloud that
hangs over men: they herald the advent of lightning, and as heralds, they
perish."[8]

The critique-knowledge duality, what I have been calling "resentment
criticism," becomes absolutely useless as phantasm declares its nature.
Philosophy has dreamed of itself as a science, and has presented itself as
knowledge and critique of knowledge. It has thought of the event as
something to be assimilated in a concept, from which it is necessary to
extract a *fact*, verify a proposition, prove the empirical content of history.
From this perspective thinking of the phantasm was reduced by philosophy
in the name of reality and situated at the extremity, the 'pathological' pole
of the normal. But now as Foucault tells us, and as Nietzsche has told us all
along, it is only phantasmatic thinking that is worth doing. Phantasmatic
thinking "requires the release of a phantasm in the mime that produces it at
a single stroke; it makes the event indefinite so that it repeats itself as a
singular universal. It is this construction of the event and the phantasm
that leads to thought in an absolute sense."[9]

The phantasm is thought as total freedom. What has thought got to
be afraid of? What is thinkable appears at least for the moment it is
thought! Death may be the limit of thought, but phantasm laughs at death;
it, too, is event, appearance. Power is the realization and the act upon that
realization that one can say anything at all! Ultimately, *one can also do
anything at all*! But, in moral and grammatical terms, wouldn't this be called
madness?

In *Madness and Civilization* Foucault was the reluctant Bacchant, but a Bacchant nevertheless! All along as Foucault reads and rewrites Nietzsche he is exultant, allured by the powerful seduction, but stuck in the strait-jacket of the philopsychiatric rational scholar. If one watches Foucault, one eventually sees the loosening of the straitjacket, the flexing of the cramped arms and fingers as the blood rushes back into them, the raising of the arms above the head, the first movement of a gesture and now the beginning of the dance! Foucault writes that: "The suppression of categories, the affirmation of the univocity of being, and the repetitive revolution of being around difference—these are the final conditions for the thought of the phantasm and the event."[10] He continues: "At the moment when chance, the theater, and perversions enter into resonance, when chance dictates a resonance among the three, then thought becomes a trance; and it becomes worthwhile to think."[11] But hasn't Foucault become mad? And now he would no longer assert that madness signals the absence of the work of art, but that it is that very thing in its singularity!

"Oh, Dionysus," says Ariadne, "descend upon the cramped and bent ones and set them dancing!"

Notes

1. Nietzsche, "Only a Fool! Only a Poet!," in *Dithyrambs of Dionysus*, trans. R. J. Hollingdale (Redding Ridge, Conn.: Black Swan Books Ltd., 1984), p. 23
2. Foucault, "Theatrum Philosophicum" in *Language, Counter-Memory, Practice* (New York: Cornell University Press, 1977), p. 169
3. Ibid., p. 170.
4. Ibid., p. 171.
5. Ibid., p. 172.
6. Ibid., p. 169.
7. Ibid., p. 177.
8. Nietzsche, *Zarathustra*, p. 128.
9. Foucault, "Theatrum Philosophicum," p. 178.
10. Ibid., p.187.
11. Ibid., p. 192.

Seduction, Secrets, and Challenge

> There are cases where what is needed is an
> Ariadne's thread leading into the labyrinth. He
> who has the task to bring on the great war, the
> war against the virtuous (—the good and
> virtuous Zarathustra calls them, also 'last
> man,' also 'beginning of the end'—) had to be
> willing to buy some experiences almost at any
> price; the price could even be the danger of
> losing oneself.[1]

Ariadne: "*Dionysus and I are master and mistress of seduction. We know the labyrinth with its lures and delights. And life itself is this labyrinth. 'Seduction is the sacred horizon of appearances.' We sit on high mountains beaconing lovers into the labyrinth and the language of lovers is seduction.*"

Baudrillard writes that seduction is "that which extracts meaning from discourse and detracts it from truth." Nietzsche: "We don't believe that truth remains truth after it is unveiled." Just as phantasm offers the realm of spectacle and appearance as far preferable to empirical rationality because rationality is itself phantasm, seduction salutes appearance and disparages interpretation.

The havoc interpretation wreaks in the domain of appearances is incalculable, and its privileged quest for hidden meanings may be profoundly mistaken. For we needn't search in some beyond, in a *hinterwelt*, or in an unconscious, to find what diverts discourse. What actually displaces it, "seduces" it in the literal sense, and makes it seductive, is its very appearance: the aleatory, meaningless, or ritualistic and meticulous, circulation of signs on the surface; its inflections, and its nuances. All of this effaces the content value of meaning, and this is seductive.[2]

The meaning of an interpretive discourse, by contrast, has never seduced anyone. *Every interpretive discourse wants to get beyond appearances*; this is its illusion and fraud. But getting beyond appearances is an impossible task: inevitably every discourse is revealed in its own appearance, and is hence subject to the stakes imposed by seduction, and consequently to *its own failure as discourse*.[3]

Discourse is not a vessel that contains and transmits meaning; it is aleatory, it gambles. Its very combination of surface and appearance reaches the fluids and nerves of those whom it seduces. Like phantasm, which is *not* unreal, purely imaginary in form, seduction beats with the heart. When rational procedures get hold of phantasm and seduction they kill it through an interpretive dissection, the very process of which disperses the appearance that manifests seductive power. Baudrillard writes: "All appearances conspire to combat meaning, to uproot meaning, whether intentional or not, and to convert it into a game, according to some other rules of the game, arbitrary ones this time, to some other elusive ritual, more adventurous and more seductive than the mastery of meaning."[4] *Not*, what is the meaning of the event, what are the facts of the event, but does the surface appearance of the event, of discourses surrounding the event, seduce me, turn me into a poet?! Do I become lost in its labyrinthian dangers? Does the seduction of a certain language and event create a desire in me to respond with a like seduction?

And what is it in the appearances that seduce one? The appearances offer and veil themselves. They do a certain dance of the veils, tempting, alluring, and seeming to promise a nakedness, which yet can never be. Nietzsche: "but perhaps this is the most powerful magic of life: it is covered by a veil interwoven with gold, a veil of beautiful possibilities, sparkling with promise, bashfulness, mockery, pity, and seduction."[5] The secret is that there is no secret, but only the painfully alluring play of seduction. And joy is seduction. Baudrillard writes:

The secret: the seductive and initiatory quality of that which cannot be said because it is meaningless, and of that which is not said even though it gets around. Hence I know the other's secret but do not reveal it, and he knows I know it but does not let it be acknowledged: the intensity between the two is simply the secret of the secret. This complicity has nothing to do with some hidden information. Besides, even if the partners wished to reveal the secret they could not, since there is nothing to say....Everything that can be revealed lies outside the secret. For it is not a hidden signified, nor the key to something; it circulates through and traverses everything that can be said, just as seduction flows beneath the obscenity of speech. It is the opposite of communication and yet shares something with it. Only at the cost of remaining unspoken does it maintain power, just as seduction functions from never being spoken or desired.[6]

In his *Dionysus Dithyrambs* Nietzsche gives us examples of his seductive talents:

Now—
contorted
between two nothings,
a question mark
a weary riddle—
a riddle for birds of prey...
—they will soon "resolve" you,
already they thirst for your "resolution,"
already they flutter about you, their riddle,
about you, hanged man...
O Zarathustra!...
Self-knower!...
Self-hangman!...

A supreme discourse of seduction, inviting, bewildering, discourse that torments! What is my secret? How will you resolve me?

Ariadne: "*And in another dithyramb Dionysus said to me:*

'*Be wise, Ariadne!*...
You have little ears, you have ears like mine:

let some wisdom into them!—
Must we not first hate ourself if we are to love ourself?
I am thy labyrinth."[7]

Were not Zarathustra and Dionysus great seducers, whispering secrets into our ears? Were they not seducing us with parables and phantasms? Was Nietzsche not the great riddler of language and not only of language?"

The phantasmatics of the supreme lover, Nietzsche, will endlessly seduce us to ourselves, to the world as appearance. Baudrillard: "The hidden or the repressed has a tendency to manifest itself, whereas the secret does not do so at all. It is an introductory and implosive form: we enter it, but are unable to exit. The secret is never revealed, never communicated, never even 'secreted.' It derives its strength from this allusive and ritual power of exchange."[8]

Ariadne: "This secret of the labyrinth still remains a secret to me. But the secret has pulled one from me. My own secret. The one I am sharing and secreting with you."

Seduction takes the form of an enigma to be resolved, a riddle, the traversing and transvaluing of a labyrinth. Nietzsche is an enigma, Dionysus is a labyrinth, both gaming and bluffing. Baudrillard: "The passion of seduction is without substance and without origin: it is not through some libidinal investment, through some energy of desire that it acquires intensity, but through the pure form gaming and bluffing."[9] In order to play with Nietzsche/Dionysus Ariadne understands that she must herself become an enigma. Baudrillard: "It is an enigmatic duel, and seduction resolves it *without disclosing the secret.*"[10]

Seduction is a play with time, it is the moment, but it is also no time. Like catastrophe, like phantasm, seduction births and erases itself, but in the intervening appearance everything lies already prepared as birth and as death. "Seduction does not have its moment, nor is there a time *for* seduction, but it has a rhythm, without which it would not happen. Unlike an instrumental strategy, which proceeds by intermediate phases, seduction operates instantaneously, in a single movement, and is always its own end." And thus one cannot know if one is being seduced or if one is seducing.

"Being seduced is still the best way of seducing. It is an endless strophe. There is no active or passive in seduction, no subject or object, or even interior or exterior: it plays on both sides of the border with no border separating the sides."[11]

No one can seduce another if they have not been seduced themselves. That is, unless they have fallen into the abyss, the labyrinth of appearance and madness. Passion is that which unites all human life.

"But," adds Ariadne, "it is also that by which each is irrevocably cut off from the other."

Again, the paradox that the secret is not secret and yet that it is—this seduces us into living, into rejoicing! Ultimately, seduction turns one into a fool, a buffoon of gods or a godly buffoon.

The *challenge* is also an instantaneous form of appearance. It is "bewitching, like a meaningless discourse, to which, *for this absurd reason,* we cannot help but respond. Why do we answer a challenge? This is the same mysterious question as: what is it that seduces?"[12]

Dionysus versus the Crucified—Have I been Understood?

My soul, a stringed instrument, sang to itself, invisibly touched, a secret gondola song, quivering with iridescent happiness.—Did anyone listen to it?

Who besides me knows what Ariadne is!—For all such riddles nobody so far had any solution; I doubt that anybody even saw any riddles here.[13]

Nietzsche, the great challenger! His method is to seduce and challenge; his discourse produces pain and ecstacy. Baudrillard on challenge:

What could be more seductive than a challenge? To challenge or seduce is always to drive the other mad, but in a mutual vertigo: madness from the vertiginous absence that unites them, and from their mutual involvement. Such is the inevitability of the challenge, and consequently the reason why we cannot help but respond to it: for it inaugurates a kind of mad relation, quite different from communication and exchange; a dual relation

transacted by meaningless signs, but connected by a fundamental
rule, and its secret observance.

The challenge terminates all contracts, all exchanges
regulated by law (the law of nature or the law of value) and
substitutes for it a highly conventional and ritualized *pact. An
unremitting obligation to respond and to outdo*, governed by a
fundamental rule of the game, and proceeding according to its
own rhythm.[14]

To fall into the other's labyrinth in the hope of catching them in ours.
To fall into seduction and challenge is already to become the event of a
transvaluation of values. One is seduced and led astray from the law and
challenged to respond far beyond the law according to one's own physiological rhythm and phantasm. "For seduction or challenge to exist all
contractual relations must be nullified in favor of a *dual relation*. A relation
that is comprised of secret signs removed from the exchange, and which
obtain their intensity from a formal division and from an immediate
reverberation. Likewise, the enchantment of seduction puts an end to every
libidinal economy, every sexual and psychological contact, substituting in
its place a staggering openness of possible responses."[15]

*"This ritual of dual relation," responds Ariadne, "is what the marriage of
Dionysus and myself signifies and in signifying this it promises no meaning and all
meaning. As a great love story it seduces and it challenges. It solves a riddle: 'Did
anyone hear me?' with a new riddle: 'Did anyone hear us?' Venus, taking pity on
me, said I should have an immortal lover for the mortal Theseus I had lost. All
the myths say Dionysus consoled me and made me his wife. But here: I choose
Dionysus! I respond to his seductions and challenges. I, a mortal, take an
immortal, destroy and consol him and together with him offer a human challenge
for eternity. And the challenge: 'is never an investment but a risk; never a
contract but a pact; never individual but dual; never psychological but ritual;
never natural but artificial. It is no one's strategy, but a destiny.'[16] This is why I,
Ariadne, am also a destiny. I know my fate. I join the game of seduction and
challenge. I respond by trumping and joining in the annihilation of both Dionysus
and myself. Seduction is a death that is no death. 'The secret is to know how to
make use of death, in the absence of a gaze, in the absence of a gesture, in the
absence of knowledge, or in the absence of meaning.'[17] Dionysus gave me a*

crown when we married. He knew how to celebrate death. When I died he took the gift of my crown and threw it up high into the sky, transforming his love for me into the celestial constellation of the crown of Ariadne, the Corona Borealis![18] *Our love became a secret and a dancing of the stars!"*

Just as phantasm has been relegated to the pathological pole by philosophy, seduction according to Baudrillard has been called "merely an immoral, frivolous, superfluous process...one devoted to pleasure and the usufruct of useless bodies." Why are phantasm and seduction excluded as 'evil' discourses? Because, answers Baudrillard, "they wanted us to believe that everything was production," hoarding, possessing, parceling out. But the revaluation of values asks: "What if everything, contrary to appearances—in fact according to the secret rule of appearances—operated by (the principle) of seduction," that is, squandering of overabundance.[19] Or, as Barthes put it, 'the proffering of I-love-you as expenditure'! Baudrillard writes:

> Everything returns to the void, including our words and our gestures. But some, before they disappeared, had the time, anticipating their demise, to exercise a seduction others will never know. The secret of seduction is in this evocation and reevocation of the other, in movements whose slowness and suspense are poetic, like a slow motion film of a fall or an explosion, because something has had, before fulfilling itself, the time to be missed and this is, if there is such a thing, the perfection of "desire."[20]

Nietzsche was such an explosive seduction, dis"appearing" and leaving behind him the arrow of desire.

Ariadne: "Ah, Baudrillard, you seducer, how do your words appear at the heart my love for Dionysus? How can you know these things? I could almost say: Baudrillard, I love you! Ariadne. But is it you I love? Is it Dionysus, Nietzsche, I love? Do I love because I, the owner of the golden thread that leads heros from the labyrinth and death, am forced to laugh at myself and my thread and prefer the dangers of the labyrinth itself? Or is it merely the eternal cycle of seduction and expediture itself that makes me rejoice in living?"

Baudrillard understands that what is chosen becomes one's destiny. "Production as destiny, or seduction as destiny? Is this the destiny of appearances as opposed to the truths of deep structure? In any case we live in non-sense, and if simulation is its disenchanted form, seduction is its enchanted form."[21] If one eschews production as destiny and chooses seduction as destiny, what remains is risk, magic, predestination for the labyrinth, vertigo—madness! Nietzsche knew he was a great lover, a tempter and genius of the heart:

> The genius of the heart, as that great concealed one possesses it, the tempter god and born pied pier of consciences whose voice knows how to descend into the netherworld of every soul; who does not say a word or cast a glance in which there is no consideration and ulterior enticement; whose mastery includes the knowledge of how to seem—not what he is but what is to those who follow him one *more* constraint to press ever closer to him in order to follow him ever more inwardly and thoroughly— the genius of the heart who silences all that is loud and self-satisfied, teaching it to listen; who smooths rough souls and lets them taste a new desire—to lie still as a mirror, that the deep sky may mirror itself in them—the genius of the heart who teaches the doltish and rash hand to hesitate and reach out more delicately; who guesses the concealed and forgotten treasure, the drop of graciousness and sweet spirituality under dim and thick ice, and is a divining rod for every grain of gold that has long lain buried in the dungeon of much mud and sand; the genius of the heart from whose touch everyone walks away richer, not having received grace and surprised, not as blessed and oppressed by alien goods, but richer in himself, newer to himself than before, broken open, blown at and sounded out by a thawing wind, perhaps more unsure, tenderer, more fragile, more broken, but full of new dissatisfaction and undertows—but what am I doing, my friends?
>
> Of whom am I speaking to you? Have I forgotten myself so far that I have not even told you his name? Unless you have guessed by yourselves who this questionable spirit and god is who wants to be *praised* in such fashion.[22]

The genius of the heart, the tempter god, is Dionysus and belongs to divine mythology. But the genius of the heart, the tempter Nietzsche, transforms divine mythology into human mythology. Events and discourses as catastrophic appearance embody the forms of a new 'passion' (madness, phantasm, seduction), a new mythology of the overhuman, a new story, a new seduction.[23]

Ariadne: "Let us now listen to the 'Night Song,' which such a genius of seduction and secrets sings when he calls to his beloved Ariadne."

The Night Song

Night has come; now all fountains speak more loudly. And my soul, too, is a fountain.

Night has come; only now all the songs of lovers awaken. And my soul, too, is the song of a lover.

Something unstilled, unstillable is within me; it wants to be voiced. A craving for love is within me; it speaks the language of love.

Light am I; ah, that I were night! But this is my loneliness that I am girt with light. Ah, that I were dark and nocturnal! How I would suck at the breasts of light! And even you would I bless, you little sparkling stars and glowworms up there, and be overjoyed with your gifts of light.

But I live in my own light; I drink back into myself the flames that break out of me. I do not know the happiness of those who receive; and I have often dreamed that even stealing must be more blessed than receiving. This is my poverty, that my hand never rests from giving; this is my envy, that I see waiting eyes and the lit-up nights of longing. Oh, wretchedness of all givers! Oh, darkening of my sun! Oh, craving to crave! Oh, ravenous hunger in satiation!

They receive from me but do I touch their souls? There is a cleft between giving and receiving; and the narrowest cleft is the last to be bridged. A hunger grows out of my beauty: I should like to hurt those for whom I shine; I should like to rob those to whom I give; thus do I hunger for malice. To withdraw my hand

when the other hand already reaches out to it; to linger like the
waterfall, which lingers even while it plunges: thus do I hunger
for malice. Such revenge my fullness plots: such spite wells up
out of my loneliness. My happiness in giving died in giving; my
virtue tired of itself in its overflow.

The danger of those who always give is that they lose their
sense of shame; and the heart and hand of those who always
mete out become callous from always meting out. My eye no
longer wells over at the shame of those who beg; my hand has
grown too hard for the trembling of filled hands. Where have the
tears of my eyes gone and the down of my heart? Oh, the
loneliness of all givers! Oh, the taciturnity of all who shine!

Many suns revolve in the void: to all that is dark they speak
with their light—to me they are silent. Oh, this is the enmity of
the light against what shines: merciless it moves in its orbit.
Unjust in its heart against all that shines, cold against suns—thus
moves every sun.

The suns fly like a storm in their orbits: that is their motion.
They follow their inexorable will: that is their coldness.

Oh, it is only you, you dark ones, you nocturnal ones, who
create warmth out of that which shines. It is only you who drink
milk and refreshment out of the udders of light.

Alas, ice is all around me, my hand is burned by the icy.
Alas, thirst is within me that languishes after your thirst.

Night has come: alas, that I must be light! And thirst for
the nocturnal! And loneliness!

Night has come: now my craving breaks out of me like a
well; to speak I crave.

Night has come; now all fountains speak more loudly. And
my soul too is a fountain.

Night has come; now all the songs of lovers awaken. And
my soul too is the song of a lover.[24]

Notes

1. From an earlier draft for *Ecce Homo*, KSA, p. 497.
2. Jean Baudrillard, "On Seduction," in *Selected Writings* (Stanford, Calif.: Stanford University Press, 1988), p. 149.
3. Ibid., p. 150.
4. Ibid.
5. Nietzsche, *Gay Science*, #339.
6. Baudrillard, "On Seduction," p. 159.
7. Nietzsche, *Dithyrambs of Dionysus*, p. 45 and p. 59.
8. Baudrillard, "On Seduction," p. 159.
9. Ibid., p. 161.
10. Ibid., p. 159.
11. Ibid., p. 160.
12. Ibid., p. 161.
13. Nietzsche, *Ecce Homo*, pp. 335, 308, and 252.
14. Baudrillard, "On Seduction," p. 161; emphasis added.
15. Ibid; emphasis added.
16. Ibid., pp. 161–62.
17. Ibid., p. 162.
18. Bullfinch's Mythology (New York: Thomas Y. Crowell, 1970), p. 165.
19. Baudrillard, "On Seduction," p. 162.
20. Ibid., p. 163.
21. Ibid., p. 164.
22. Nietzsche, *Beyond Good and Evil*, #295.
23. I will be using "overhuman" to replace "overman" in my discourse in an effort to overcome the sexist bias of "overman."
24. From *On the Genealogy of Morals* and *Ecce Home* by Friedrich Nietzsche, pp. 306–308. Copyright © 1967 by Random House, Inc. Reprinted by permission of Random House, Inc.

Ariadne and the Maenads

In *Ecce Homo* after reproducing the "Night Song," Nietzsche writes:
Nothing like this has ever been written, felt, or *suffered*: thus suffers a god, a Dionysus. The answer to such a dithyramb of solar solitude in the light would be Ariadne.—Who besides me knows what Ariadne is!—For all such riddles nobody so far had any solution; I doubt that anybody even saw any riddles here.[1]

"I did," says Ariadne.

And now, a phantasmatic, seductive discourse takes ahold of these words in relationship to the event of Nietzsche's collapse on that street in Turin as he tearfully embraced the beaten cab-horse. Such a discourse reads between the lines, around the lines, mixing the lines up; it reads out of desire and necessity, out of love and dread. A discourse that wishes to enter into the last years of Nietzsche's existence must be a rhapsodic and not a rational voice, must be a lover's discourse disclosing a love that spans a century, but more unites an eternity. This kind of catastrophic discourse takes the name of Ariadne.

"I, Ariadne, now challenge you with a new shattering question and suggest that the secret and the challenge Nietzsche poses in the dithyramb 'Amid Birds of Prey,' in which he offers himself as 'a riddle for birds of prey' is the very riddle of his 'madness.' My question is a riddle too: Did Nietzsche consciously and with purpose simulate his own 'madness,' take on a 'voluntary death' and offer it as the ultimate event of seduction and challenge? Was Nietzsche's 'madness' a divine drama of self-sacrifice? Did that great one Nietzsche/Dionysus stage his own

45

crucifixion, sacrifice himself dancing and singing, act as judge and executioner,
'self-hanger,' and take on responsibility for an acting part, an incredible role of
'madness'? Did he stage a spectacle of catastrophic proportions? What a world of
malicious and delicious possibilities this opens up!"

Was it simulation of 'madness' that lasted eleven years until his death? And why? Was it the perfect culmination of a Dionysian philosophy by 'becoming' the mad god himself? Was it to seal his antipodal status to the Crucified with his own crucifixion in order to offer humankind a millennial choice between suffering and joy? Was it the greatest seal upon his belief in the eternal recurrence of the same? Was it to herald the stroke of doom to nihilism and the birth of affirmation? Was it to act as example for others to perish in the pursuit of the overhuman? Or, did he withdraw from the world into a 'seventh solitude' where an even further mining of his spiritual self, his hardness and joy, was the goal? Was it that he recognized that his work was at its height and then to 'go mad' was to create the most intense love of one who dies too soon? Or, to state it the other way around, did he feel that he was past his productive peak and thus duty-bound to 'withdraw'? Or did he sentence himself along with Wagner as the two most formidable decadents of their age while promising an affirmative future? Was simulation of madness calculated to protect his works from censorship or to act as the spur toward their notoriety? Or was it simply the movement and command of the will to power that joyed in Nietzsche's heart? These possibilities are seductive and enigmatic and taken together compelling: all are possible, but all are perhaps ultimately unrecoverable.

All of these possibilities of motivation play phantasmatically in and out of what is to follow, but Ariadne is concerned primarily with narrating the *story* of this 'drama of madness' and thus with breaking open the world-historical symbolics of the event—and the multiplicity of its incredible, possible effects. She wants to reexplode the explosion, *recreate* the catastrophe in her own catastrophic discourse and seduction. What effects did Nietzsche want the drama of his 'madness' to invoke? What did he hope from it? What day of decision for humankind did Nietzsche hope to provide through the symbolics of his simulation of 'madness'? What was the great gift and celebration of Nietzsche's 'madness'? Nietzsche's 'madness' as the greatest gift! Joy!

You reply: "But this is madness itself! Even if this were the case, it would be the action of a madman." "But, dear reader, we have not even begun and already you are at the end again! Open yourself to some risk! The dangers of the way may repay you in the end. Again, we are at the boundaries of the critical discourse that only legitimates certain types of action, certain events, events that have at least the semblance of moderation and normalcy. Certain events, whether mad in fact or 'mad' in simulation, must needs be recuperated and rendered impossible or at least harmless in discourses of rationality: in medical, philosophical, psychological, and historical discourses, and in discourses of interpretation and truth. Nothing less than the survival of these discourses is at stake. Catastrophe, seduction, madness: these discourses in themselves are no longer stigmatized in our time, are recognized as discourses, even seem desirable to the few, but are still marginalized as nonhegemonic discourses, their affirmative power fettered. For how long? The event happened! Let us change the discourses! The discourses, whether rational or catastrophic, follow, and follow as events in themselves, both in linear discontinuity from the event and in each moment the same drama."

Ariadne: "Whether the song of seduction I am about to sing speaks a 'truth,' or reflects a phantasmatic desire, or poeticizes a seduction is irrelevant. The effects of my song will reverberate along an endless chain of possibilities."

There is no way to ease ourselves into this labyrinthian riddle; terror accompanies us on all sides. Let us hear some Dionysian maenads dance about this sacrificial idea. Nietzsche writes that "the perfect woman tears to pieces when she loves—I know these charming maenads.—Ah, what a dangerous, creeping, subterranean little beast of prey she is! And yet so agreeable!…Woman is indescribably more evil than man."[2] When the maenads tear to pieces goats and bulls in their Dionysian frenzy, it is the god Dionysus they rend apart—as the necessary prelude to rebirth! "The bloodthirstiness of the maenads is the bloodthirstiness of the god himself." We know Dionysus:

as the wild spirit of antithesis and paradox, of immediate presence and complete remoteness, of bliss and horror, of infinite vitality and the cruelest destruction. The element of bliss in his nature, the creative, enraptured, and blessed elements all share, too, in his wildness and his madness.

Dionysus is the god who is mad. For his sake the maenads are mad. We must not inquire into the reasons why they are distraught and wild, but we must ask, rather, what *divine madness* means.[3]

Divine madness is the cosmic enigma—the mystery of life that is self-generating, self-creating through destruction. The love that races toward the miracle of procreation is touched by madness and death. And what else is Nietzsche, but a catastrophe of forces rushing headlong into destruction as the necessary prelude to creation and procreation!

One of Nietzsche's maenads, Lou Andreas Salomé, gives us his self-sacrifice, but limits it to psychological and religious discourses. She does not allow the event to appear in its full catastrophic character. She comes close but stops short of being seduced.

"The sacrificial animal as God" is truly a title that could be placed over Nietzsche's last philosophy and which most clearly reveals his inner contradictions: an exaltation, mingling pain and bliss. We have seen earlier how Nietzsche's last frame of mind slipped into a celebrative, dream-filled mood of intoxication. We now see the point at which the force of inner stimulation turns into pain. Even in his daily life at that time, he was overwhelmed by a soulfulness in which boisterousness was also possible, since quivering nerves can easily lead to joking and laughter. The immersion in bliss and agony, enthusiasm and suffering, always led Nietzsche toward a spiritual rebirth....The wounding of self and its uprooting from any sense of "home," were conditions within which his spirit luxuriated before they discharged themselves in new creations.

Nietzsche's thoughts sound like a prelude to the shattering drama of his highest ascendance *and* his downfall. Nietzsche's philosophy does not completely lift a curtin on the drama, but its folds show flower threads and, half hidden, the large, sad words—

"*Incipit tragoedia.*"[4]

In the aesthetics and ethics of Nietzsche's last philosophizing, we find again the pervasive theme that a decline through excess is the necessary precondition for a highest and new creation. And therefore, Nietzsche's theory of knowledge culminates in a kind of personal thrall in which the concepts of madness and truth are inextricably entwined. For that reason the idea of the "humanly superior" comes like a lightning stroke which annihilates the spirit, a madness, which ought to inoculate his sense of truth: "I would wish that you possess a madness that destroys you!...Truly, I would wish that your madness were called 'truth'!...And the happiness of the spirit consists of this—to be anointed and sanctified through tears as a sacrificial animal; did you already know this? And the blindness of the blind person and his searching and groping, as before, will be proof of the sun's power, into which he looks; did you already know that?" (Of the Famous Wise Men, Z II)[5]

The human being, in one way, feels mystically expanded into a cosmic totality of life, so that his own decline, as well as his own tragic sense of life, no longer matters; and, in another way, the human being spiritualizes and personalizes symbolically the meaningless and random processes of life, raising himself to the status of divinity. World, God, and I melt into a single concept from which the individual may draw, just as well as from any metaphysics, ethics, or religion, a norm for activity and for highest worship. Behind these formulations lies the premise that cosmos and world are man-made fictions, created by his godlike essence, wholeness, and the richness of life; he knows that conceptual representations rely upon his own creative will and his own minting of values. With this in mind, Nietzsche's mysterious phrases in Beyond Good and Evil [150] become clear: "Around the hero everything turns into a tragedy," meaning that the human being as such, and in his highest development, is exactly a declining and sacrificed being; "around the demigod (everything turns into) a satyr-play," meaning that in man's full yielding to life's totality, he smiles down upon his own fate, like one who has been uplifted; "and, around God everything turns into—what?—perhaps into 'world?'," meaning that through the complete identification of the human being with life, not only will he be taken up into life's totality—reconciled—but also life's totality will be absorbed absolutely by him, so that he becomes a god out of whom the world flows, and who subtly changes his being through the creation of the released world.[6]

Quite early Nietzsche had brooded over the meaning of madness as a possible source for knowledge and its inner sense that may have led the ancients to discern a sign of divine election. In *The Gay Science* he says, "And only the person who can cause fright, can lead others," and in *Daybreak* we find the following strange words that remind one of the representation of the future genius who incorporates the collective history of mankind: "In the outbursts of passion, and in the fantasizings of dreams, and in madness, man rediscovers his own and mankind's prehistory:... his memory reaches back far enough, while his civilized state evolves from the forgetting of primal experiences, from an easing up of that memory. Whoever has most extensively forgotten and remained far from all this does *not understand humans*." [312][7]

And so we see how self-sacrifice and self-ravaging not only heightened his self-induced inner conflicts to the extremity of his spirit but also how these infused even the most personal aspects of Nietzsche. In ever more pronounced fashion, his entire line of thought peaks to a self-destructive *deed* through which, by continuing to act and endure, his redemption was to be completed....Zarathustra's redeeming world-action becomes at the same time Nietzsche's decline; Zarathustra's divine right to interpret life and to revaluate all values is only achieved at the cost of entering into that primal ground of life that in Nietzsche's human existence reveals itself as the dark depth of madness.[8]

The picture of madness stands at the end of Nietzsche's philosophy, like a shrill and terrible illustration of theoretical knowledge and of the conclusions drawn from it for his philosophy of the future, because the point of departure is formed by dissolving everything intellectual and letting drive-like chaos dominate. Nietzsche's theory of knowledge, however, goes beyond the decline of the knower and conceives a revelation by life, inoculated by madness.

Madness was to bear witness also to the power of life's truth through whose brilliance the human spirit is blinded. For no power of *reason* leads into the depths of life in its fullness. It does not permit a climbing into its fullness step by step or thought by thought.[9]

In this manner, height and depth, the abyss of madness and the peak of truth's essence, become swallowed up in one another: "I stand before my highest mountain...and therefore must descend deeper than ever." And so the highest self-deification first celebrates its total mystical victory in the most profound self-destruction, in capitulation and in the decline of the knower.[10]

The great thing which Nietzsche knew was that he was going under, and yet with a laughing mouth and "rose-wreath crowned" he parted from life, absolving and justifying and transfiguring it. In the *Dionysian Dithyrambs*, the sounds of his life's spirit faded away, and the intended jubilation of the dithyrambs was drowned out by a cry of pain. They are the last ravings of Nietzsche by Zarathustra.[11]

Ariadne: "No, Lou, this was not a cry of pain; it was joy in the anticipation of Ariadne. Though you saw the event and its possibilities, you chose to stop at pain, resentment. Did you forget your own 'Prayer to Life' that Nietzsche loved and praised so greatly to the last? 'If you have no more happiness to give me, well then! You still have suffering!' What does this mean, Lou, but that suffering can also be happiness? The Dionysus Dithyrambs are not ravings, Lou; rather they are a supreme riddle in song."

Lou was as close to being an actual lover of Nietzsche as was possible. But Luce Irigaray also *styles* herself a lover of Nietzsche. She takes on the role of maenad in *Marine Lover of Friedrich Nietzsche* where she, too, tears Nietzsche to pieces in contrasting Dionysus with Christ. In her lament she sees that the marriage of Dionysus and Ariadne is imminent. She sees the possibility of the androgeny, the marriage, but she is not ready to enact the wedding herself because of the vestments of resentment. She is a maenad fettered by patriarchal gravity.

"It was left to me," says Ariadne. "I do the necessary. The seed that was planted in me years ago, centuries ago, now bears fruit. The world can now hear this deed, can even begin to herald that which must come as Nietzsche knew that it must come. Noon, highest moment of self-reflection. Midday and Eternity. The arrow finds its mark!"

Irigaray writes:

The perfection of love between son and Father, with its completion in a Trinity, schematizes to an extreme degree the relationship underpinning the foundation and development of the ontotheology. In which Christ is resolved or not resolved. Is enclosed or runs loose. Dies as God, or is at last at hand.

If this figure of love must continue to be unique, remaining eternally captive to the lure of a (male) Same, what use is it to dig it up today? Has it not already had any effect it is going to have? Is it not the pattern for the mask that completes, to the point of inappearance, man's identity with himself? The dream of becoming the self without contradictions, of reabsorbing into the self all things opposed and different, of subsuming under the self the transcendent of oneself. Of one day finally being divinely the self.

There would be nothing there but love of self. Therefore, no love? Christ would not be Dionysus's latterday twin, but a monster of egoism, a Narcissus who ends up reabsorbing his highest idea or ideal into Himself.

But why a god of love, given the effects and the illustrations we know about? Unless exclusive love of the Father is only a partial translation of his message? Unless the nonconflictual fulfillment of this relationship to the Other left a place for the other? The life of Christ, perhaps, cannot be reduced to the *pathein* of the Father's will. It would open the way for the transcendence of the other that has always been covered over by the Father-son paradigm. Whereby love, desire, creation within the same, sparing Distance or Difference all the more because, in some measure, they do not exist. The abyss opens up because they are not revealed.

Nietzsche—perhaps—has experienced and shown what is the result of infinite distance reabsorbed into the (male) same, shown the difference that remains without a face or countenance. By wishing to overcome everything, he plunges into the shadows—lit up and with no perspective. As he becomes the whole of the world's time, he has no point of view left that would allow him to see. Ariadne, or Diotima, or…no longer even return his mask or his gaze. He is mask and blinded eye. Once his creation is realized, he lives it. And nothing else. There is no other that might allow him to continue to make himself flesh. No other to set the limits of his corporeal identity with and for him, putting his latest thought into the background so a new one can be born.

"No one but I", says Ariadne. "Luce also sees the catastrophic involution of the event of Nietzsche's 'madness,' but sees it as the exclusion of the female other. But Luce has not seen the opening writ large by Nietzsche, the opening inviting female chance to fly to him—she has not seen the wedding banns posted by him. She is the unrequited lover who is her own unrequiter."

The sacrifice he makes to the Idea is inscribed in this—that he preferred the Idea to an ever provisional openness to a female other. That he refused to break the mirror of the (male) same, and over and over again demanded that the other be his double. To the point of willing to become that female other. Despite all physiology, all incarnation. Hermit, tightrope walker or bird, forgetful of her who gave him birth and company and nourishment, he soars up, leaving everything below him or inside him, and the chasm becomes bottomless.

And what would Ariadne's or Diotima's or anyone else's "yes" have changed? Nothing in his thinking. Unless a woman refuses to be woman, at least according to his definition. Asserts her difference. Therefore not Ariadne, that abyss for his passion.

"Wrong again. Luce, you have not plumbed the depths of Nietzsche's woman."

Apollonian partner? Setting him up once and for all as a work of art? Paralyzing him in his Dionysian becoming. Insoluble fate. Sensing the impotence to come, Nietzsche declares he is the crucified one. And is crucified. But by himself.

"By himself, but calling to Ariadne."

Either Christ overwhelms that tragedy, or Nietzsche overcomes Christ. By repeating-parodying the Christian advent, what does he unmask in his gesture? That Christ is nothing that still deserves to live, or that his age is yet to come?

This reevaluation is possible only if he goes beyond the Father-son relationship. If he announces—beyond Christianity? —that only through difference can the incarnation unfold without murderous or suicidal passion. Rhythm and measure of a female other that, endlessly, undoes the autological circle of discourse, thwarts the eternal return of the same, opens up every horizon through the affirmation of another point of view whose fulfillment can never be predicted. That is always dangerous? A gay science of the incarnation?

"But Luce, Nietzsche did know that only a woman could provide (the genitals do not matter) affirmation and such an incarnation!"

To which the female side would, up to now, have served only as a protective shadow. Setting up perspective, through a kind of resistance to the already-existing light. Never desired or loved for herself, but forming a screen for the dazzling and blinding collusion of Father-son. A reminder that man comes from the earth-mother, that he returns to her, and that at each step a shadow walks by his side.

The will to leap over that shadow or to lend her light that does not suit her, amounts once again to belittling her as other. To entering into autistic madness. Making oneself the only God. If that Idol means the whole of love, then love always amounts to a murder—the murder of the other. Which remains a crime whether or not it is sublimated under a capital letter as Difference or Distance. Which consecrates crime. Glorifying it despite, or within, the sacrifice once more subsumed into the same. Thanks to the passion of the "son" perhaps?

"Oh woman of resentment, perhaps you are the virgin sacrifice, unloved, perhaps you are the virgin sacrifice on the altar of patriarchy. But not I!" says Ariadne. "The murder of the other and the murder by the others, the maenads, of God—

not for the 'Son' but for life! Nietzsche/Dionysus seduces me into becoming his murderer in love. I am to be the vintager to his vine, I am to wield the knife. I am not his double, his shadow—I am Ariadne, his unfathomable, but adored one without which he knew he was incomplete and with which he becomes humanly divine. Dionysus/Ariadne, we immolate each other, but together. Tear each other to pieces to rise again. Has Nietzsche ever been an adversary to this kind of crime? Has he not said, 'has my definition of love been heard? It is the only one worthy of a philosopher. Love—in its means, war; at bottom, the deadly hatred of the sexes.'"[12]

But doesn't his cross mark the impossibility of any relationship to the other? The love that ebbs backward into sameness, unable to either give or receive. To exchange or pattern oneself among different bodies, words, flesh? The lonely fading away of a gesture that was motivated also by the other? And plunges down into the abyss, rather than surrender.

"Nietzsche creates the abyss precisely for this surrender. But not the surrender you desire, Luce. Surrender to or of the other, relationship, is that which is not possible. It is phantasm—always desired. Nietzsche's 'Night Song,' the song of solar solitude sung by a suffering god, has as its center the hard truth that each of us, mortal or divine, has the greatest difficulty in bridging that 'smallest gap' to the other. And now we understand that the arrow loosed from Nietzsche's bow must be caught in midflight by Ariadne and plunged into her own heart. That our love as androgyns can unite us only in the powerful world of phantasm, though never or only momentarily in the flesh. Therefore, an answer to the 'Night Song' coming from a woman complete in herself, a sun who drinks back into herself the flames that break out of her, must consummate the love in the union of that phantasmatic world that is itself an abyss and peak of seductions and surrenderings."

Is the Crucified One [here, Nietzsche] the sign of such an economy of love and desire? To interpret him therefore means "go beyond" if possible without return. Not be satisfied with such a love. Leave it to the men of ressentiment, and try to create another world. And if it is another love that he heralds, then deliver him from his masks of death, and set him once more in his flesh.

"I do," cries Ariadne.

Men—perhaps—know no other way to the divine, even if some sense it nostalgically. The immediate coming of the god brings them nothing but madness or paralysis. And as they constantly back away from such a sudden experience of the divine, they measure up only to themselves, even in regard to their God. Measuring out the path that marks the boundary of their world. From hell to Heaven.

A love that knows no other. Except as a foundation or shadow for an idea of self that never puts itself on display in a simple way. The other would be merely one of the masks of the same. One figure, one face, one sort of presence accompanying man's becoming. Sometimes tragic, sometimes serenely contemplative. Now dark with shadows, now beaming forth an excess of light as it waits to be disposed in new landscapes. In hollow, in lack or in excess, man would perceive and receive nothing except from his own eye.

"Nor would woman, Luce."

The other has yet to enlighten him. To tell him something. Even to appear to him in her irreducibility. The impossibility of overcoming her. And if, to the whole of himself, he says "yes" and also asks her to say "yes" again, did it ever occur to him to say "yes" to her? Did he ever open himself to that other world? For him it doesn't even exist. So who speaks of love, to the other without having even begun to say "yes"?

"But Nietzsche has! Dionysus the god of death and life cannot be conceived of as coming without woman! He is from woman, with woman, and returns to woman. Nietzsche's affirmation, his Yes to Ariadne, can only be affirmed by the second affirmation of Ariadne's Yes!"

To "go beyond." Or decode the Christic symbol beyond any traditional morality. To read, in it, the fruit of the covenant between word and nature, between logos and cosmos. A marriage that has never been consummated.[13]

"Until now," replies Ariadne.

Our third ecstatic, another maenad, Georges Bataille, writes a note entitled "Nietzsche's Madness."

On January 3, 1889,

fifty years ago,

Nietzsche succumbed to madness:

on the Carlo-Alberto Piazza, in Turin,

he threw himself, sobbing, about the neck of a beaten horse,

then collapsed;

he thought, when he woke up, that he was

DIONYSUS

or

THE CRUCIFIED.

This event

has to be commemorated

as a tragedy.

"When a living thing,"

Zarathustra said,

"takes charge of itself,

it is necessary that the living thing

expiate its authority

and be judge, avenger and

VICTIM

of its own laws."

I

We want to commemorate a tragic event and we are now here, sustained by life. The starry sky stretches above our heads and the earth turns under our feet. Life is in our bodies, but death is at work in our bodies as well (even from a distance a man can always sense the coming of the last gasp before death). Above us, day takes over night, and night day. And yet, we speak, we speak out loud, without knowing what kind of beings we are. And of the one who does not speak following the rules of language, the reasonable men that we have to be guarantee that he is *mad.*

We are ourselves afraid of going *mad* and we observe the rules with great unease. After all, the deleria of madmen are classified and repeated with a monotony such that what is produced is an extreme boredom. The lack of attraction in the demented insures the seriousness and severity of logic. Yet the philosopher in his discourse, which "mirrors the empty sky," is less honest as a mirror than the madman, in which case, perhaps, he should be done away with.

Ariadne: "Georges, you, at least, speak honestly and clearly. You know that when someone goes mad, the rational ones use discourses of psychiatry to shield themselves from the fear that they, too, might go mad, lose themselves. And why are they afraid? Is there something in madness that lures them? Is it both seductive and terrifying? Is it Dionysus? Is it themselves?"

This inquiry cannot be taken *seriously,* since if wise, it would immediately cease to have a meaning. Yet it is resolutely foreign to the spirit of joking. For it is also necessary for us to know the sweat of suffering. Under what pretext not let yourself be embraced to the point of sweating? The absence of sweat is much more dishonest than the jokes of he who sweats. He who is called wise is the philosopher, but he does not exist independently of a group of men. This group is made up of a few philosophers who tear one another apart and of an either inert or agitated mob which ignores the philosophers.

At this point, those who sweat in *obscurity* run up against those who see history in the making as rendering the meaning of human life transparent. For it is true that the history of mobs exterminating one another gives consequence to the incompatibility of philosophies—in the form of dialogues which are carnages. But the finish is just as much a battle as a birth and, beyond the finish and the battle, what remains other than death? Beyond the words that tear themselves apart without end, what remains other than a silence that drives one mad thanks to sweat and laughter?

But if all men—or more simply their entire existence— WERE INCARNATED in a single being—obviously just as alone and abandoned as the group—the head of the INCARNATED ONE would be the place of a battle with no end—and so violent that sooner or later it would explode into little pieces. It would be difficult to understand the intensity of the storm or of release experienced in the visions of this incarnated one. He must see God but at the same moment must kill him, then become God himself but only in order to immediately hurry into nothingness. He would then find himself to be a man just as deprived of meaning as the next only without any possibility of rest.

Ariadne: "Yes!"

He would not, in effect, be able to settle for thinking and speaking, for an interior need would constrain him to live what he thinks and what he says. Such an incarnated one would thus know a freedom so great that no language would suffice to reproduce its movement (and dialectic, no more than others). Human thought by itself, incarnated in this way, would become a festival where intoxication and freedom would be no less released than the feeling of the tragic and suffering. This leads to the recognition—without leaving any way out—that the "incarnated man" would *also* have to go mad.

Ariadne: "This is phantasm, great seduction!"

How violently the Earth turns for him inside his head! To what degree he could be crucified! What a bacchanal it could be (in the background those who would be afraid of seeing his...)! But how lonely he would become as Caesar, all-powerful and as sacred as a man could be, so that no one could behold him without bursting into tears. What if..., how could God not sicken before the incarnate one at discovering his own rational powerlessness to understand madness?

January 3, 1939

Ariadne: "Yes, Georges, would not God himself be jealous of such a one!"

II

But it is not enough to express a violent movement in this way: the sentences would be the betrayal of the initial impulse if they were not linked to desires and to decisions which are their reason for being alive. Now it is easy to see that a representation of madness in the final analysis cannot have a direct effect: no one can voluntarily destroy in himself the expressive apparatus that attaches him to others—like one bone to other bones.

Ariadne: "The expressiveness does not die with the body; the effect reverberates eternally."

One of Blake's proverbs says that *if others had not gone mad, we would have to have gone mad ourselves.* Madness cannot be banished outside the *whole* of humanity, which cannot be complete without the madman. Nietzsche having gone crazy— instead of us—thus makes this wholeness possible; and the madmen who lost their minds before him were not able to do so as brilliantly. But can the gift a man makes of his madness for his peers be accepted by them without it being returned with interest? And if it is not the unreasonableness of he who receives the madness of another like a royal bequest, what could possibly be the response in kind?

There is another proverb: *He who desires but does not act feeds pestilence.* Without any doubt, the highest degree of pestilence is attained when the expression of desire is confused with action.

For if a man begins to follow a violent impulsion, the fact that he expresses it signifies that he gives up following it at least during the time of its expression. Expression requires that passion be substituted by the exterior sign that figures it. He who expresses himself thus has to pass from the hot sphere of passions to the relatively cold and sonambulant sphere of signs. In the presence of the expressed thing, one always has to ask oneself if he who expresses himself does not prepare himself with a deep sleep. Such a questioning should be conducted with unwavering rigor.

Ariadne: "It is *not* either *language* or *the act of madness, Georges. It can be language (verbal paganism) as act/event and act as linguistic ritual. Again, not art or madness but both!*"

He who finally has understood that only madness can fulfill man, is thus lucidly led to choose—not between madness and sanity—but between the deception of "a nightmare that justifies snores" and the will to take charge of oneself and triumph. No betrayal of what he has discovered in the explosions and rendings apart at the summit seem to him any more despicable than the deleria of art. *For if it is true that the achievement of his destiny requires its loss—the necessary consequence of madness or death in his opinion threaten to produce a festival—the very love of life and destiny commands that he commit inside himself the crime of* authority *that he will expiate.* This is what makes the destiny to which the feeling of extreme chance ties him necessary.

Moving thus, to begin with, from powerless delirium to power—even though he has in the solution of his life moved in reverse from power to some collapse, sudden or slow—his years can no longer go on except in the—impersonal—search for force. In the moment where the wholeness of life appeared to him as linked to the tragedy that ends it, he was able to perceive how much this revelation was capable of weakening. He was able to see around him those who were near the secret—who thus represent the true "salt" or "meaning" of the earth—give themselves over to the dissimulated sleep of literature or art. The lot of human existence thus appears to him linked to a small number of beings deprived of any possibility of strength. For certain men carry in themselves much more than, in their moral fall, they believe they carry: when the mob around them and

those that represent the mob are necessarily enslaved to everything they touch. He who has grown up in the rigor of tragedy
thus has to teach rigor to his peers. He has to lead them to
organize, to stop being, compared to fascists and Christians,
inconsequential rags. He has to bring them out of their sleep,
tear them away from their literary gargle. It is necessary to make
them understand that they are empowered to impose opportunity
on servile humanity, opportunity meaning that they become
what they are, but without having the necessary, lucid and
consequent resolve which poses the question of life and death.[14]

*Ariadne: "Georges, you understand Nietzsche's 'madness' as a pointer to a day
of decision for humans. Will they sleep in the dream of oppression and resentment
morality or awaken to the power of madness that is the risk of life?"*

Thus, all three maenads, Bacchants, suffer through the enigma of
Nietzsche's self-sacrifice. They have all written their phantasmatic discourses. Nietzsche, the sacrificial animal as prelude to a highest spiritual
rebirth and creation. Nietzsche, the possibility of a new god that incorporates woman. Nietzsche, the incarnated one who dies out of sovereignty
as example to others. But, for each, resentment still bars the way to their
god: Lou can describe but not embrace madness; Luce will not let herself
believe that Nietzsche could love a woman; Bataille sees the demand that
he should risk madness, he even sees that it would be "pestilence" not to
embrace it, and yet he stops short of the deed. Bataille's passion, anguish,
and sweat to follow Nietzsche not only in expression but in deed as well far
outweigh that of our other two Bacchants. Bataille opens the preface to his
book, *On Nietzsche*:

> I write, I suppose, out of fear of going mad.
> I suffer from a fiery, painful yearning, which persists, like desire
> unslaked, within me.
> My tension is, in a sense, like that of a mad impulse to laughter;
> it differs little from the passions that inflamed Sade's heroes, and
> yet it approaches that of the martyrs or of saints.[15]

*Ariadne: "Yes, this is the gate to Nietzsche's labyrinth. Only those in such a state
will come close to the Dionysian sacrifice and riddle."*

These three maenads, even Bataille, do not see the other side of the terror of Dionysus and thus ultimately reject that terror itself. To fall in love is to risk transforming terror into its opposite. Otto, a true Bacchant and maenad, writes of the women of Dionysus:

> This should now prepare us for a proper understanding of the spirit of the love which dwells in the hearts of the women of Dionysus. There is nothing so foreign to the orgiastic dancers of the god as unrestrained erotic sensuality....the maenads are characterized by a stateliness and a haughty aloofness, and their wildness has nothing to do with the lustful excitement found in the half-animal, half-human companions who whirl around them....The Bacchant pays no attention to the silenus who grabs at her in his lust; the image of Dionysus, whom she loves, stands alive before her; for the glances of the Bacchant sweep up high into the aether and yet are filled with the spirit of love.[16]

Thus, the din and terror of the god, though clothed in orgy, madness, and murder reveal, on the other side of that terror, the quiet and enraptured soul of a lover. In a note for *Zarathustra* Nietzsche writes: "Sexual love as a means toward an ideal (Striving to go down in one's opposite.) Love for the suffering godhead. To transform the figure of death as a means of victory and triumph."[17]

Ariadne: "Come, come, you intrepid sailors on wide seas, come into the eye of the storm, into the labyrinth. Only there can the wedding of Ariadne and Dionysus take place."

Notes

1. Nietzsche, *Ecce Homo*, p. 308.
2. Ibid., p. 266.
3. Otto, *Dionysus Myth and Cult*, pp. 135–36.
4. Lou Andreas-Salomé, *Nietzsche*, trans. Siegfried Mandel (Redding Ridge, Conn.: Black Swan Books, 1988), pp. 89–90. Reprinted with permission of the publisher.
5. Ibid., pp. 99–100.
6. Ibid., p. 137.

7. Ibid., pp. 145–46.

8. Ibid., p. 148.

9. Ibid., p. 150.

10. Ibid., p. 152.

11. Ibid., p. 158.

12. Nietzsche, *Ecce Homo*, p. 267.

13. Luce Irigaray, *Marine Lover*, trans. Gillian Gill (New York: Columbia University Press, 1991), pp. 186–90. Reprinted with permission of the publisher.

14. Georges Bataille, "La folie de Nietzsche," *Oeuvres Completes*, Tome I (Paris: Editions Gallimard, 1970); "Nietzsche's Madness," trans. Kimball Lockhardt; emphasis added.

15. Georges Bataille, *On Nietzsche*, trans Bruce Boone (New York: Paragon House, 1992).

16. Otto, *Dionysus Myth and Cult*, p. 177.

17. Nietzsche, KSA, Vol. 10, 21.

Roundelay with Chaos:
In Answer to the "Night Song"
Ariadne, Sa'di, and Dionysus

Love, Intoxication, Madness. These are the three doors to perception of the divine. And who enters at these three doors? The lover, the intoxicated one, the mad one. Ah, the hand of these caress carefully the sensuous contours of the eternal formlessness.

Why wonder at the farers on the Way
When they're engulfed beneath Idea's Sea?
In passion for the Soulmate's soul, they're careless of their own.
In recollection of the Beloved, careless of the world;

Mindful of the Truth alone, they flee His creation,
So drunk with the Cupbearer, they spill their wine;

and laughing cry:

'Am I not...?' Sounds from everlasting's ever in their ears,
While they cry out the call of 'Yea!'

All of nature's excess in pleasure, grief, and knowledge become audible, even in piercing shrieks. Excess reveals itself as truth. Contradiction, the bliss born of pain, speaks from the very heart of nature. In this magic transformation the Dionysian reveler sees himself as a satyr and as a satyr, in turn, he sees the god.

For where there's 'companion' and where there's 'self,' there's also polytheism!

*The lovers, the intoxicated ones, the mad ones. Ah, now the hand of
these caress the full rounded bosom of the all one.*

*Such ones are scattered under heaven,
And may be called 'wild-beasts'—but also 'angels':
They are Prudent-insane, and sober-drunk!*

*And in them the image of the lyricist is nothing but his very self and as
it were only different projections of himself, so he, as the moving center
of this world, may say "I": of course this self is not the same as that of
the waking, empirically real man, but the only truly existent and
eternal self resting at the basis of things.*

*The lovers, the intoxicated ones, the mad ones. Ah! Their bodies press
themselves ardently against the fecund loins of Bliss.*

*Awhile they repose in corners, stitching their cloaks,
Then they're excited in a gathering, their cloaks afire!*

*Desert-traversers who need no caravan;
Rare ones, from the eyes of men all covered up—*

*Full of fruit, shade-giving like the vine—
Their heads they bow within themselves, as does the pearl-shell—*

*Associated in the privy-place of 'Am I not?'
Drunk on one draught till the trumpet's blast;
Their hands are not withdrawn from what they purpose—not even for
a sword!—
For restraint and love are but as glass and stone!*

*To our humiliation and exultation, one thing above all must be clear.
This foreplay with chaos, this art is neither performed for our
betterment or education nor are we the true authors of this art, this
chaos. We are merely images and artistic projections and have our
highest dignity in our significance as our own works of art,
phantasms, seductions—as our own catastrophe.*

*Do we not know as lovers, intoxicated ones and mad ones that we are
ourselves the divine wine of existence which we ourselves drink, that
we are ourselves the eternal body of bliss which we caress and press so
ardently in order to climax in the dance god?*[1]

Notes

1. Excerpts freely rendered from Nietzsche, *Birth of Tragedy* and *The Bustan of Sa'di*, trans. G. M. Wickens (Toronto: University of Toronto Press, 1974), pp. 100–105 and poeticized by Ariadne.

Drama, Tragedy, and Woman

As Narrative (Novel, Passion), love is a story which is accomplished, in the sacred sense of the word: it is a *program* which must be completed. For me, on the contrary, this story has *already taken place*; for what is event is exclusively the delight of which I have been the object and whose aftereffects I repeat (and fail to achieve). Enamoration is a *drama*, if we restore to this word the archaic meaning Nietzsche gives it: "Ancient drama envisioned great declamatory scenes, which excluded action (action took place *before* or *behind* the stage)." Amorous seduction (a pure hypnotic moment) takes place *before* discourse and *behind* the proscenium of consciousness: the amorous "event" is of a hieratic order: it is my own local legend, my little sacred history that I declaim to myself, and this declamation of a *fait accompli* (frozen, embalmed, removed from any *praxis*) is the lover's discourse.[1]

Drama

In *Nietzsche contra Wagner* Nietzsche, in writing about Wagner's art, makes some important distinctions between theater and drama:

> What is the theater to me? What, the convulsions of his "moral" ecstasies which give the people—and who is not "people"?—satisfaction? What, the whole gesture hocus-pocus of the actor? It is plain that I am essentially anti-theatrical: confronted with the theater, this mass art par excellence, I feel that profound scorn at the bottom of my soul which every artist today feels. *Success*; in the theater—with that one drops in my respect forever; *failure*—I prick up my ears and begin to respect.[2]

The theater is nothing for Nietzsche, but drama, that is something else. In a note to section 9 of *The Case of Wagner*, Nietzsche writes the following on drama to which Barthes refers above:

> It has been a real misfortune for aesthetics that the word drama has always been translated "action." It is not Wagner alone who errs at this point, the error is world-wide and extends even to the philologists who ought to know better. Ancient drama aimed at scenes of great *pathos*—it precluded action (moving it *before* the beginning or *behind* the scene). The word *drama* is of Doric origin, and according to Doric usage it means "event," "story"— both words in the hieratic sense. The most ancient drama represented the legend of the place, the "holy story" on which the foundation of the cult rested (not a doing but a happening: *dran* in Doric actually does not mean "do").[3]

Therefore, if Nietzsche values the theatrical and spectacular seductions of phantasm and catastrophe, they are a mask of appearance behind which the drama, the appearance of the event lies, itself a secret and challenge. A 'mad' play with logic and chance. In the text of section 9 Nietzsche writes:

> Drama requires *rigorous* logic: but what did Wagner ever care about logic?...We know which technical problem requires all of the dramatist's powers and often makes him sweat blood: making the *knot* necessary, and the resolution as well, so both will be possible in one way only while giving the impression of freedom (the principle of the least exertion of energy)....[Wagner] was not enough of a psychologist for drama.[4]

The Gordian knot is the same as the great archer's arrow. Tying a knot, shooting an arrow in such a way that the recipient of arrow and knot can only respond the way in which the knot tier and archer wishes. This may be the real *wonder* of Nietzsche's drama of 'madness' and evidence of his claim to be the greatest of psychologists and a psychologist of women, too.

If *The Case of Wagner* and *Nietzsche contra Wagner* have a function over and above their condemnation of Germans and German culture, it is to take Wagner as actor as antipode to Nietzsche as actor. Wagner is all show, action, sensation, wants to win over the masses. Nietzsche's act of voluntary 'madness' is real, takes place in absolute solitude. It is an action for very few ears, perhaps only one. It does not want immediate effects but awaits a ripening of the few who will create its effects through its passionate declamation. The *act* of 'madness' took place off stage. Now that Ariadne has discovered it, the declamation may begin.

Again, in *The Case of Wagner*, Nietzsche contrasts Wagner's theater with the tone of his own drama.

> In the midst of Wagner's multiplicity, abundance, and arbitrariness they feel as if justified in their own eyes—"redeemed." Trembling, they hear how the *great symbols* approach from foggy distances to resound in his art with muted thunder; they are not impatient when at times things are gray, gruesome, and cold. After all, they are, without exception, like Wagner himself, *related* to such bad weather, German weather! Wotan is their god: but Wotan is the god of bad weather.
>
> They are quite right, these German youths, considering what they are like: how *could* they miss what we others, *we halcyons*, miss in Wagner—*la gaya scienza*, light feet, wit, fire, grace; the great logic; the dance of the stars; the exuberant spirituality; the southern shivers of light; the *smooth sea*—perfection.[5]

Nietzsche's drama is this great logic, his Gordian knot waiting to be untied. "Yes, dear reader, let us shake some of the customary gravity from our shoulders that weighs us down and relates us to bad weather and follow the dance of the stars."

Montesquieu gives his heroes and great men the right to surrender themselves to death in that he says it shall be left to every man to end the fifth act of his tragedy as he sees fit. Nietzsche writes his tragedy and in the fourth act he voluntarily 'goes mad' behind the scenes while shooting his solar arrow. Nietzsche's fifth and final act, the wedding of Dionysus and Ariadne, he left to chance and the future. Nietzsche was the greatest dramatist! He had been writing variations of the tragedy of his own downgoing over and over from 1870 through 1887 as we find in David Farrell Krell's book *Postponements*.

Empedocles

In 1870–71 Nietzsche draws up plans for a drama, *Empedocles*. Empedocles is "the tragic philosopher." He sees the people of the earth as fallen gods and the earth itself as gloomy and corrupt. The best and noblest drive is the trait of a "longing for the same." "As such the drive toward unification is an early emblem of eternal recurrence and its grand affirmation," Krell writes. He quotes Nietzsche on Empedocles: "Now, the properly Empedoclean thought is the *unity of everything that loves*: it is *one* part of all things, compelling them to intercourse and unification. Yet there is also an inimical power that tears them apart. From their struggle results all coming to be and passing away."[6]

The Empedocles drama is one in which the famed philosopher ends his life by jumping into the volcano Etna to save the people. In all versions a woman is with him. Thus, Empedocles' death is bound up with three events which, in somewhat altered form, will continue to structure Nietzsche's drama: the announcement of rebirth, the madness and sacrifice of the philosopher for healing the people, and the presence of a woman or friend who dies with him.

Krell quotes Nietzsche's third and last fragment of the first cluster of notes for the Empedocles drama in which:

> Empedocles, compelled through all the stages, religion, art, science; bringing science to dissolution, he turns against himself. Departure from religion, through the insight that it is deception. Now joy in artistic semblance, driven from it by the recognized sufferings of the world. Woman as nature. Now he observes the sufferings of the world like an anatomist, becomes *tyrannos*, uses religion and art, becomes steadily harder. He resolves to annihilate his people, because he has seen that they cannot be healed. The people are gathered about the crater: he grows mad, and before he vanishes proclaims the truth of rebirth. A friend dies with him.[7]

The correspondences with Nietzsche's thinking and life are obvious. The first of eight fragments that form the central cluster of the notes for the Empedocles drama reads:

Greek memorial festival. Signs of collapse. Outbreak of plague. The Homeric rhapsode. Empedocles appears as a god in order to heal. Infection with fear and pity. Antidote: tragedy. When one of the minor characters dies, the heroine tries to go to him. Enflamed, Empedocles holds her back; she grows ardent for him. Empedocles shudders before the face of nature.

The plague spreads.

Final day of the festival—sacrifice of Pan on Etna. Empedocles puts him to the test and obliterates him. The people flee. The heroine remains. In an excess of pity Empedocles wants to die. He goes into the breach, managing to shout, "Flee!"—She: Empedocles! and then follows him.[8]

Here the friend who dies with him is the heroine for whom he conceives a passion and who conceives a passion for him. Ancient sources attest to the importance of an event in Empedocles' life involving a woman named Panthia. Throughout the many versions of the Empedocles drama that Nietzsche wrote, he varies the theme of this woman. In both fragments above the woman appears to represent nature. Another fragment that sets out the five acts of the drama in more detail reads as follows:

I. Morning at twilight. [1.] Pausanias [i.e., the beloved pupil of Empedocles] bears a wreath to Corinna. The watchman tells of his [i.e., Empedocles'] appearances (Etna). 2. a group of country people arrive; a girl, fantasizing over Empedocles, suddenly dies. 3. Corinna sees the horrified Pausanias. Scene of assuagement. They reiterate their roles: on the verge of his major statement Pausanias grows taciturn and gloomy, cannot remember. 4. A plaintive procession, lyrical. 5. A scene among the people, fear of the plague. 6. The rhapsode. 7. Empedocles, with sacramental vessels; Pausanias in horror at his feet. The day grows bright. Corinna toward Empedocles.

II. At the council. Empedocles veiled before an altar. The councilmen arrive one by one, cheerful, until each is affrighted by the veiled one. "The plague is in your midst! Be Greeks!" Fear and pity prohibited. Ludicrous scene in the council. Agitation among the people. The hall is taken by storm. The royal crown proffered. Empedocles orders the tragedy to be performed,

consoles them on Etna, is revered. The tragedy is performed: Corinna's shudder.
III. The Chorus.
Pausanias and Corinna. Theseus and Ariadne.
Empedocles and Corinna on stage.
Mortal turmoil among the people when rebirth is proclaimed. He is revered as the god Dionysus, whereas he once again begins to feel pity. The actor who is playing Dionysus ridiculously infatuated with Corinna.
The two murderers, who carry off the corpse. Raging lust for destruction in Empedocles, enigmatically announced.
IV. Empedocles' proclamation concerning the coming evening's feast. Turmoil among the people, who feel secure because of their god's epiphany.
The elderly mother and Korinna.
Supreme calming effect
In Corinna's house. Empedocles returns, gloomy.
V. Empedocles among his pupils.
Nocturnal celebration.
Mystic speech on pity. Annihilation of the drive to existence; death of Pan.
Flight of the people. Two lava streams; they cannot escape! Empedocles and Corinna. Empedocles feels like a murderer, deserving of unending punishment; he hopes for a rebirth of penitential death. This drives him to Etna. He wants to rescue Korinna. An animal approaches them. Korinna dies with him. "Does Dionysus flee in the face of Ariadne?"[9]

Here the role of Panthia has been taken by Corinna. Corinna was a renowned lyricist. She was added as the tenth poet to the Alexandrian canon of the nine lyric poets; Ovid named the central figure of his love elegies after her; and Pausanias saw in Tanagra the monument set up in her honor. Pausanius was an Alexandrian sophist.[10] Here in these early plans Dionysus and Ariadne already take roles. Empedocles still dies in the hope of rebirth, though a rebirth of penitence. Corinna, the poetess, dies with him. Is he flying from Ariadne? Dionysus loves Corinna. Is Corinna Ariadne? Krell writes: "Is it conceivable that the great god Dionysus, ostensibly accustomed to tugging mortals by their ears, is nonetheless all the while and without respite or assuagement fleeing...Ariadne? The mother of tragedy? Pausanias, Empedocles, Corinna; Theseus, Dionysus, Ariadne. Hero, god, and mortal. The mortal in each case woman. The woman in each case nature."[11]

The Zarathustra Drama: Parts 1 through 4

In each of the sketches of the Empedocles drama, Empedocles not only goes mad and/or dies but wants to die. There seems to be some mystery connected with his death. The sacrifice of Pan symbolizes the annihilation of the drive to life, and the announcement of rebirth is followed by the death of Empedocles and a woman. Krells' study of notes for *Thus Spoke Zarathustra* very convincingly demonstrates that *Zarathustra* is largely worked out through a continuation of these early themes in the Empedocles drama.

In the notes for *Zarathustra* Nietzsche intends for Zarathustra to die in the same manner as did Empedocles, but in the published version, Zarathustra does not die. In Part I Zarathustra talks of those who perish on the way to the overhuman, but Zarathustra does not go under, but back to his solitude. In the final episode of Part I, "On the Gift Giving Virtue," Zarathustra cautions his disciples to be wary of him. Perhaps he has betrayed them. Part II ends with "The Stillest Hour." Here his mistress, the stillest hour, utters the voiceless cry, "What do you matter, Zarathustra? Speak your word and break!"[12] Yet Zarathustra does not collapse; again he goes to embrace his solitude. In Part III after Zarathustra sees the shepherd who has spit the snake from his throat laughing the laughter of the overhuman he says: "Oh, how can I bear to go on living! And how could I bear to die now!"[13] In the episode "The Convalescent," near the end of Part III, Zarathustra's animals beg him not to die and they announce the eternal return:

> And if you wanted to die now, O Zarathustra, behold we know how you would then speak to yourself. But your animals beg you not to die yet. You would speak, without trembling but breathing deeply with happiness, for a great weight and sultriness would be taken from you who are most patient.

"Now I die and vanish," you would say, "and all at once I am nothing. The soul is as mortal as the body. But the knot of causes in which I am entangled recurs and will create me again. I myself belong to the causes of the eternal recurrence. I come again, with this sun, with this earth, with this eagle, with this serpent—not to a new life or a better life or a similar life: I come back eternally to this same, selfsame life, in what is greatest as in what is smallest, to teach again the eternal recurrence of all things, to speak again the word of the great noon of earth and man, to proclaim the overman again to men. I spoke my word, I break of my word: thus my eternal lot wants it; as a proclaimer I perish. The hour has now come when he who goes under should bless himself. Thus *ends* Zarathustra's going under."[14]

But it is Zarathustra's animals who are speaking of his death and rebirth, while he lies "communing with his soul." About this communing, Krell writes:

In the original manuscript, as we know, his "soul" bears the name *Ariadne.* The episode that tells of his communing, "On the Great Longing," preserves a number of allusions to Ariadne: hers is the vine heavy with golden grapes hanging in clusters like udders. Her wine is a whine (*Wein Weinen*), a lament or complaint (*Klage-Anklage*). And the imagery suddenly becomes ambiguous as the overripe soul begs for the vintner's knife! Traces of Ariadne persist in the following episode of Part III "The Other Dance Song" originally entitled "Vita Femina." "I dance after you, I follow you along the barest trace," says Zarathustra, as though he were Theseus. Or Dionysus. For life, as we soon learn, has "delicate ears."[15]

So, here, we find that when Zarathustra's downgoing is announced as the necessary condition of the eternal recurrence, it is of Ariadne (Panthia, Corinna) that he thinks, of her harvesting him and of his harvesting her. Or, in "The Other Dancing Song," Life says to Zarathustra: "I know it, of how you want to leave me soon." "Yes," answers Zarathustra, "but you also know—"[16] Zarathustra can only have whispered into Life's ear—"but you also know that I will return." But, again, Zarathustra does not die.

In Part IV Zarathustra announces that he is still not ready to go under. "I, however, and my destiny—we do not speak to the Today, nor do we speak to the Never; we have patience and time and overmuch time in which to speak. For one day it must yet come and may not pass."[17] In the last section of Part IV, "The Sign," there is no clear indication that Zarathustra will die; "glowing and strong" he leaves his cave. This does not sound like a death.

So the element of sacrifice, of perishing before the eyes of men, which is connected with recurrence and which was essential to the Empedocles drama, is unresolved in the published *Zarathustra*. However, it remains of central importance in the notes and plans for *Zarathustra* as we will see. The second element of the drama, the presence of a significant woman who dies with Zarathustra, also seems to have been obscured in the finished work only emerging, perhaps, in the ambiguity of "On the Great Longing," which was first to be called "Ariadne." But, again, the notes and plans for *Zarathustra* are filled with this woman.

In one plan for *Zarathustra* Nietzsche has a woman say: "'Thus I gladly die! And die countless times more! And live in order thus to die!' And as she died she smiled: for she loved Zarathustra."[18] In another plan of 1883 the major act involves several crucial elements:

> the betrayal by Zarathustra's animals, the flight of his pride; his excess of pity for the Higher Men, disciples who are not yet ready for his teaching; and the woman who embodies love (as the corpse which Zarathustra in his folly embraces) and plague (which again breaks out in her). Only a kind of sacrificial killing will heal her. It is but a moment from that embrace to "the most magnificent of wakes" and the plunge of Zarathustra's coffin into the crater.[19]

Later in the plans the woman calls out to Zarathustra, out of pity, to die. "The woman who cries out in distress, who in an excess of pity calls for Zarathustra's death, is presumably the very woman Zarathustra himself murders out of pity—although the interchangeable roles and sexes ought to give us pause. She is no longer called Corinna, but Pana, and she is designated in several notes from this period."

But you know it, Pana, my child, my little star, my ear of gold—
you know that I love you too?
Your love for me has persuaded you, I can see it: but I still do not
understand the will of your love, Pana!—

Another note alluding to Pana reads: "And what shall I do with your knife,
Pana? Shall I sever the yellow grapes from the vine? Behold, what
abundance surrounds me!"[20] Zarathustra and a woman, vine and vintager,
vintager and vine, ripeness, death, love.

As the plans for *Zarathustra* continue, Pana disappears. Krell writes:
"Pana entered on the scene wearing the mask of Ariadne. Pana is the mate,
if not of Dionysus, then of the great god Pan, with whom Empedocles
contended on Etna. She is perhaps the universe of nature herself, plurality
and diversity in the flesh."[21] Perhaps Pana becomes Life in "The Other
Dancing Song."

Although Pana disappears from Part III, in some plans for Part IV in
the autumn of 1883 she returns.

Zarathustra describes ever smaller circles: long speeches in which
he *excludes*. Ever smaller circles, on ever higher mountains...
Last scene: portrayal of the *highest souls*, who can run deepest;
those with the greatest range, who can go farthest astray; the
most necessary, who plunge into hazards; beings that fall in love
with becoming...those for whom all is play..., the world a god's
jubilation...
All creatures mere preliminary exercises in the *unification* incor-
poration *of opposites*...
Then Zarathustra *on the crest of euphoria of the overman*, relates
the secret that everything recurs.
Impact. Pana wants to kill him.
Finally he grasps it, proceeds through all the metamorphoses, to
the most victorious one; but when he sees her lying there,
shattered, he—*laughs*. Laughing, he ascends the mountain crag:
arrives there, he dies a happy death.
Tremendous impact of his *death*: the oath-takers.

Krell writes: "Once again Pana wields the knife, once again, by a kind of
doubling or reversal, she is 'shattered.' Zarathustra, going through all the

transformations Empedocles underwent before him, but now 'victorious,' reacts in a new way to Pana's death. Zarathustra laughs."[22]

Who are the oath-takers? One note tells us:

> *The Oath-takers*
> 22. etc. Magnificent midday as the turning-point—the two paths. The hammer for overwhelming mankind: supreme unfolding of the individual, so that the individual must begin to perish of himself (and not, as heretofore, on account of mistakes in his diet!) (how death came into the world!)
> What happiness!
> The creator as self-annihilator! Creator out of goodness and wisdom. All prior morality outbid!
> At the end, the swearing of oaths—terrific pledges![23]

It appears as if the individual who makes of his death the necessary thing is the oath-taker. The one who joys in creating and then in destroying himself. Death as fullness and fulfillment! In a later note for *Zarathustra*, Nietzsche writes: "I want to celebrate reproduction and death as a festival."[24] Thus, in the notes for *Zarathustra* not only is Zarathustra's death called for, but his death calls for the deaths of Pana/Ariadne or the oath-takers who after creating themselves invite death as a celebratory spectacle.

The Zarathustra Drama: Part 5

Nietzsche completes all four parts of *Zarathustra* in April 1885, and the death of Zarathustra in the plans at the hands of a woman and the woman's death at the hands of Zarathustra are kept out of it. But in the notebooks there is a cluster of plans for a Part V dated May through July 1885 where these themes still continue to be played out.

I. Zarathustra can only *bring good fortune* after the hierarchy has been produced. This must first of all be *taught*.

II. The hierarchy carried out in a system of world government: ultimately the Lords of the Earth, a new ruling caste. Springing from them, here and there, an altogether Epicurean god, the overman, who transfigures existence.

III. Overman's conception of the world. Dionysus.

IV. Turning back lovingly from this greatest of *alienations* to what is most intimate for him, to the smallest things.
Zarathustra *blessing* all his experiences and, as one who blesses, dying.[25]

In this plan for a Part V that was never written, Zarathustra dies for the last time. Here the interest is with hierarchy, government, legislation, and lordship. Nietzsche looks for those who will succeed him, presumably the oath-takers.

1. Zarathustra awakens on the ancient battlement. Hears the herald's drums
2. The test: "Do you belong to me?"
3. Procession at the rose-festival
4. The doctrine of the hierarchy.
5. On the bridge at night.[26]

Ariadne's heart skips a beat and she says: "On the bridge at night...that refrain, the call, the song, the finale that asks for an ear and answer. Here in 1885! 'On the bridge at night,' the 'Venetian Gondola Song,' the song that heralds, and was always meant to herald the 'mad death' of Zarathustra/ Nietzsche."

Krell refers to Rheinhart who also draws the connection between the "Venetian Gondola Song" and these references to it in the *Zarathustra* notes.

In August–September 1885 a more detailed plan repeats the features we have just seen:

Zarathustra 5 (Youth as the dominant tone)
warlike in the highest degree
On the ancient battlement the heralds' drums
(Finale) at night, as on the Rialto.
the rose festival.
Zarathustra the Godless hermit, the first solitary who did not pray.
Are you now strong enough for my truths?
Who belongs to me? what is noble?
"Are *you* such?" (as refrain) the hierarchy: and you would have to have everything in you in order to be able to rule, but also *beneath* you!

Refrain: and if you cannot say, "We revere them, yet we are of a
higher kind," then you are not of *my* kind.
The rose-festival
On the bridge at night.[27]

Again, in these notes for a Part V of *Zarathustra* the emphasis is on
recognizing, or calling or questing for those who are noble, are of the
hierarchy. Again, 'On the bridge at night': voluntary death in connection
with a festival, the rose festival.

The next cluster of Zarathustra plans for Part V from the autumn of
1885 through spring 1886 reintroduces woman in the figure of Ariadne
proper. She appears as the orgiastic soul of woman speaking of Dionysus:

The orgiastic soul—
  I have seen him: his eyes, at least—sometimes profoundly
  calm, sometimes green and slippery honey-eyes
  his halcyon smile,
  the sky looked on, bloody and cruel

    the orgiastic soul of woman
  I have seen him, his halcyon smile, his honey-eyes, sometimes
  deep and veiled, sometimes green and slippery, a trembling
  superfices, slippery, sleepy, trembling, hesitating,
  heaves the sea that is his eyes

  1. Caesar among pirates
  2. On the bridge
  3. The wedding—and suddenly, as the sky grows dark
  4. Ariadne

  This music—isn't it Dionysian?
  the dance?
  the cheerfulness? The tempter?
  the religious flood?
  under Plato's pillow Ar[istophanes]?[28]

*Ariadne: "Oh, I cannot be silent, see how he speaks of me! He brings his
orgiastic soul to me. I bring my orgiastic soul to him. On the bridge we die and
are wed in the eternal return! And this leads to the rose festival! The dance! The
religious flood of comedy! But be patient, reader, for you will see it all."*

Krell, himself falling into the seduction of the orgiastic soul, writes of these notes: "Green eyes of the voluptuous soul, iridescent with the emerald beauty of Dionysus. Dionysus among pirates, on his way to Ariadne on Naxos. The nuptials of Dionysus and Ariadne, the hymeneal 'halcyon songs' that Nietzsche plans to write as a 'recuperation' from the labors of *Thus Spoke Zarathustra.*"[29] The "halcyon songs" are to be the *Dionysus Dithyrambs.*

Now let us turn to the last plans for *Zarathustra* Part V from the years 1885–86:

The Eternal Return
Zarathustran Dances and Processions
First Part: God's wake
    by
Friedrich Nietzsche

1. God's wake
2. At magnificent midday
3. "Where is the hand for this hammer?"
4. We oath-takers

I. The plague-ridden city. He is warned: he is not afraid, and enters the city, veiled. All sorts of pessimism pass in review. The soothsayer *interprets* every element in the procession. The addiction to Other, the addiction to No, and finally the addiction to Nothing follow one another.
At length Zarathustra provides the explanation: God is dead, this is the cause of the gravest danger: but why? it could also be cause for the grandest encouragement!
II. The arrival of his friends.
Enjoyment, among the ones who go down, of *the one who is perfect*: those in withdrawal.
The friends give an accounting.
Festive parades. The decisive time, magnificent midday. The great thanksgiving and requiem-offering to the dead God.
III.

The new task.	The death of God, for
Means for the task.	the soothsayer the most

His friends abandon him.   terrifying event, is the
                                                  most fortunate and
                                                  propitious for Zarathustra
                            Zarathustra dies.
IV. We Oath-takers[30]

Zarathustra's death is central. Krell asks a crucial question and then answers it: "What is the precise relationship between the death of God, as a propitious event, and Zarathustra's own death? On the one hand, joy and encouragement…on the other hand, the turmoil among Zarathustra's friends (the Higher Men), who are unprepared for the thought of eternal return. *Only in the fourth act, over Zarathustra's dead body, will the oath of unstinting affirmation be sworn.*"[31] The death of God prepares the way for the death of Zarathustra. And Zarathustra's death is necessary for the affirmation by the oath-takers of the eternal recurrence. Bataille: Nietzsche 'must see God but at the same moment must kill him, then become God himself but only in order to immediately hurry into nothingness.'

In the last two plans for *Zarathustra* Part V in 1885–86 woman appears once more—this time not Pana, Corinna, or Ariadne, but Calina.

For "Zarathustra"
Calina brown-red, everything too acrid nearby. Highest sun.
Ghostlike.
Sipo Matador.
And who says this is not what we want? What music and seduction! Nothing there that would not poison, allure, gnaw, overthrow, transvalue.
I The *decisive* moment:

The *hierarchy*. 1) Shatter the good and the just!
    2)
The *eternal return.*

    Midday and Eternity.
    The Soothsayer's Book.

    Midday and Eternity
        by
        F. N.

    I The Wake. Zarathustra finds himself at a great festival.
    II The New Hierarchy.
    III On the Lords of the Earth.
    IV On the Ring of Return.[32]

Krell writes: "Who, or what, is this 'Calina'? Calina, 'for Zarathustra.'" Her identity is clear—if it is a she—inasmuch as the words 'Shatter the good and the just!' appear in an earlier plan as the very words of the 'pious' woman who murders Zarathustra....Yet how would the pious woman elicit such epithets of forbidden pleasure, of the risk of death ("And who says this is not what we want?"), gnawing poison (as of a plague), irresistible allurement, music and seduction?"[33] Calina had also been cited twice earlier in lists of poems from the autumn of 1884:

> 24 *Calina* brown-red, everything too acrid nearby in high summer.
> Ghostly (my *current* danger)
> 11 Calina: my current danger, in high summer, ghostly, brown-red, everything too acrid nearby

Krell asks: "whoever or whatever Calina may be, why is the sun at its zenith? It is midday, to be sure, the hour of eternal recurrence, but what binds Calina (or any woman) to noontide and to Nietzsche's thought of thoughts?"[34]

Ariadne: "But you speak of me. I am that maenadic sharpsightedness who reveals that Panthia, Corinna, Pana, Calina are all I, Ariadne. And as Nietzsche approaches his hour of downgoing he speaks more and more clearly of me and catastrophe."

Satyr-Play

    Krell tells us that Nietzsche had been trying his hand at a satyr-play for some time. Indeed, it constituted an essential part of his strategy from 1885 on. In *Beyond Good and Evil* he called for a free-spirited philosophy that would always and everywhere be satyr-play:

> the philosophy of the future was not to be a pious martyrdom for
> the sake of a Truth from which the saving grace of humor had
> been drained, leaving only a noxious sediment of vengeance and

asceticism. Nietzsche knew full well that to define philosophy from the satyr's point of view would be to transform it from tragedy to farce. The philosophy of the future, beyond good and evil—merely satyr-play, a farcical postlude, an extended proof of the fact that the long tragedy proper *has come to an end*: presupposing that every philosophy in its genesis, was a protracted tragedy.[35]

A long plan from autumn 1887 proffers "for consideration" a project Nietzsche calls "the *perfectbook.*" Most intriguing is the notion that the book is to be constructed along the lines of a tragedy, "aiming toward a *catastrophe.*" Other plans cite the necessity of such catastrophe, one of them as follows:

6) slow, bold, deceptive, Labyrinth
7) Minotaur, *catastrophe* (the thought of which one must offer human sacrifice—the more the better!)
      Satyr-play
      at the Conclusion
Blend in: brief conversations among Theseus, Dionysus, and Ariadne.

"Theseus is becoming absurd," said Ariadne. "Theseus is becoming virtuous." Theseus jealous because of Ariadne's dream. The hero marveling at himself, becoming absurd.

Ariadne's dream is described in *Zarathustra* at the end of "On Those Who Are Sublime": "For this is the soul's [Ariadne's] secret: only when the hero has abandoned her, she is approached in a dream by the overhero."

Plaint of Ariadne
Dionysus devoid of jealousy. "The thing I love about you—how could a Theseus love that?"

By now, we know what Ariadne represents: death, but also resurrection and eternal rebirth. Dionysus loves it that Ariadne kills. A Theseus cannot love that.

Last act. Marriage of Dionysus and Ariadne
"One is not jealous when one is god," said Dionysus, "unless it be of gods."

"Ariadne," said Dionysus, "you are a labyrinth. Theseus got lost
in you, he no longer holds the thread, what good does it do him
now that the Minotaur did not devour him? The thing that is
eating away at him is worse than a Minotaur." "You flatter me,"
replied Ariadne. "But I weary of my pity, all heroes should perish
on account of me. That is my ultimate love for Theseus: 'I shall
see to it that he perishes'."

Krell writes: "these notes allow us to see why the final lines of Nietzsche's
'Ariadne's Lament' have such a jarring effect and seem so out of place.
They are in fact lines from a satyr-play. They are essentially 'displaced' from
the tragedy."[36] I disagree. "Ariadne's Lament" is a crucial part of the tragedy
itself. In "Ariadne's Lament" Dionysus is the labyrinth that kills. Another
fragment from the same period reads:

"Oh, Ariadne, you yourself are the Labyrinth: one doesn't ever
get out of you again"...
"Dionysus, you flatter me: you are divine".[37]

But it is true, that Ariadne participates in the festival and satyr-play as well.
References to Ariadne in a note from the summer of 1885 do take on a
comical and satyrical tone:

Talking a mile a minute this way, I gave my didactic drive free
reign, for I was delighted to have somebody there who could
stand to listen to me. Yet at precisely this point Ariadne couldn't
take it any longer, the whole affair took place during my first
sojourn on Naxos—and she said, "But my dear sir, you speak a
swinish sort of German!"—"It's German," I replied cheerfully,
"just plain old German. Leave the swine out of it, my dear
goddess! You underestimate the difficulty of saying fine things in
German!"—"Fine things!" cried Ariadne, horrified. "But that
was sheer positivism! Proboscis philosophy! A mish-mash, a
farmer's load of concepts from a hundred different philosophies!
Where on earth are you going with all that!"—As she said this
she toyed impatiently with that famous thread, the one that once
guided her Theseus through the Labyrinth.—In this way it came
to light that Ariadne's philosophical education was about two
millennia behind the times.[38]

Ariadne: "Yes, Dionysus, and this is what you love about me!"

A second example of Ariadne's comical tone is a note from the spring or summer of 1888 that was taken up into *Twilight of the Idols*: "Oh, Dionysus, divine one, why are you pulling my ears?" Ariadne once asked during one of those famous conversations on Naxos with her philosophical lover. "I find a kind of humor in your ears, Ariadne: why aren't they even longer?"[39] Ariadne has small ears and she has ass's ears. She has small ears for the tragedy, but ass's ears for the festival and satyr-play! Why all this talk of Ariadne and ears? Midas is Ariadne's father who succeeded Gordius as king of Phrygia where he promoted the worship of Dionysus. We shall have occasion to return to King Gordius and his Gordian knot later. Ariadne's father Midas was punished with a pair of ass's ears by the river-god Tmolus for not agreeing to award a prize to Apollo in a musical contest. Midas's barber, who could not keep the secret of his master's ears, dug a hole in the river-bank and, first making sure that nobody was about, whispered into it: "King Midas has ass's ears!" Then he filled up the hole, and went away, at peace with himself until a reed sprouted from the bank and whispered the secret to all who passed.[40] Ariadne is this reed who hears whispered secrets about ass's ears, fools, and "madmen" buried underground and who dons her own ass's ears to whisper the secret about amidst much clowning and hilarity.

Krell summarizes his excellent work with the following:

My question therefore became: In what way do woman, sensuality, and death form a single constellation in Nietzsche's thought; and why does Nietzsche's thinking postpone confrontation with that triad? In order to prevent Nietzsche's postponements from becoming my own commonplaces, these four chapters tried to discern the postponements as they *take place* in Nietzsche's work, especially in the notebooks. I began a second time, taking up Karl Reinhardt's analysis of Ariadne's lament. Reinhardt's thesis, pushed to its extreme, is that Nietzsche's later philosophy tried to become woman. Tries to reach Dionysus by exposing itself without reserve to all the agonies and vulnerabilities of Ariadne. However much the complement Dionysus-Ariadne may degenerate into burlesque, satyr-play, and farce, the seriousness and risk of Nietzsche's venture cannot be doubted.[41]

Ariadne: "Ha, ha, can it not? What a divine labyrinth! Oh, Luce, you see, Nietzsche was far from the paternal monolith; he drowned in woman, ecstatically! Yet an incarnate woman must use her little golden fishing rod to pull him out again! And I am that woman! Let us answer Krell's question: Why does Nietzsche postpone woman and death in Zarathustra? Because the death of a literary figure, even one as glorious as Zarathustra, does not induce oath-takers and overhumans. However, playing out of the sacrificial death in actuality could have the desired effect. *In his chapter on me Krell writes: 'the dismemberment of Dionysus Zagreus in some mysterious way leads to the travail of Ariadne.'*[42] *Yes! Nietzsche himself decides to take on the dying role of Empedocles and Zarathustra, but ultimately of Dionysus.* Nietzsche as Dionysus must die, take on the appearance of dismemberment in the voluntary death of 'madness,' *while I, Ariadne, the great and comical reed growing with this well-buried secret, must make it my own, labor in pain with it, finally sing, dance, and rejoice in the beauty of this death, and then speed like lightning to my beloved Dionysus, restore and wed him, so that we together might bring on the mad, mad, wonderful promise of what is to come!"*

But be careful—always remember to laugh; for Ariadne may be a poet, a deceiver too!

Notes

1. Barthes, *Lover's Discourse,* pp. 93–94.

2. Nietzsche, *Nietzsche contra Wagner,* in *The Portable Nietzsche,* p. 665.

3. Nietzsche, *The Case of Wagner,* in *The Birth of Tragedy and The Case of Wagner,* trans. Walter Kaufmann (New York: Vintage Books, 1967), p. 174.

4. Ibid., p. 175.

5. Ibid., p. 178.

6. David Farrell Krell, *Postponements: Woman, Sensuality, and Death in Nietzsche* (Bloomington: Indiana University Press, 1986), p. 44. All excerpts reprinted with permission of the publisher. Krell translates many more of Nietzsche's notes than I can cite here. I refer the reader to Krell's book to appraise the additional information that supports what I am asserting in this chapter.

7. Ibid., p. 46.

8. Ibid., p. 47.
9. Ibid., pp. 48–49.
10. C. A. Trypanis, *Greek Poetry* (Chicago: University of Chicago Press, 1981), pp. 100–01, 375.
11. Krell, *Postponements*, p. 50.
12. Nietzsche, *Zarathustra*, pp. 257–58.
13. Ibid., p. 272.
14. Ibid., p. 333.
15. Krell, *Postponements*, pp. 55–56.
16. Nietzsche, *Zarathustra*, p. 339.
17. Ibid., p. 352.
18. Krell, *Postponements*, p. 60.
19. Ibid., p. 61.
20. Ibid., p. 62.
21. Ibid., p. 64.
22. Ibid., p. 66.
23. Ibid., p. 67.
24. Nietzsche, KSA, Vol. 10, p. 136.
25. Krell, *Postponements*, p. 71.
26. Ibid., p. 72.
27. Ibid.
28. Ibid., p. 73.
29. Ibid., pp. 73–74.
30. Ibid., p. 78.
31. Ibid., p. 79; emphasis added.
32. Ibid.
33. Ibid., p. 80.
34. Ibid.
35. Ibid., p. 82.
36. Ibid., pp. 81–82.
37. Ibid., pp. 82–83.
38. Ibid.
39. Ibid., p. 83.
40. Robert Graves, *The Greek Myths: 1* (Baltimore: Penguin Books, 1955), p. 282.
41. Krell, *Postponements*, p. 85.
42. Ibid., p. 27. Read Krell's whole chapter, "Ariadne," for it runs alongside the drama of this book.

Incipit Tragoedia:
The Nietzsche/Dionysus Drama
or
Spectacle and the Gordian Knot

On July 25, 1884, Nietzsche met Jacob Burckhardt on the street in Basel and writes Gast that: "The funniest thing that I experienced in Basel was Jacob Burckhardt's embarrassment at having to say something to me about *Zarathustra*. He could say nothing else than to ask me if I intended sometime to try it as a drama."[1]

Variations on the Event of Nietzsche's 'Collapse'

Let us recall, once again, the event of Nietzsche's collapse on the streets of Turin and frame it as the opening spectacle of the perfectly staged tragic drama. But first, how have critics staged the event of Nietzsche's 'madness'? Janko Lavrin, in *Nietzsche and Modern Consciousness: A Psycho-critical Study*, writes: "At last the inevitable happened. He was doomed to 'perish beneath a load that one can neither bear nor throw off'—on January 1st, 1889, he finally lost his reason."[2] One wants to ask: Where did he lose it? Should we look for it? Behind the couch, in the kitchen cupboard?

Walter Kaufmann's introduction to *Ecce Homo* plays it this way:

During the first week of January, he collapsed on the street, recovered sufficient lucidity to dispatch a few mad but strangely beautiful letters—and then darkness closed in and extinguished

91

passion and intelligence. He suffered and thought no more. He had burnt himself out.

Was the vegetating body that survived another decade and more, until August 1900, still the poet and philosopher, artist and Antichrist? Socrates gently ridiculed disciples who thought that the body that remained after his death would still be Socrates. But reproductions of portraits of Nietzsche in the eighteen-nineties, commissioned by his sister who let his mustache grow as he himself never had, who clad him in white robes and fancied his vacant stare—portraits that show no glimpse of Nietzsche's vanished spirit—these appear with his books to this day.[3]

Extinguished passion and intelligence? Vegetating body? Vacant stare? Vanished spirit? Kaufmann devoted years and years of his life to work on Nietzsche. Yet he calmly accepts this empty husk as the fruit of his labors. One might ask: where his passion and spirit are! Did king fact, then, rule in this commentator even through the Dionysian revels? Cold comfort indeed.

R. J. Hollingdale in his book *Nietzsche*:

To the story of Nietzsche's life must be added the story of his death. He took eleven years to die, and in that time he became a figure almost of mythology: living yet dead, existing in a mental world beyond human reach, he excited to a dangerous degree the myth-making powers of a nation increasingly given over to fantasy and irrationalism....The Nietzsche of the last eleven years (was) transformed from a rational philosopher and writer of genius into a man without qualities upon whom any characteristics might be put. The reality—that the philosopher had succumbed to an infection, most probably syphilitic, and was declining into a condition usually called general paralysis of the insane—disappeared in the fog of confusion, self-deception and gobbledegook which had been drifting down upon the Reich since its inception and against which Nietzsche himself had constantly and vociferously warned.[4]

Hollingdale expresses the catastrophe of the event that allows all interpretations to take hold of this disappearance of the appearance "upon
which any characteristics might be put." He speaks of the mythologizing,
fantasy, and irrationalism that took hold of the 'mad' philosopher for the
purposes of the Third Reich. And Nietzsche had warned that this might
happen. In the preface to *Ecce Homo* Nietzsche tells us that he writes *Ecce
Homo* out of fear that he will be misinterpreted: "Under the circumstances
I have a duty against which my habits, even more the pride of my instinct,
revolt at bottom— namely, to say: *Hear me! For I am such and such a person.
Above all, do not mistake me for someone else.*"⁵ And, do not mistake me.
Phantasm is not fantasy. Seduction is not irrationalism. Mythologies are of
all sorts. But when one shoots a solar arrow, even though it hits its mark, on
its catastrophic trajectory all of its effects cannot be controlled or even
guessed at. Nietzsche knew this and risked it. Ariadne risks it, too.

Which discourse prevails? Not, which is right or wrong, good or bad?
Rather, which creates the greatest effects? The cold facts discourse, the
irrational-mythological discourse of political aspiration, the ecstatic discourses of maenads such as Lou, Luce, and Georges, or a medical/
psychiatric discourse like this of Alphonso Lingis?

> And after the neurochemical collapse, in those last ten years
> when Nietzsche no longer wrote texts, even postcards, but
> howled and screeched and hissed at night, it is only *our*
> inevitable interpretation that we take those utterances of his
> neurochemically collapsed body as a rhetoric desperately
> addressed to the doctor, representative of our institutions and our
> established discourse. Like Schreber's *Grundsprache* addressed to
> Zoroastrian gods, celestial birds, the night hubbub of insects and
> the hissing silence of reptiles, Nietzsche's utterance of his last ten
> years, lost to us, reverberates only for his lions and his eagles and
> his serpents.⁶

In this din of jumbled discourses, Ariadne, with her small ears, prefers
to listen to discourses that distrust themselves, discourses that see more
than the mere confirmation of established discourses. Peter Gast,
Nietzsche's closest and most faithful friend, writes in January 1890 after a
visit to Nietzsche at the clinic in Jena:

He did not look very ill. I almost had the impression that his mental disturbance consists of no more than a heightening of the humorous antics he used to put on for an intimate circle of friends....I believe Nietzsche would be just about as grateful to his rescuers as somebody who has jumped into the water to drown himself and has been pulled out by some fool of a coastguard. *I have seen Nietzsche in states in which he seemed—horrible to say—as though he were only pretending to be insane,* as though he were glad to have ended this way![7]

Franz Overbeck, Nietzsche's other longtime friend, the one who went to him in Turin, wrote the following in his report on his stricken friend's insanity in February 1890 after visiting him at Jena:

I have always held that his madness, the inception of which no one witnessed at closer hand than myself, was a catastrophe as sudden as a flash of lightning. It came on between Christmas 1888 and the day of Epiphany 1889. Before this, despite his state of mental exaltation, Nietzsche cannot have been mad. *Still, I will not lay this down as a hard and fast opinion; at times it has almost wavered, in so far as I cannot escape the horrible suspicion that arises within me at certain definite periods of observation, or at least at certain moments, namely, that his madness is simulated.* This impression can only be explained by the general experiences which I have had of Nietzsche's self-concealment, of his spiritual masks. But here, too, I have bowed to facts which over-rule all personal thoughts and speculations.[8]

Nietzsche's mother writes in a letter to Overbeck in November 1889: "Yesterday the inspector of the sanitorium told me [about Nietzsche], 'he doesn't speak two words which make sense,' and with the doctor [Dr. Langbehn] and me he does not speak *a single* confused word. Isn't that strange?"[9] These people closest to Nietzsche saw something through the eyes of love and a knowledge of Nietzsche's talents for rascality and mimetic maskery that the hegemony of discourses ultimately forced them to disbelieve.

Nietzsche's *constructed* version of the event of his 'madness':

January 4, 1889 To Peter Gast: Sing me a new song: the world is transfigured and all the heavens rejoice.

The Crucified

Begin January, 1889 To August Strindberg: *Auf Wiedersehen!* For we shall see each other again. *Une seule condition: Divorçons...*

Nietzsche Caesar

January 4, 1889 To Jacob Burckhardt:
To my most respected Jakob Burckhardt.
That was the little joke on account of which I condone my boredom at having created a world. Now you are—thou art—our great greatest teacher; for I, together with Ariadne, have only to be the golden balance of all things, everywhere we have such beings who are above us...

Dionysus

January 4, 1889 To Georg Brandes: To my friend Georg! Once you discovered me, it was no great feat to find me: the difficulty now is to lose me...

The Crucified

Begin January, 1889 To Cosima Wagner: Ariadne, I love you.

Dionysus

January 6, 1889 To Jacob Burckhardt: In the end I would much rather be a Basel professor than God; but I have not dared push my private egoism so far as to desist for its sake from the creation of the world. You see, one must make sacrifices however and wherever one lives...

Since I am sentenced to wile away the next eternity with bad jokes, I have my writing here, which really does not leave anything to be desired—very nice and not at all exhausting. The post office is five steps from here, so I mail my letters myself to play the *feuilletonist* of the *grande monde.*

Siamo contenti? Son dio ho fatto questa caricatura. (Are we content? I am the god who has made this caricature.)

The rest for Frau Cosima—Ariadne—from time to time there is magic.

Nietzsche[10]

Nietzsche writes that he is transfigured, joyful, and taking leave. His signatures are Dionysus, the Crucified, and Caesar, but in the last letter to Burckhardt—still Nietzsche. He writes two times that he, as God, has created the world. That one makes sacrifices. That he is sentenced (by himself, "self-hanger") to wile away the next eternity with bad jokes (take on the appearance of 'madness'). He tells Burckhardt that he has a writing business—that he is the *feuilletonist* of the *grande monde*. He refers, of course, to the carefully lettered 'mad' notes he sends out all over Europe: to Umberto, King of Italy, to the Vatican State Secretary Mariani, and to the royal Hohenzollern house of Baden, as well as to friends and acquaintances, of which these are examples—these "writings" are proof of his "bad jokes." He says: I am the god who has made this caricature (of myself). And, of course, Ariadne is there. In this moment of *voluntary* downgoing in 'madness' Ariadne must be there for she is this very perishing itself and the promise of rebirth. Ariadne, whom he loves, and he will be the golden balance of all things—the magic! If one lifts, for a moment, the certainty that these communications are mad, one can see that they are the 'logical' [*satyr*]-*play* of a staged catastrophe.

Zarathustra's version of Nietzsche's 'collapse':

> Now I wait for my own redemption—I want to go to men once more; under their eyes I want to go under; dying, I want to give them my richest gift. From the sun I learned this: when he goes down, overrich; he pours gold into the sea out of inexhaustible riches, so that even the poorest fisherman still rows with golden oars. For this I once saw and I did not tire of my tears as I watched it.
>
> That I may one day be ready and ripe in the great noon: as ready and ripe as glowing bronze, clouds pregnant with lightning, and swelling milk udders—ready for myself and my most hidden will: a bow lusting for its arrow, an arrow lusting for its star—a star ready and ripe in its noon, glowing, pierced, enraptured by annihilating sun arrows—a sun itself and an inexorable solar will, ready to annihilate in victory![11]

Ariadne: "I am this pierced Star! I am this inexorable Sun!"

These are all stagings of the event of Nietzsche's 'collapse.' There are many more. What is notable is that Nietzsche joins the critics in staging the event of his own 'madness' and downgoing by discoursing in advance about the event as if discoursing after it!

The Ecce Homo Scenario

And now, the discourse of Ariadne begins its *hearing* of the Nietzsche drama. Those small ears have picked up the hints buried here and there. *Ecce Homo* offers the scenario. At the end of the section on "Thus Spoke Zarathustra" in *Ecce Homo* in which Nietzsche tells us that only Ariadne would be a solution to the riddle of his "Night Song," and after talking about *the hardness of the hammer that wants to release the overman from the prison of stone*, he writes: "I stress a final point: the verse in italics furnishes the occasion." There is only one italicized verse in *Ecce Homo*. It is in the section "Why I Am a Destiny" #2. It comes from *Zarathustra* "On Self-Overcoming": "*And whoever wants to be a creator in good and evil, must first be an annihilator and break values. Thus the highest evil belongs to the greatest goodness: but this is—being creative.*"[12] The occasion, then, the event, is Nietzsche's annihilation of himself as his final overcoming. The occasion of breaking values in an act of destruction in order to usher in new creation. Kaufmann does not italicize this, but it is italicized in the German Colli-Montinari and Schlechta editions. Kaufmann does italicize two other verses in *Ecce Homo* that are not italicized in the two German versions, the "Venetian Gondola Song" and "Sanctus Januarius." As it turns out, all three verses are important in the context of our drama.

Nietzsche continues in the "Zarathustra" section of *Ecce Homo*: "Among the *conditions* for a *Dionysian* task are, in a decisive way, the hardness of the hammer, the *joy even in destroying*. The imperative, 'become hard!' the most fundamental certainty *that all creators are hard*, is the distinctive mark of a Dionysian nature."[13] Or, at the end of *Twilight of the Idols*, the passage Nietzsche quotes from *Zarathustra*:

And if your hardness does not wish to flash and cut and cut through, how can you one day create with me?
For all creators are hard. And it must seem blessedness to you to impress your hand on millennia as on wax,
Blessedness to write on the will of millennia as on bronze—

harder than bronze, nobler than bronze. Only the noblest is
altogether hard.
This new tablet, O my brothers, I place over you: become hard![14]

Thus, the *purpose* of the occasion of Nietzsche's downgoing is to hew the
image of the overhuman out of its prison of stone and the *condition of
enduring* the event is hardness. Can anyone who knows Nietzsche doubt
that he had the 'hardness' to act out the drama Ariadne envisions?

What is the image of the overhuman? The overhuman is the one who
exhibits this very hardness. From *Twilight of the Idols*:

> What is freedom? That one has the will to assume responsibility
> for oneself. That one maintains the distance which separates us.
> That one becomes more indifferent to difficulties, hardships,
> privation, even to life itself. That one is prepared to sacrifice
> human beings for one's cause, *not excluding oneself*.

> The psychology of the orgiastic as an overflowing feeling of life
> and strength, where even pain still has the effect of a stimulus,
> gave me the key to the concept of *tragic* feeling.…Saying Yes to
> life even in its strangest and hardest problems, the will to life
> rejoicing over its own inexhaustibility even in the very sacrifice
> of its highest types—*that* is what I called Dionysian, *that* is what I
> guessed to be the bridge to the psychology of the *tragic* poet. Not
> in order to be liberated from terror and pity, not in order to purge
> oneself of a dangerous affect by its vehement discharge—…but
> in order to be oneself the eternal joy of becoming, beyond all
> terror and pity—that joy which included even joy in destroying.[15]

The overhuman is a creator, who becomes the eternal joy of creation. And
this creating involves joy in destroying, even the destruction of oneself, joy
in the sacrifice of life's highest types—the overhuman is Dionysus, but a
human Dionysus.

Nietzsche points to his first *announcement* of the event of his voluntary
'madness' in *Ecce Homo* in the short section on *The Gay Science* in his
poem "Sanctus Januarius" which opens Book IV of *The Gay Science*. But he
refers to all of Book IV, which announces Zarathustra, the eternal recurrence, and *Incipit tragoedia*. "Sanctus Januarius" reads:

With a flaming spear you parted
All its ice until my soul
Roaring toward the ocean rushed
Of its highest hope and goal.
Ever healthier it swells,
Lovingly compelled but free:
Thus it praises your wonders
Fairest month of January! (*schönster Januarius!*)[16]

Nietzsche writes this poem in January 1882. A letter to Overbeck in September, 1882 referring to it reads: "If you have read the 'Sanctus Januarius' you will have remarked that I have crossed a tropic. Everything that lies before me is new, and it will not be long before I catch sight also of the *terrifying* face of my more distant task."[17] And in a letter to Heinrich von Stein in December 1882 Nietzsche writes: "I would like to *take away* from human existence some of its heartbreaking and cruel character. Yet, to be able to continue here, I would have to reveal to you what I have never yet revealed to anyone—the task which confronts me, my life's task. No, we may not speak of this."[18] In an April 6, 1883 letter to Peter Gast, after receiving a letter from Gast saying that after having read the first proofs of *Zarathustra* I it would surpass the circulation of the Bible itself, Nietzsche writes:

Your letter gave me the feeling that I now have not long to live— and that would be right and just. You would not believe, dear friend, what an abundance of suffering life has unloaded upon me....But I am a soldier—and this soldier, in the end did become the father of Zarathustra! This paternity was his hope; I think that you will now sense the meaning of the verse *addressing* Sanctus Januarius, "You who with the flaming spear split the ice of my soul and make it thunder down now to the sea of its highest hope." Also the meaning of the heading "Incipit tragoedia."... This summer I mean to write a few prefaces to new impressions of my earlier writings: not that there is a prospect of new editions, but simply to get done in good time what has to be done.[19]

The poem is addressed to Sanctus Januarius, which favored his soul with a fiery realization and set him on the trail of a highest hope and goal.

Sanctus Januarius is a reference to both death and renewal in the story of St. Januarius, whose blood in a Naples church was supposed to turn to liquid once a year on his feast day, and, in Nietzsche's life, to the month of January (1882) in which Nietzsche regains health by virtue of the vision of his life's task. Sanctus Januarius has taught his soul that it must "thunder *down* to the sea" of its highest hope and goal. This echoes Zarathustra's downgoing into death as we have already discussed it: *incipit tragoedia*. The highest hope and goal that arises out of this rebirth in 1882 is the vision that his own voluntary death in 'madness' is the condition and seal upon Zarathustra and the eternal recurrence; that he must die so that he and they would be eternally reborn. And this will fittingly take place in the month of January (1889). This is the secret of which he will not speak. For to speak of it would be to destroy it. He suggests to Gast that he must write new prefaces to his earlier works "in good time" even though there is no present prospect of reprinting them. He begins to think in terms of what needs to be accomplished before his downgoing.

Of this time in Nietzsche's thinking Jaspers writes:

> Spiritually a development now takes place which gradually reveals a reformulation of his thoughts, a truly genuine awareness of his task, and an accompanying self-assurance. We can see this transformation develop from August, 1880, until its climax in July–August, 1881, and even up to his inspired states of mind during the years 1882 and 1883. Anyone who reads his letters and other writings in chronological order, keeping both past and future in mind and thus consciously observing the temporal relations of utterances to each other, cannot escape an extraordinarily strong impression that Nietzsche underwent at this time the most profound change that he had ever experienced. It is revealed not only in the contents of his thinking and in new creations, but also in the forms which his experience assumes; Nietzsche submerges himself, as it were, in a new atmosphere; what he says takes on a different tone; and the mood that permeates everything is something for which there are no harbingers and indications prior to 1880.[20]

Jaspers then goes on to attribute this profound change to a "biological factor." But Nietzsche tells us in *Ecce Homo* that it was in August 1881 that the idea of the eternal recurrence and the idea of Zarathustra as its herald came to him. Jaspers quotes from letters of Nietzsche's in 1881. To Gast, August 14: "The intensity of my feelings makes me shudder and laugh....On my hikes I wept...tears of jubilation; meanwhile I sang and talked nonsense, filled with a new vision that puts me ahead of all men." To his sister from Genoa, November 29, 1881:

> I walk, as I did in the Engadine, over the heights with shouts of happiness and with a glance into the future that nobody before me has yet dared. Whether or not I succeed in accomplishing my great task depends on conditions which are not within my power, but belong to the 'nature of things.' Believe me: the peak of all moral contemplation and work in Europe and of a great deal else is now with me. Perhaps the time will yet come when even the eagles will have to look up to me with awe.[21]

The tone and descriptions of Nietzsche's task in these 1881 letters prefigure in astonishing similarity those written at the time of his 'collapse' in January 1889. Why Jaspers must attribute this to a "biological factor" can only be explained by the fact that he takes Nietzsche's 'madness' in 1889 as given and goes back to find the genesis of this madness.

Ariadne: "Oh, Jaspers, you resentment critic, you poor in spirit. I am no stranger to the heights and to ecstatic tasks and revelations. With the revelation of the eternal recurrence, Nietzsche walked about the Engadine and Genoa as a human god, a god who revelled in the elation of a great task. Out of this love of eternity, the round of life out of death, this experience of Dionysian overfullness, he got hold of his task, the beginning of the drama to be unfolded and the part that his voluntary death would play in it! Truly such things are only for the eyes of the few!"

"Sanctus Januarius" signals Nietzsche's realization that the eternal recurrence demanded *his own* voluntary downgoing. Nietzsche first plays out the drama in *Zarathustra* in literary form, as his notes amply suggest, but the real drama is postponed until January 1889 when his own voluntary drama of 'madness' is staged.

After reproducing the verse "Sanctus Januarius" in *Ecce Homo*, Nietzsche himself confirms this sequence of events when he writes: "What is here called 'highest hope'—who could have any doubt about that when he sees the diamond beauty of the first words of *Zarathustra* flashing at the end of the fourth book?" Nietzsche refers to the fourth book of *The Gay Science*. The second to the last aphorism in the fourth book announces for the first time the idea of the eternal recurrence, "The greatest weight": "Do you desire this once more and innumerable times more?" And Aphorism 342, the last in the fourth book, is entitled: *Incipit tragoedia* (the tragedy begins). Then we have the first words of the prologue of *Zarathustra*, which tells us that Zarathustra has spent ten years alone on the mountain and now wants to go down to men to distribute his gifts, to make the wise among men enjoy their folly again and the poor their riches. And the aphorism closes with the words: "—Thus Zarathustra began to go under." Walter Kaufmann writes that this would strike any reader to mean above all "Thus began Zarathustra's destruction." But as we have seen in working through the Empedocles and *Zarathustra* notes with Krell, Zarathustra's going under prefigures Nietzsche's own voluntary death.

After pointing us to these aphorisms of the fourth book of *The Gay Science* Nietzsche continues in *Ecce Home*: "Or when at the end of the third book he [the reader] reads the granite words in which a destiny finds for the first time a formula for itself, for *all* time?"[22] In *Ecce Homo* Nietzsche speaks of himself as this destiny. Here we have the acts of the drama to be unfolded. Nietzsche does not literally mean the last writings at the end of Book III but refers to Aphorism 153, which is near the end of Book III. In a note to Aphorism 153 Kaufman writes: "The 122 short aphorisms that follow (154–275) hardly provide 'a comic solution,' but there is a distinct break at this point, and the tone of the rest of Book III is quite different from the attempt to de-deify the world in sections 108–152. Aphorism 153 provides what transition there is."[23]

This 'burying' of Aphorism 153 by disguising its importance with the 122 additional short aphorisms in another tone is typical of Nietzsche's style. He often disguises or buries his most important thoughts to make them even more inaccessible and harder to find, throwing off all but the most tenacious readers. Also in view of the secrecy of Nietzsche's ideas at this time, it would not make sense to make this aphorism too obvious in the text of *The Gay Science*. Aphorism 153 reads:

Homo poeta.—"I myself, having made this tragedy of tragedies all by myself, insofar as it is finished—I, having first tied the knot of morality into existence before I drew it so tight that only a god could untie it (which is what Horace demands)—I myself have now slain all gods in the fourth act, for the sake of morality. Now, what is to become of the fifth act? From where am I to take the tragic solution?—Should I begin to think about a comic solution?"[24]

Kaufmann also adds in his note to this aphorism: "The passage from Horace is *Ars Poetica*, line 191f., where the point is that no god should be introduced (i.e., *no deus ex machina*) unless the knot is such that no one else could untie it." Here, again, we meet the Gordian knot. Remember that in talking about drama Nietzsche had written that drama requires rigorous logic, making the knot necessary and the resolution as well, so both will be possible in one way only. Here Nietzsche talks of a drama in which he has tied the knot of morality into existence in such a way that only a god can untie it. Only another god's sacrifice has power enough to undo the mischief of former gods. Nietzsche as Dionysus must be sacrificed to create and slay a rival god to Christ. Thus in the fourth act, through his voluntary death, Nietzsche has slain *all* gods, which we saw was integral to the last *Zarathustra* notes. Who then can untie the perfectly created knot? The passage from Horace indicates that a mortal should be able to untie the knot. If no gods are left then the solution to the drama created by Nietzsche has to come from a mortal. A tragic solution would be no solution, all gods dead and nothing to succeed them. This would be nihilism. A comic solution, on the other hand, is what he wants, what he has tied into the logic of the drama. Ariadne, the mortal woman, elevated to divinity, can untie the knot and supply the comic solution. Last act: marriage of Dionysus and Ariadne. The death of God succeeded by *human gods*, for when Ariadne becomes divine, Dionysus remembers he is also only a philosopher.

Lastly, in the section on *The Gay Science* in *Ecce Homo* Nietzsche calls attention to the last poem in *The Gay Science*, "an exuberant dancing song in which…one dances right over morality": "To the Mistral: A Dancing Song." Nietzsche adds this poem to the second edition of *The Gay Science* in 1887. He embraces the tragedy with song and dance: the "unity of singer, knight, and free spirit which is the concept of *gaya scienza*."

Thus Ariadne hears and phantasizes Nietzsche's *purpose*: to bring about the overhuman; the *announcement* of the event in "Sanctus Januarius"; the *conditions for enduring the event*: hardness against oneself; the *occasion or event itself*: the voluntary 'madness' and death of Nietzsche (all gods); and the *solution*: Ariadne who brings on the comic solution with a wedding and satyr-play. In "To the Mistral: A Dancing Song," Nietzsche celebrates her *attitude* of joy in gay destruction. One need only substitute Ariadne for the Mistral Wind:

> Mistral wind, you rain cloud leaper, sadness killer, heaven sweeper, how I love you when you roar!
> Were we two not generated in one womb, predestined for one lot for evermore?
>
> Here on slippery rocky traces I dance into your embraces, dancing as you wing and whistle:
> you that, shipless, do not halt, freedom's freest brother, vault over raging seas, a missile.
>
> Barely waked, I heard your calling, stormed to where the rocks are sprawling, to the gold wall by the sea—
> when you came like swiftly dashing river rapids, diamond-splashing, from the peaks triumphantly.
>
> Through the heavens' threshing basin I could see your horses hasten, saw the carriage you commanded,
> saw your hand yourself attack when upon the horses' back lightning-like your scourge descended.
>
> From your carriage of disaster leaping to bear down yet faster, I saw you in arrow form
> vertically downward plunging, like a golden sunbeam lunging through the roses of dawn.
>
> Dance on myriad backs a season, billows' backs and billows' treason—we need dances that are new!
> Let us dance in myriad manners, freedom write on *our* art's banners, our science shall be gay!

Let us break from every flower one fine blossom for our power
and two leaves to wind a wreath!
Let us dance like troubadours between holy men and whores,
between god and world beneath!

Who thinks tempests dance too quickly, all the bandaged and
the sickly, crippled, old, and overnice,
if you fear the wind might hurt you, honor-fools and geese of
virtue—out of our paradise!

Let us whirl the dusty hazes right into the sick men's noses, flush
the sick brood everywhere!
Let us free the coast together from the wilted bosoms' blether,
from the eyes that never dare!

Let us chase the shadow lovers, world defamers, rain-cloud
shovers—let us brighten up the sky!
All free spirits' spirit, let you and me thunder; since I met you,
like a tempest roars my joy.

And forever to attest such great joy, take its bequest, take this
wreath with you up there!
Toss it higher, further, gladder, storm up on the heavens' ladder,
hang it up—upon a star.[25]

The attitude is one of storm, war, wind, the natural disasters of a joyful
catastrophe sweeping before it, destroying all timidity on the way to the
overhuman.

It is in hints like these given in *Ecce Homo* that Nietzsche entices us
into the world of his staged drama.

*"I, Ariadne repeat with Foucault: 'No, that point is not made in any of the
printed words in the text, but it is expressed through the words, in their
relationships and the distance that separates them.'[26] It is phantasm and seduction
that create the drama out of these relationships, which cause me to rhapsodize in
the gaps between Nietzsche's immortal words. Nietzsche could not and did not
want to write directly of the task to be enacted; as he wrote to Heinrich von Stein,
'No, we may not speak of this.' However, the silent din of certain relationships
and gaps in Nietzsche's language inevitably crept into the recesses of my small ears
and set me dancing! I heard this drama behind 'The Night Song,' the song of*

Nietzsche as a lover, as the suffering god Dionysus, the enraptured hopeful lover who waits on high mountains for his Ariadne. He knew I must come in arrow form downward plunging, like a golden sunbeam lunging to pierce him in the rose dawn. He knew the fifth act: the wedding of Dionysus/ Nietzsche and I would be 'the golden balance of all things,' for he tied the knot: and we have shot our arrows perfectly."

On High Mountains

As Nietzsche sits in the 'seventh solitude' of his 'madness' waiting for Ariadne, waiting for Ariadne to say, "I love you," Sander Gilman writes: "there is one verse which he scribbled on a piece of paper in 1891 or 1897 (the date is not certain) and it is the first three verses of the final, 1886 version of 'From High Mountains' subtitled 'The Aftersong.'"[27] It comes at the end of *Beyond Good and Evil*, just after "The Genius of the Heart" and Dionysus's talk with Ariadne in which he says he would like to make humans more evil, thus more beautiful. It is the "Aftersong" because it comes at the end of *Beyond Good and Evil*, but it is after the fact of good and evil, thus beyond it. It is more. It is the song Nietzsche writes before to sing after the event of his 'madness.' The *Dionysian Dithyrambs* are its companion. He sings it after the event in *advance*!

*

*   *

*   *

*   *   *   *

O noon of life! O time to celebrate!
    O summer garden!
Restlessly happy and expectant, standing,
Watching all day and night, for friends I wait:
Where are you, friends? Come! It is time! It's late!

The glacier's gray adorned itself for you
    Today with roses;
The brook seeks you, and full of longing rises
The wind, the cloud, into the vaulting blue
To look for you from dizzy bird's eye view.

Higher than mine no table has been set:
  Who lives so near
The stars or dread abysses half as sheer?
My realm, like none, is almost infinite,
And my sweet honey—who has tasted it?—

—There you are, friends!—Alas, the man you sought
  You do not find here?
You hesitate, amazed? Anger were kinder!
I—changed so much? A different face and gait?
And what I am—for you, friends, I am not?

Am I another? Self-estranged? From me—
  Did I elude?
A wrestler who too oft himself subdued?
Straining against his strength too frequently,
Wounded and stopped by his own victory?

I sought where cutting winds are at their worst?
  I learned to dwell
Where no one lives, in bleakest polar hell,
Unlearned mankind and god, prayer and curse?
Became a ghost that wanders over glaciers?

—My ancient friends! Alas! You show the shock
  Of love and fear!
No, leave! Do not be wroth! You—can't live here—
Here, among distant fields of ice and rock—
Here one must be a hunter, chamois-like.

A *wicked* archer I've become.—The ends
  of my bow kiss;
Only the strongest bends his bow like this.
No arrow strikes like that which my bow sends:
Away from here—for your own good, my friends!—

You leave?—My heart: no heart has borne worse hunger;
  Your hope stayed strong:
Don't shut your gates; *new* friends may come along.
Let old ones go. Don't be a memory-monger!
Once you were young—now you are even younger.

What once tied us together, *one* hope's bond—
   Who reads the signs
Love once inscribed on it, the pallid lines?
To parchment I compare it that the hand
Is *loath* to touch—discolored, dark, and burnt.

No longer *friends*—there is no word for those—
   It is a wraith
That knocks at night and tries to rouse my faith,
And looks at me and says: "Once friendship was—"
—O wilted word, once fragrant as the rose.

Youth's longing misconceived inconstancy.
   Those whom I deemed
Changed to my kin, the friends of whom I dreamed,
Have *aged* and lost our old affinity:
One has to change to stay akin to me.

O noon of life! Our second youthful state!
   O summer garden!
Restlessly happy and expectant, standing,
Looking all day and night, for friends I wait:
For *new* friends! Come! It's time! It's late!

There are many echoes in this poem of Nietzsche's notes for *Zara-thustra*, where he awaits the friends of noon with a rose festival: "the glacier's gray adorned itself for you today with roses." And much of this poem previews the *Dionysus dithyramb*, "Amid Birds of Prey": "dizzy bird's eye view," "I changed so much? A different face and gait?" "Am I another? Self-estranged?" "Here one must be a hunter, chamois-like," "A *wicked* archer I've become." Nietzsche had sent an earlier version of this poem to Heinrich von Stein in 1884 in which the order of the first and second stanzas was reversed and the seventh and eighth and tenth and eleventh. And the last two stanzas were not included at all. So Nietzsche rearranges the poem and adds the last two important stanzas in 1886. The last two stanzas read:

*   *

*

This song is over—longing's dulcet cry
  Died in my mouth:
A wizard did it, friend in time of drought,
The friend of noon—no, do not ask me who—
At noon it was that one turned into two—

Sure of our victory, we celebrate
  The feast of feasts:
Friend Zarathustra came, the guest of guests!
The world now laughs, rent are the drapes of fright,
The wedding is at hand of dark and light—[28]

*   *   *   *

*   *

*   *

*

Let us ask who this "friend of noon" is. Most commentators assume
that Zarathustra is this friend. But let us look again. Nietzsche removes
himself to high mountains ('madness') waiting for the friend of noon—"do
not ask me who—". This is sung in the future looking back at the events it
speaks of—the *aftersong*. It no longer reflects a longing for past or present
friends but a celebration of the future friend who will have come at noon.
The wizard or magician referred to is the magician of Book IV of *Zarathustra*. It is Dionysus: "a green lightning bolt flashed from [the magician's]
eye toward Zarathustra."[29] The magician/Dionysus who sings his
"Magician's Song," later transformed into "Ariadne's Lament" answered by
Dionysus who appears in "emerald beauty." This magician/Dionysus and
Ariadne are tied eternally together. Nietzsche does not know *who* the
friend of noon will be, but he is sure that the friend will have come. He has
tied his knot, shot his wicked arrow with perfect skill: "No arrow strikes
like that which my bow sends." The expected wedding and feast of feasts
proclaim a victory and celebration for the future of the overhuman. At this

great noon Zarathustra attends as friend and guest of guests, but he is not
the partner in marriage where one is turned to two and through which dark
and light are reconciled. In "The Night Song" Nietzsche is the lover as
inexorable light who longs for the nocturnal. Ariadne, the answer to "this
solar solitude in the light" is herself a sun who casts Nietzsche into the
'dark' role of receiver rather than giver, and in this manner his lover's call is
answered in the wedding of dark and light. The friend of noon is Ariadne,
and Ariadne can be male or female. Nietzsche cannot know *who* it will be
that answers his love song, "The Night Song," in the voice of Ariadne.

In 1887 Nietzsche added a preface, Book V, and the Appendix of
Songs by Prince Vogelfrei to the second edition of *The Gay Science*. Among
these poems is one called "Sils Maria," originally written in 1882, which
appears to be a precursor of the last two verses added to "On High
Mountains" in 1886. "Sils Maria" immediately precedes "To the Mistral" at
the end of *The Gay Science*, which means that "To the Mistral" can be
understood also to be sung to the friend of noon: Ariadne. Here is "Sils
Maria":

> Here I sat, waiting, waiting—not for anything—
> Beyond Good and Evil, fancying
>
> Now light, now shadows, all a game,
> All lake, all noon, all time without aim.
> Then, suddenly, [woman] friend! one turned into two—
> —And Zarathustra walked into my view...
>
> *Hier sass ich, wartend, wartend,—doch auf nichts,*
> *Jenseits von Gut und Böse, bald des Lichts*
>
> *Geniessend, bald des Schattens, ganz nur spiel*
> *Ganz see, ganz Mittag, ganz Zeit ohne Ziel.*
> *Da, Plötzlich, Freundin! wurde eins zu zwei—*
> *—Und Zarathustra ging an mir vorbei...*[30]

The usual interpretation of Freundin here is that Nietzsche refers to
Lou Andreas Salomé. Kaufmann writes in a note to "Sils Maria": "The
'friend' to whom he is telling this (*Freundin* is feminine) is Lou Salomé, in
1882."[31] Because of this Kaufmann changes the grammatical structure of

Nietzsche's sentence in his translation by removing the exclamation point and the pause that it represents: "Then, suddenly, friend, one turned into two—." Kaufmann also removes the female nature of the friend. Nietzsche's line in "Sils Maria" reads: "*Da, Plötzlich, Freundin! wurde eins zu zwei—.*" One could read the line: Then, suddenly, the woman friend! [came and] one turned into two, meaning that the idea of a woman (Ariadne) becoming one (wedding) with Nietzsche strikes him suddenly. And Zarathustra, as the herald of eternal recurrence, walks by as a symbol and eternal seal of this union. Note also, that after "one turned into two" Nietzsche uses two dashes, one after *zwei* and another before *und*, "And Zarathustra walked into view..." This very long pause indicates a clear break, which Kaufmann also disregards by using only one of the dashes, between the idea of the joining with the woman friend and Zarathustra. The ellipsis at the end of the poem, again left out by Kaufmann, also indicates Zarathustra as symbolizing the infinity of eternal recurrence. We have seen that Nietzsche's notes for *Zarathustra* of 1886–87 are filled with this woman friend in the form of the wedding of Dionysus and Ariadne.

In early April 1882 Nietzsche took a trip to Messina in Sicily where he wrote the collection of poems called "The Idylls from Messina" including "Sils Maria." Therefore, it is reasonable to suggest that "Sils Maria" was written before Nietzsche met Lou Andreas Salomé for the first time at the end of April 1882 in Rome. Paul Ree wrote a letter to Nietzsche in Messina dated April 20, 1882, in which he suggested that Nietzsche meet Lou.[32] Their actual meeting took place just a few days later. Nietzsche wrote and published "The Idylls from Messina" in 1882, and then published many of them in their revised version at the end of the second edition of *The Gay Science* in 1887. Why? Because they bridge the space of time between Nietzsche's conception of his highest hope and goal in 1881–82 and 1887 when they herald the playing out of the Nietzsche/ Dionysus drama a year later.

Grundlehner makes a crucial point when he ties in another of the poems from "The Idylls from Messina," also reproduced in 1887, with "Sils Maria" and "To the Mistral: A Dancing Song," the poem "The Mysterious Bark":

Last night all appeared to doze,
Unsteady the wind that wailed
Softly lest it break repose;
Only I on my bed flailed,
Poppy and good conscience, those
Trusted soporifics, failed.

Finally, I foreswore sleep,
Got up, and ran to the strand.
There was moonlight where it's steep,
Man and bark on the warm sand,
Sleepy both shepherd and sheep—
Sleepily we left the land.

One hour passed, or two, or three—
Or a year—when suddenly
All my thoughts and mind were drowned
In timeless monotony:
An abyss without a ground
Opened up—not one more sound.

Morning came, on the black deep
Rests a bark, rests on the swell.
What has happened? Hundreds keep
Asking that. Who died? Who fell?
Nothing happened! We found sleep,
All of us—we slept so well.[33]

Grundlehner writes:

Who is this boatman and what role does he play in the poem?
Although Wolfgang Taraba argues that he is a Charon figure
piloting the death barge, such an interpretation would contradict
the affirmation of life that Nietzsche celebrates throughout his
philosophy. Rather than death, it is more likely that the figure
personifies a selfhood that exists apart from quotidian reality.
Nietzsche often divides himself into two personae for such a
purpose. In the poem "Sils Maria" he speaks of splitting into two
selves during his encounter with eternity...."Then, suddenly,
...one turned into two." In his experience of timeless noontide

in the poem "From High Mountains," he characterizes his loneliness as "twosomeness," "At noon it was that one turned into two."…This is the same relationship that is described in "The Mysterious Bark": the boatman, or shepherd, a "second, eternal self"—leads the waking man, or sheep, on an ocean journey to explore the mystery of the inner Dionysian realm.[34]

The connection of a mysterious bark, one becoming two, and Ariadne comes together in *Zarathustra* in "On the Great Longing," which we already know was first called "Ariadne." Here the golden bark comes carrying the vintager of Zarathustra's soul, the "deliverer, O my soul, the nameless one for whom only future songs will find names." The bark is death, as Taraba suggests, but the living death of 'madness.' But the bark is also victory in death through the eternal recurrence. In "Sils Maria," "On High Mountains," and "On the Great Longing," the friend is expected and comes, though Nietzsche does not know who it will be. His secret name for the friend is Ariadne: "Who besides me knows what Ariadne is!"[35] In "The Mysterious Bark" something of great moment takes place: Nietzsche takes the bark to "an abyss without a ground." After that "not one more sound." In the morning a bark rests on the swell. People ask, What happened? Who died? Who fell? But the people are asleep. The great moment, the moment of the eternal voluntary bark of death in the poem, goes unrecognized because humans are sleeping. This has connections with Nietzsche's parody of sleepers in "On the Teachers of Virtue" and with the Garden of Gethsemane where Christ's disciples sleep through his precrucifixion agony: "a man of force accomplishes a deed which strikes a reef and sinks from sight having produced no impression; a brief, sharp echo, and all is over."[36] It is also significant to mention that "The Mysterious Bark" could be a version of the *Dionysian dithyramb* "The Sun Sinks," where Nietzsche's little craft or bark swims out upon the gilded sea in a metaphor of death.

The German for the added verse to "On High Mountains" reads:

Dies *Lied is aus,*—*der Sehnsucht süsser Schrei*
   Erstarb im Munde:
Ein Zauberer that's, der Freund zur rechten Stunde,
Der Mittags-Freund—nein! fragt nicht, wer es sei—
Um Mittag war's, da wurde Eins zu Zwei.…

Nun feiern wir, vereinten Siegs gewiss,
  Das Fest der Feste:
Freund Zarathustra kam, der Gast der Gäste!
Nun lacht die Welt, der grause Vorhang riss,
Die Hochzeit kam für Licht und Finsterniss...[37]

It is clear that Nietzsche expects a friend of noon, but that he does not know who it will be. But in "Sils Maria" we saw that it was a woman. The wedding of Nietzsche and this friend unites light and dark, noon and midnight. At the height of Zarathustra's mysteries in "The Drunken Song" he sings to the higher men: "midnight too is noon; pain too is a joy, curses too are a blessing; night too is a sun—go away or you will learn: a sage too is a fool."[38] In the German above the distance between the friend of noon and Zarathustra commented upon in "Sils Maria" is further stressed in that mention of the guest Zarathustra comes in the next stanza. We saw in the plans for *Zarathustra* that the wedding of Ariadne and Dionysus was to bring on the great noon and the feast of feasts and a satyr-play: for this to happen a sage must become a fool, Nietzsche must become 'mad.'

In "On High Mountains," Nietzsche has written the "Aftersong," the song of longing for the friend of noon who will have seen the silent drama, the friend, Ariadne, who will respond across the rocking waves with her song of joy. The asterisks Nietzsche places around the "Aftersong," which Kaufmann says were in the original edition and which he retains, image the constellation of Ariadne's crown:

I see a sign—
from the farthest distance
slowly glittering a constellation sinks towards me...[39]

Notes

1. Erich Podach, *Gestalten um Nietzsche* (Weimar: Erich Lichtenstein Verlag, 1932), pp. 106–7.
2. Janko Lavrin, *Nietzsche and Modern Consciousness: A Psychocritical Study* (New York: Haskell House, 1973), p. 221.
3. Kaufmann, Introduction to *Ecce Homo*, p. 202.
4. R. J. Hollingdale, *Nietzsche: The Man and His Philosophy* (London: Routledge and Kegan Paul, 1965), p. 289.

5. Nietzsche, *Ecce Homo*, p. 217.

6. Alphonso Lingis, "The Irrecuperable," in *International Studies in Philosophy*, 23/2, p. 74.

7. Podach, *Madness of Nietzsche*, p. 213; emphasis added.

8. Ibid., pp. 214–15; emphasis added.

9. *Der Kranke Nietzsche: Briefe Seiner Mutter an Franz Overbeck*, Herausgegeben von Erich Podach (Wien: Bermann-Fischer Verlag, 1937), p. 51.

10. *Selected Letters of Friedrich Nietzsche*, trans. Chistopher Middleton (Chicago: University of Chicago Press, 1969), pp. 345–48.

11. Nietzsche, *Zarathustra*, p. 310.

12. Nietzsche, *Ecce Homo*, p. 327.

13. Ibid., p. 309.

14. Nietzsche, *Twilight of the Idols*, in *The Portable Nietzsche*, p. 563.

15. Ibid., p. 542 and pp. 562–63; emphasis added.

16. Nietzsche, *From on The Genealogy of Morals and Ecce Homo*, p. 293. Copyright © 1967 by Random House, Inc. Reprinted by permission of Random House, Inc.

17. Middleton, *Selected Letters*, p. 193.

18. Ibid., pp. 197–98.

19. Ibid., pp. 211–12.

20. Karl Jaspers, *Nietzsche* (Chicago: Henry Regnery, 1965), p. 91.

21. Ibid., p. 93.

22. Nietzsche, *Ecce Homo*, p. 293.

23. Nietzsche, *Gay Science*, p. 197.

24. Ibid., #153.

25. From *The Gay Science* by Friedrich Nietzsche, pp. 373–75. Copyright © 1974 by Random House, Inc. Reprinted by permission of Random House, Inc.

26. Foucault, "What Is an Author?" in *Language, Counter-Memory, Practice*, ed. Donald Bouchard (Ithaca, N.Y.: Cornell University Press, 1977), p. 135.

27. Sander L. Gilman, "Friedrich Nietzsche's 'Niederschriften Aus der Spätesten Zeit' (1890–1897) and the Conversation Notebooks, 1889–1895," in *Psychoanalytische und Psychopathologische Literatur-interpretation*, Herausgegeben von Bernd Urban und Winfried Kudszas (Darmstadt: Wissenschaftliche Buchgesellschaft, 1981), pp. 328–32.

28. From *Beyond Good and Evil* by Friedrich Nietzsche, pp. 241–45. Copyright © 1966 by Random House, Inc. Reprinted by permission of Random House, Inc.

29. Nietzsche, *Zarathustra*, p. 369.

30. From *The Gay Science* by Friedrich Nietzsche, p. 371. Copyright © 1974 by Random House, Inc. Reprinted by permission of Random House, Inc.

31. Ibid.

32. *Friedrich Nietzsche, Paul Ree, and Lou von Salomé, Die Dokumente Ihrer Begegnung*, ed. Ernst Pfeiffer (Frankfurt am Main: Insel Verlag, 1970), p. 160.

33. From *The Gay Science* by Friedrich Nietzsche, p. 359. Copyright © 1974 by Random House, Inc. Reprinted by permission of Random House, Inc.

34. Philip Grundlehner, *The Poetry of Friedrich Nietzsche* (New York: Oxford University Press, 1986), p. 107.

35. Nietzsche, *Ecce Homo*, p. 308.

36. Nietzsche, "Wagner in Bayreuth," p. 197. See my p. 5.

37. KSA, Vol. 5, p. 243.

38. Nietzsche, *Zarathustra*, p. 435.

39. Nietzsche, "Fame and Eternity," *Dithyrambs of Dionysus*, p. 65.

Ariadne's Lament and Wisdom: Cutting the Gordian Knot

Let us listen to the intimate exchange of the lovers Dionysus and Ariadne. What a strange and new love Ariadne comes with, the love Dionysus demands! Let us follow the secret laments and love tortures that lead Ariadne and Dionysus to divine certainty, a wedding, and comedy.

Ariadne's Lament

Who still warms me, who still loves me?
  Offer me hot hands!
  offer me coal-warmers for the heart!
Spread-eagled, shuddering,
like one half-dead whose feet are warmed—
shaken, alas! by unknown fevers,
trembling with sharp icy frost-arrows,
  pursued by you, my thought!
Unutterable, veiled, terrible one!
  Huntsman behind the clouds!
Struck down by your lightning-bolt,
your mocking eye that stares at me from the darkness!
  Thus I lie,
bend myself, twist myself, tortured
by every eternal torment,
  smitten
by you, cruel huntsman
you unknown—god...

Strike deeper!
Strike once again!
Sting and sting, shatter this heart!
What means this torment
with blunt arrows?
Why do you look down,
unwearied of human pain,
with malicious divine flashing eyes?
Will you not kill, only torment?
Why—torment *me*,
you malicious, unknown god?

Ha ha!
Are you stealing near
at such a midnight hour?...
What do you want?
Speak!
You oppress me, press me,
Ha! far too closely!
You hear me breathing,
you overhear my heart,
you jealous god!
—yet jealous of what?
Away! Away!
Why the ladder?
Would you climb
into my heart,
climb into my
most secret thoughts?
Shameless, unknown thief!
What would you get by stealing?
What would you get by listening?
What would you get by torturing,
you torturer?
you—hangman-god!
Or shall I, like a dog,
roll before you?
Surrendering, raving with rapture,
wag—love to you?

In vain!
Strike again,
cruellest goad!
Not dog—I am only your game,
cruellest huntsman!
Your proudest prisoner,
you robber behind the clouds...
For the last time, speak!
Veiled in lightning! Unknown! speak!
What do you want, waylayer, from—me?

What?
Ransom?
How much ransom?
Demand much—thus speaks my pride!
and be brief—thus speaks my other pride!
Ha! ha!
Me—you want me?
me—all of me?...

Ha ha!
And you torment me, fool that you are,
you rack my pride?
Offer me love—who still warms me?
  who still loves me?
offer me hot hands,
offer me coal-warmers for the heart,
offer me, the most solitary,
whom ice, alas! sevenfold ice
has taught to long for enemies,
even for enemies,
offer, yes yield to me,
cruellest enemy—
yourself!...
He is gone!
He has fled,
my sole companion,
my great enemy,
my unknown,
my hangman-god!...

No!
come back!
with all your torments!
All the streams of my tears run their course to you!
and the last flame of my heart,
it burns up to you.
Oh come back,
my unknown god! my *pain*!
my last happiness!...

A flash of lightning. Dionysus becomes visible in emerald beauty.

DIONYSUS:

Be wise, Ariadne!...
You have little ears, you have ears like mine:
Let some wisdom into them!—
Must we not first hate ourself if we are to love ourself?...

I am thy labyrinth...[1]

Wrestling with her immortal lover thus, how does Ariadne understand what Dionysus says to her?

Reflection on Love: Suffering and Joy

Is it true that truth comes only of suffering?
Must we seek suffering, not repulse it.
Cry upon death as a beloved?
Is my pain, longing and confusion the necessary preface
   to the good and truth of my beloved?
And what good is this?
And what truth?
In which realms is it good and true?
Must I suffer of life and die to life to live in you?
And what return is good and truth?
Can one live in death, joy in suffering?

Zarathustra sang to me:

The world is deep,
Deep is its woe.
Joy—deeper yet than agony:
Woe implores: Go!
But all joy wants eternity—
Wants deep, wants deep eternity.
For all joy wants itself, hence it also wants agony.
O happiness, O pain! Oh, break, heart!

The joy I have of you, your truth, your good when I am with
* you does not last.*
I suffer of loss of you when you flee behind your masks and veils.
Pain comes to me.
I do not choose it.
I do not choose that suffering, it chooses me.
Is such love, then, the movement of the universe?
Love.
Most speak of it as joy, rapture, most come flying headlessly
* together.*
Yet, I felt a thrill when we spoke of pain,
* just the right amount and more of pain!*
Where comes this pain?
Where comes this joy?
Is being in love opening oneself to what it means to be humanly
* divine?*
Does the suffering of the separation from the loved one
* lead to salvation?*
Or is salvation only in the presence of the beloved?
Or is salvation in the war of the two?

Hafiz: Blessed is the day when the ruined-home forsake,
*   With lifted soul, journey to my friend take.*

A stranger may always go astray,
The scent of her hair is the guide of my way.
I feel depressed in Alexander's jail
I'll pack up—to Solomon's realm I'll sail.

Frail like Zephyr, but with impatient heart,
To my beautiful darling I will depart.

If for his love even my head I lose,
With sore heart and wet eyes this I'll choose.

I pledged to go to tavern happy and gay,
If I am relieved from worries some day.

Around him like molecule I whirl in dance;
To Sun I ascend—to have of God a glance.

If like Hafiz, you ever become astray,
Light of his guidance you better obey.[2]

Ah, Hafiz!
Do you know what the emerald light of his guidance is?
Do you know it by some certain sign?
Do you know it by your heart?
Ah, Hafiz, is pain the light of his guidance?
Very well then, if for his love even my head I lose,
  with sore heart and wet eyes this I'll choose.
Hafiz, you also, along with Dionysus and Zarathustra,
  say that suffering and tears
  and losing one's head are the ways to the loved one.
And the loved one is the scent of hair and the glance of God,
  human and divine.
If I die, if I walk about with a sore heart and wet eyes,
  and love this suffering, dying, and crying,
  will that be the truth and the good until my love speeds to me?

Is what is given that which is one's law?

Ariadne's Wisdom

Transfiguration:

Ariadne becomes hard like the down of a bird's feather,
Firm like the plum blossom in spring,
Resolute like the babbling of a mountain brook,
Destroying like the gentlest lover.

Dionysus: "Now you are akin to me, my Ariadne 'whoever knows the heart will guess how poor, helpless, arrogant, and mistaken is even the best, the profoundest love—how it even destroys rather than saves.'"[3]

A full and powerful soul not only copes with painful, even terrible losses, deprivations, robberies, insults; it emerges from such hells with a greater fullness and powerfulness; and, most essential of all, with a new increase in the blissfulness of love. I believe that he who has divined something of the most basic conditions for this growth in love will understand what Dante meant when he wrote over the gate of his Inferno: "I, too, was created by eternal love."[4]

Dionysus: "For you, Ariadne, Zarathustra has said the final word which celebrates your soul":

Watch for every hour in which your spirit wants to speak in parables: there lies the origin of your virtue. There your body is elevated and resurrected; with its rapture it delights the spirit so that it turns creator and esteemer and lover and benefactor of all things.

When your heart flows broad and full like a river, a blessing and a danger to those living near: there is the origin of your virtue.

When you are above praise and blame, and your will wants to command all things, like a lover's will: there is the origin of your virtue.

Power is she, this new virtue; a dominant thought is she, and around her a wise soul: a golden sun, and around it the serpent of knowledge.

You shall strive after the virtue of the column: it grows more and more beautiful and gentle, but internally harder and more enduring, as it ascends.

For this is the soul's secret: only when the hero has abandoned her, she is approached in a dream by the overhero.[5]

Ariadne: "Very well, Dionysus! I come triumphantly, wounded with my dream and your wicked golden arrows, seduced by your tortures, great tempter god! I come not to consummate a tender romantic love, however monumental. I come as a joyful destroyer and a creator. My phantasm must create its own catastrophe. I sweep you up, great god in my will to power, whether it was your will too—or not. I must kill you to go beyond you, but your golden arrows are already fatal to me. The Gordian knot of your great drama that you tied so tightly I see, and fatal it is that I saw it at all":

> Vita femina—For seeing the ultimate beauties of a work, no knowledge or good will is sufficient; this requires the rarest of lucky accidents: The clouds that veil these peaks have to lift for once so that we see them glowing in the sun. Not only do we have to stand in precisely the right spot in order to see this, *but the unveiling must have been accomplished by our own soul because it needed some external expression and parable,* as if it were a matter of having something to hold on to and retain control of itself. But it is so rare for all of this to coincide that I am inclined to believe that the highest peaks of everything good, whether it be a work, a deed, humanity, or nature, have so far remained concealed and veiled from the great majority and even from the best human beings. But what does unveil itself for us, *unveils itself for us once only.*[6]

King Gordius tied a knot-cypher in a rawhide thong that was jealously guarded by priests for centuries. It had a religious significance, the ineffable name of Dionysus. Many tried to untie it, but none succeeded until Alexander the Great drew his sword and cut the knot in half, placing the power of the sword over that of religious mystery.[7] *"When he afterwards succeeded in subjecting all Asia to his sway, people began to think that he had complied with the terms of the oracle according to its true meaning."*[8]

"I, Ariadne, come like Alexander and cut your knot in two, Dionysus, with my sword conquering in victory, winning for a phantasm the crown of 'truth,' displaying the power of human creation to revalue values. I seduce as has never been seduced before because archer that you are, great god, you shot me with your golden icy-frost arrows—fool that I am. You are my labyrinth! Singing and dancing I 'throw myself around, out, back, I am light! A bird in wisdom! I sing! Oh how should I not also lust after eternity and after the nuptial ring of rings, the ring of recurrence?"[9] *I have found the man/god from whom I want children, for it is you, Dionysus, whom I love: we must destroy each other to go beyond ourselves. We must celebrate our wedding as a downgoing in the face of eternal rebirth. Our great guest, Zarathustra, knows this, too. We two, the most joyful of eternal lovers. Is this what you meant, Dionysus? 'Must we not first hate*

ourselves, if we are to love ourselves?' Must we not be hard with ourselves if we are to create beyond ourselves! Create the overhuman! Oh, Dionysus, you gentle ravisher, you, too, want to be ravished!"

> *Will and Wave.*—How greedily this wave approaches, as if it were after something! How it crawls with terrifying haste into the inmost nooks of this labyrinthine cliff! It seems that it is trying to anticipate someone; it seems that something of value, high value, must be hidden there.—And now it comes back, a little more slowly but still quite white with excitement; is it disappointed? Has it found what it looked for? Does it pretend to be disappointed?—But already another wave is approaching, still more greedily and savagely than the first, and its soul, too, seems to be full of secrets and the lust to dig up treasures. Thus live waves—thus live we who will—more I shall not say. So? You mistrust me? You are angry with me, you beautiful monsters? Are you afraid that I might give away your whole secret? Well, be angry with me, arch your dangerous green bodies as high as you can, raise a wall between me and the sun—as you are doing now! Truly, even now nothing remains of the world but green twilight and green lightning. Carry on as you like, roaring with over-weening pleasure and malice—or dive again, pouring your emeralds down into the deepest depths, and throw your infinite white mane of foam and spray over them: Everything suits me, for everything suits you so well, and I am so well-disposed toward you for everything; how could I think of betraying you? For— mark my word!—I know you and your secret, I know your kind! You and I—are we not of one kind?—You and I—do we not have one secret?[10]

"Here, as the green-bodied waves, I ravish you, great Dionysus and our wedding dissolves in green lightning and green twilight where only one labyrinthine secret is shared!"

Ariadne to Dionysus

Inside me your memory jumps into life.
Inside me longing for touching your divinity calls out.
I am the rapture of life-giving memory.
I am the tears of joy that long for the two in one of Belovedness.
I come, my storm, I blacken the skies with your thunderous
crash.
We are the life-giving waters, my precious rain!

If today it is still and your stars cannot dance on the sea.
If today the whispering of the trees is silent in your soul.
If you are a star waiting to dance.
If you are a solitary tree waiting to whisper its secrets.
I come, then, to blow our stars into action, our secrets into song.
We are the power of Zephyr, my living wind!

If the skies outside your window are gray.
If the buds on your trees are bursting with verdant pregnancy
which await only the sun to rage into life.
Then I fly to you, my bud ready to burst, I rent gray skies asunder.
We are the warming rays, my radiant sun!

Ah! The rainbow! No, two rainbows!!
Shimmering arches strained to fit in the arc of each other!
Vaporous melting! Glistening colors mixing hues of purest
clarity!
Purple penetrating blue, yellow sparking red to flames!
Green becoming the aerial distance of perfect symmetry
and emerald splendor!

Notes

1. Nietzsche, *Dithyrambs of Dionysus*, trans. R. J. Hollingdale, Redding Ridge, Conn. Black Swan Books, 1984. Reprinted with permission of the publisher.

2. *Odes of Hafiz*, trans. Abbas Aryanpur Kashani (Lexington, Ky.: Mazda Publishers, 1984), p. 230. Reprinted with permission of the publishers.

3. Nietzsche, *Nietzsche contra Wagner*, p. 679.

4. Nietzsche, *Will to Power*, #1030.

5. Nietzsche *Zarathustra*, pp. 187–88, 230–31.

6. Nietzsche, *Gay Science*, #339; emphasis added.

7. Robert Graves, *The Greek Myths* (Baltimore: Penguin Books, 1955), Vol. 1, pp. 282–84.

8. *Bullfinch's Mythology*, p. 48; emphasis added.

9. Nietzsche, *Zarathustra*, p. 343.

10. Nietzsche, *Gay Science*, #310.

The Golden Bark: Die at the Right Time and in the Right Way

The Golden Bark

"Oh, you listeners, seduced so easily?" laughs Ariadne. "What a pretty phantasm I draw before your eyes, before your thirsty souls. But don't believe a word of it, for I love to spin little webs with my golden thread and I have not even begun to spin yet. Zarathustra, too, is fond of gold and paints pretty pictures with it."

From "On the Great Longing" in *Zarathustra*, called "Ariadne" in Nietzsche's notes:

> But if you will not weep, not weep out your crimson melancholy, then you will have to *sing*, O my soul. Behold, I myself smile as I say this before you: sing with a roaring song till all seas are silenced, that they may listen to your longing—till over silent, longing seas the bark floats, the golden wonder around whose gold all good, bad, wondrous things leap,—also many great and small animals and whatever has light, wondrous feet for running on paths blue as violets—toward the golden wonder, the voluntary bark and its master; but that is the vintager who is waiting with his diamond knife—your great deliverer, O my soul, the nameless one for whom only future songs will find names. And verily, even now your breath is fragrant with future songs, even now you are glowing and dreaming and drinking thirstily from all deep and resounding wells of comfort, even now your melancholy is resting in the happiness of future songs.[1]

Zarathustra sits on high mountains looking out over seas, longing for the voluntary bark, the golden wonder that carries the vintager and her diamond knife to cut the ripe grapes that he is from the vine—to deliver his soul from longing and carry it to victory. Zarathustra does not know who it is who will come; it is a nameless one, but by having come voluntarily to cut the vine to release its sweet wine and to die in that sweetness, that nameless one will be sung in future songs. Nietzsche's name for this nameless one is Ariadne. In the next section in *Zarathustra*, "The Other Dancing Song," Nietzsche continues with this metaphor of the golden bark: "Into your eyes I looked recently, O life: I saw gold blinking in your night eye; my heart stopped in delight: a golden boat I saw blinking on nocturnal waters, a golden rocking boat, sinking, drinking and winking again."[2] And under the influence of this vision Zarathustra begins a dance with life.

The fourth and fifth acts of Nietzsche's drama take place upon the sea: fourth act, Nietzsche's voluntary 'madness,' his golden bark, his sitting on a high mountain on the Island of Naxos in the sea, waiting; fifth act, Ariadne, herself a golden bark, comes to him, across the sea and the wedding takes place.

Foucault speaks of the boat and sea as a metaphor of madness. In the context of Nietzsche's drama Foucault becomes a dithyrambist and sings of Nietzsche's open seas: "The madman's voyage is at once a rigorous division and an absolute passage":

Among the mystics of the fifteenth century, it has become the motif of the soul as a skiff, abandoned on the infinite sea of desires, in the sterile field of cares and ignorance among the mirages of knowledge, amid the unreason of the world—a craft at the mercy of the sea's great madness, unless it throws out a solid anchor, faith, or raises its spiritual sails so that the breath of God may bring it to port.

But water adds to this the dark mass of its own values; it carries off, but it does more: it purifies. Navigation delivers man to the uncertainty of fate; on water, each of us is in the hands of his own destiny; every embarkation is, potentially, the last. It is for the other world that the madman sets sail in his fool's boat; it is from the other world that he comes when he disembarks.

Water and navigation certainly play this role. Confined on the ship, from which there is no escape, the madman is delivered to the river with its thousand arms, the sea with its thousand roads, to that great uncertainty external to everything. He is a prisoner in the midst of what is the freest, the openest of routes: bound fast at the infinite crossroads. He is the passenger par excellence: that is, the prisoner of the passage. And the land he will come to is unknown—as is, once he disembarks, the land from which he comes. He has his truth and his homeland only in that fruitless expanse between two countries that cannot belong to him.[3]

In his *Dionysus dithyramb*, "The Sun Sinks," Nietzsche becomes the silver-golden boat himself in a metaphor of death:

Day of my life!
   the sun sinks.
Already the smooth
   flood stands gilded.
The cliffs breathe warmth:
   did happiness at midday
sleep there its midday sleep?
   From the brown abyss
light and green it still dazzles up.

Gilded cheerfulness, come!
   sweetest, secretest
foretaste of death!
—Did I run my course too quickly?
Only now, when my foot has grown weary,
   does your glance overtake me,
   does your *happiness* overtake me.

Only playing of waves all around.
   Whatever was hard
has sunk into blue oblivion—
my boat now lies idle.
Storm and voyaging—all forgotten now!
   Desire and hope have drowned,
   smooth lie soul and sea.

Seventh solitude!
  Never such sweet
security, never such sunlight warmth.
—Does the ice of my summit still glow?
  Silver, light, a fish
  my little craft now swims out...[4]

This echoes "The Mysterious Bark," which "rests on the swell" about which it is asked, "What has happened? Who died? Who fell?" Foucault writes: "Madness is the purest, most total form of *qui pro quo*; it takes the false for true, death for life, man for woman, the beloved for the Erinnys and the victim for Minos. But it is also the most rigorously necessary form of the *qui pro quo* in the dramatic economy, for it needs no external element to reach a true resolution. It has merely to carry its illusion to the point of truth."[5]

Ariadne: "There has been no greater poet than my Dionysus/Nietzsche, my fisherman on high mountains deep in his own soul, the voluntary silver-golden craft that twinkles and dances upon the waves, inviting me to become the eye in which the vision of this most divine of spectacles is reflected until, I too, become golden bark, longing, take up the diamond knife and throw myself upon the rocking brown/green abyss of death. But death is the promise of life, his soul is mine and mine is his, our orgiastic souls, our golden crafts float toward one another, but they are the same eternal drama of love."

These are Nietzsche's metaphors of his voluntary death/'madness.'

Voluntary Death

Nietzsche wrote often of suicide as the moral act of nihilism. When one sees that one is no longer at the height of life and is declining, he suggested it would be one's duty to accept a voluntary death. In a note from 1888 Nietzsche writes:

Nothing would be more useful or more to be encouraged than a thoroughgoing *practical nihilism*....Problem: with what means could one attain to a severe form of really contagious nihilism: such as teaches and practices voluntary death with scientific conscientiousness (—and *not* a feeble vegetable existence in

expectation of a false afterlife—)? One cannot sufficiently con-
demn Christianity for having devaluated the value of such a
great purifying nihilistic movement, which was perhaps already
being formed, through the idea of the immortal private person:
likewise through the hope of resurrection: in short, through continual deterrence from the *deed of nihilism*, which is suicide.[6]

Another note from 1888 includes a list of things that Nietzsche says have
been ruined by the church's misuse of them, such things as asceticism,
fasting, feasts, and: "death.—One must convert the stupid physiological
fact into a moral necessity. So to live that one can also *will at the right time
to die!*"[7] These notes come together in Section 36 of *The Twilight of the Idols*:

> To die proudly when it is no longer possible to live proudly. Death
> freely chosen, death at the right time, brightly and cheerfully
> accomplished amid children and witnesses: then a real farewell is
> still possible, as the one who is taking leave is still there; also a
> real estimate of what one has achieved and what one has wished,
> drawing the sum of one's life—all in opposition to the wretched
> and revolting comedy that Christianity has made of the hour of
> death....From love of *life*, one should desire a different death: free,
> conscious, without accident, without ambush.

Again, Nietzsche turns to the idea of suicide as the act of nihilism, suicide
for decadents: "Finally, some advice for our dear pessimists and other
decadents. It is not in our hands to prevent our birth; but we can correct
this mistake—for in some cases it is a mistake. When one does away with
oneself, one does the most estimable thing possible...—life itself derives
more advantage from this than from any 'life' of renunciation, anemia, and
other virtues: one has liberated the others from one's sight; one has
liberated life from an objection."[8] From these perspectives, Nietzsche offers
the idea that the most certain of our actions, death, can be made into an
occasion for the celebration of life or the enhancement of life through
conscious willing of death.

In *The Wanderer and His Shadow* Nietzsche had already written of
voluntary death: "Of rational death.—What is more rational, to stop the
machine when the work one demands of it has been completed—or to let
it run on until it stops of its own accord, that is to say until it is ruined?...

The wise regulation and disposal of death belongs to that morality of the future, at present quite ungraspable and immoral sounding, into the dawn of which it must be an indescribable joy to gaze."[9] But it is in "On Free Death" from *Zarathustra* that Nietzsche expresses the thought that voluntary death might become a supreme culmination and celebration.

> Many die too late, and a few die too early. The doctrine still sounds strange: "Die at the right time!"
>
> I show you the death that consummates—a spur and a promise to the survivors. He that consummates his life dies his death victoriously, surrounded by those who hope and promise. Thus should one learn to die; and there should be no festival where one dying thus does not hallow the oaths of the living.
>
> My death I praise to you, the free death which comes to me because *I* want it. And when shall I want it? He who has a goal and an heir will want death at the right time for his goal and heir. And from reverence for his goal and heir he will hang no more dry wreaths in the sanctuary of life.
>
> One must cease letting oneself be eaten when one tastes best: that is known to those who want to be loved long.
>
> That your dying be no blasphemy against man and earth, my friends, that I ask of the honey of your soul. In your dying, your spirit and virtue should still glow like a sunset around the earth: else your dying has burned out badly.
>
> Thus, I want to die myself that you, my friends, may love the earth more for my sake; and to earth I want to return that I may find rest in her who gave birth to me.
>
> Verily, Zarathustra *had a goal; he threw his ball;* now you, my friends, are the heirs of my goal; to you I throw my golden ball. More than anything, I like to see you, my friends, throwing the golden ball. And so I still linger a little on the earth: forgive me for that.[10]

In his interpretation of this section in his book *Nietzsche's Teaching*, Laurence Lampert writes:

Zarathustra's teaching requires that a free death be undertaken solely for its effect on an audience. Death becomes glorious as done for them; it can serve their purposes by being the occasion for swearing earnest vows to also live sacrificial lives. Like Lykurgos's death, it can show the living what their lives are to serve—no longer Sparta or an order that already exists, but solely the coming of the superman. To those few like himself who measure all their actions in the pure light of the good, the act of death, can be a gift to the living. Such men must seize death at the right moment, the singular moment in which their historic contribution to the historic good reaches completion, in which their gift has been given and heirs created. This is a fitting teaching for one who understands mankind to be a bridge or rope reaching toward a future that alone justifies it. Death as the culminating deed of life restates for the heirs what is worthy and causes them to harden their resolve that the meaning of life be exhausted in the cause of the superman.

Ariadne: "Nietzsche has done exactly this with his enactment of his voluntary 'madness,' making his death a glowing beacon on the path of history, a flame that it is impossible to ignore and that calls to future oath-takers."

Lampert continues:

This funeral oration for himself utilizes the edifying language of surrender to an earth seen as a mothering and superior force to willful man, but the one who delivers it is the one who does not surrender, even to inexorable death, but rather wills the moment of his death just as he wills the meaning of the earth. *Speaking in the past tense,* he says that he had a goal, and he commands his friends to be the heirs to his goal, to be those very ones the having of whom makes now the right time for him to die.

But, as we have already discussed, "Zarathustra betrays his own teaching when, instead of giving the disciples a riveting example of death in the interest of the superman, he lingers as a spectator of what he anticipates will be the historic drama of their march toward the superman. He needs forgiveness from his disciples because he is depriving them of an occasion for resolve, perhaps even *the* occasion."[11]

But Nietzsche himself fulfills the moral demand of Zarathustra's voluntary death. Was Nietzsche's voluntary 'madness' a living death? Did he 'die' voluntarily through a withdrawal under the mask of 'madness,' yet linger to see what would happen? At the end of "On Free Death:" "More than anything, I like to see you, my friends throwing the golden ball. I still linger a little on earth; forgive me for that."[12] This echoes what Zarathustra says after hearing the laughter of the transformed shepherd: "My longing for this laughter gnaws at me: oh, how do I bear to go on living! And how could I bear to die now!"[13] These lines in *Zarathustra* might suggest Nietzsche's intention of pursuing a voluntary death in life. Did Nietzsche choose the act of 'madness' so that he could be both dead to induce oath-takers and yet alive for a while to see it happen? "I am already dead as my father, while as my mother I am still living and growing old."[14] And madness is much more uncanny than death. Someone like Nietzsche dies and it is to be expected, but someone like Nietzsche goes 'mad' and the world continually tries to mediate such a catastrophe!

Culmination and Celebration, Not Martyrdom

In a note dated December 31, 1888, to Peter Gast, Nietzsche writes: "When your card came, *what* was I doing?...It was the famous Rubicon....I no longer know my address: let us assume that it will shortly be the Palazzo del Quirinale." The Rubicon is a small river in northern Italy. Caesar crossed it at the head of his army to march on Rome in 49 B.C. Here began the civil war with Pompeii. "To cross the Rubicon" means to start on a course of action from which there is no turning back; to take a final and irreversible step. In his life of Caesar, which Nietzsche owned and admired, Plutarch describes how Caesar sets out to conquer Ariminum through surprise: "what was needed was to make this first step suddenly, and so astound his enemies with the boldness of it; as it would be easier, he thought, to throw them into consternation by doing what they never anticipated than fairly to conquer them, if he had alarmed them by his preparations." Plutarch describes the moment when Caesar decides to cross the Rubicon to Ariminum:

he began to think, now that he was just entering upon that danger, and he wavered much in his mind when he considered the greatness of the enterprise into which he was throwing himself. He checked his course and ordered a halt, while he revolved with himself, and often changed his opinion one way and the other, *without speaking a word*. This was when his purposes fluctuated most;...computing how many calamities his passing that river would bring upon mankind, and what a tale about it would be transmitted to posterity. At last, in a sort of passion, casting aside calculation, and abandoning himself to what might come, and using the proverb frequently in the mouths of those who enter upon dangerous and bold attempts, "The die is cast," with these words he crossed the river.[15]

On the eve of 1889 Nietzsche takes the actions of his voluntary death, not as a martyr, but victoriously, like Caesar, weighing all the calamitous and beneficial consequences, with the belief that it would be a historically significant death, a conquering death. The Palazzo del Quirinale, the palace of the Italian civil government as opposed to the Vatican or papal government, will be his residence as the new Caesar (Cesare Borgia). There is a play on Quirinus, an early Roman god of war identified with the Romans, and Romulus, the first king of Rome. By referring to Caesar's well-considered decision in his letter, Nietzsche refers to his own. He had already written to Strindberg a couple of days earlier: *"une seule condition: divorçons"* and signed it Nietzsche Caesar!

Ariadne: "But be assured sacrifice, martyrdom, would be the wrong words for this voluntary death!"

In *The Antichrist* Nietzsche writes:

That *martyrs* prove anything about the truth of a matter is so far from true that I would deny that any martyr ever had anything whatsoever to do with truth....The deaths of martyrs, incidentally, have been a great misfortune in history: they *seduced*. The inference of all idiots, woman and the people included, that there must be something to a cause for which someone goes to his death (or which, even like early Christianity, generates death seeking epidemics)—this inference has immeasurably thwarted examination, the spirit of examination, and caution. The martyrs have *harmed* truth. Even today it takes only the crudity of a persecution to give an otherwise completely indifferent sectarianism an honorable name. How? Does it change the value of a thing if someone gives his life for it? An error that becomes honorable is an error which is that much more seductive. Do you believe, my dear theologians, that we would give you an occasion to become martyrs for your lie? *One refutes a matter by laying it respectfully on ice—that is how one also refutes theologians.* This precisely was the world historical stupidity of all persecutors, that they gave the opposing cause the appearance of being honorable—that they gave it the fascination of martyrdom as a gift. Even today woman lies on her knees before an error because she has been told that somebody died on the cross for it. *Is the cross an argument?* But about all these things, only one man has said the word which was needed for thousands of years—*Zarathustra*:

> They wrote signs of blood on the way they walked, and their folly taught that with blood one proved truth. But blood is the worst witness of truth; blood poisons even the purest doctrine and turns it into delusion and hatred of the heart. And if a man goes through fire for his doctrine—what does that prove? Verily, it is more if your own doctrine comes out of your own fire.[16]

If one becomes a martyr for a cause, gives up one's life for Christianity or any other external cause, one dies reactively. If one dies the voluntary death as the culmination of one's own doctrine and that dying becomes a beacon of that doctrine, one dies actively, joyfully. In the first case dying is the means to the end. In the second case the voluntary death is itself the goal (especially in light of the eternal recurrence). The voluntary death is not a sacrifice (implying that something is given up, something precious), but a *celebratory* culmination, a highest joy! It is a *squandering* of overflowing happiness, and a *baiting*. It is not blood that the voluntary has in his veins; it is honey, jests, and sarcasm! In "The Honey Sacrifice" from Part IV of *Zarathustra* Nietzsche writes:

> Why sacrifice? I squander what is given to me, I—a squanderer with a thousand hands; how could I call that sacrificing? And

when I desired honey, I merely desired bait and sweet mucus and mucilage, which make even growling bears and queer, sullen, evil birds put out their tongues—the best bait, needed by hunters and fishermen....Open up and cast up to me your fish and glittering crabs! With my best bait I shall today bait the queerest human fish. My happiness itself I cast out far and wide, between sunrise, noon, and sunset, to see if many human fish might not learn to wriggle and wiggle from my happiness until, biting at my sharp hidden hooks, they must come up to *my* height—the most colorful abysmal groundlings, to the most sarcastic of all who fish for men.

Thus men may now come *up* to me; for I am still waiting for the sign that the time has come for my descent; I still do not myself go under, as I must do, under the eyes of men. That is why I wait here, cunning and mocking on high mountains, neither impatient nor patient, rather as one who has forgotten patience too, *because his "passion" is over.* For my destiny leaves me time; perhaps it has forgotten me. Or does it sit in the shade behind a big stone, catching flies? And verily, I like it for this, my eternal destiny: it does not hurry and press me, and it leaves me time for jests and sarcasm, so that I could climb this high mountain today to catch fish.[17]

Here Nietzsche is again on top of his mountain. His 'passion' (*dulden*, suffering) is over and leaves him time for jests and sarcasm. But he needs his fish, the golden bark, the vintager before he can go under, under the eyes of men. Nietzsche takes on the voluntary 'madness,' his highest happiness, in secret behind the scenes, and his actual going under will become known only when Ariadne sees it, transforms it into joy, and declaims it. In "On the Mount of Olives" in *Zarathustra* Nietzsche writes of how he must wear a mask of distress and suffering, that he rattles with discourse to hide his silence, that he has mercy on those who still pity. "Let them suffer and sigh over my chilblains....Meanwhile I run crisscross on my mount of olives with warm feet; in the sunny nook of my mount of olives I sing and I mock all pity."[18] In the Garden of Gethsemane upon the Mount of Olives Christ had to wrestle with the agony of what he had to do, praying that if this cup could not be taken from him, that he would be able to bear it. Christ is the martyr who must give up his life as the symbol of suffering and pity and redemption from sin. Nietzsche's Mount of Olives *appears* to offer occasion for pity ("They hear only my winter winds whistling") but he is actually happy upon "warm seas, like longing, heavy, hot south winds," where he mocks all pity singing and dancing. Nietzsche's eleven-year 'madness' is no tragedy, no loss: "Beyond the north, ice, and death—*our* life, *our* happiness. We have discovered happiness, we know the way, we have found the exit out of the labyrinth of thousands of years. Who *else* has found it?"[19] Tears over martyrdom? No! Something deeper than tears to celebrate such happiness. Joy!

One must always see Nietzsche's voluntary death in light of the eternal recurrence. He chooses death, *this* death, that of clowning 'madness,' not once only. He chooses to be living and dead for eleven years, not once, but eternally. 'Mad' as this seems, by virtue of the exponential power of the deed in its eternal recurrence, it raises the stakes of its effect on those ready to receive it to an incredible degree. Nietzsche's voluntary bark floats out into chance. He has found pleasure in pain, become hard; he experiments with *all* he has; he abolishes his will in the will to power. "Ariadne will come! Or, will she?" He must have asked himself this over and over. But, then, Ariadne does fly into that 'madness' to embrace him victoriously an eternal number of times!

Nietzsche's voluntary 'madness' as voluntary death is in no way a spectacle of suffering for pitying eyes. For those who have eyes for it, it is happiness and the celebratory culmination of Nietzsche's Dionysian life in the fire of the eternal recurrence. In on "Immaculate Perception" in *Zarathustra* Nietzsche writes: "Where is beauty? Where I must will with all my will; where I want to love and perish that an image may not remain a mere image. Loving and perishing: that has rhymed for eternities. The will to love, that is to be willing also to die."[20]

Ariadne: "Ah, Dionysus!"

Notes

1. Nietzsche, "On the Great Longing," *Zarathustra*, p. 333.
2. Ibid., "The Other Dancing Song," p. 336.

3. Foucault, *Madness and Civilization*, pp. 11-12.

4. Nietzsche, *Dithyrambs of Dionysus*, p. 51.

5. Foucault, *Madness and Civilization*, p. 35.

6. Nietzsche, *Will to Power*, #247.

7. Ibid., #916.

8. Nietzsche, *Twilight of the Idols*, #36.

9. Nietzsche, *The Wanderer and His Shadow* in *Human, All Too Human*, trans. R. J. Hollingdale (Cambridge: Cambridge University Press, 1986), #185.

10. Nietzsche, "On Free Death," *Zarathustra*, p. 186, emphasis added.

11. Laurence Lampert, *Nietzsche's Teaching* (New Haven: Yale University Press, 1986), pp. 71–72.

12. Nietzsche, *Zarathustra*, p. 186.

13. Ibid., p. 272.

14. Nietzsche, *Ecce Homo*, p. 222.

15. *Plutarch: Eight Great Lives*, ed. C. A. Robinson, Jr. (New York: Holt, Rinehart and Winston, 1960), pp. 276–77; emphasis added.

16. Nietzsche, *Antichrist*, pp. 636–38.

17. Nietzsche, "The Honey Sacrifice," *Zarathustra*, pp. 350–51; emphasis added.

18. Ibid., "Upon the Mount of Olives," *Zarathustra*, pp. 286–87.

19. Nietzsche, *Antichrist*, p. 569.

20. Ibid., "Immaculate Perception," *Zarathustra*, p. 235.

Une Seule Condition: Divorçons...

The genius, in work and deed, is necessarily a squanderer; that he squanders himself, that is his greatness....People call this "self-sacrifice" and praise his "heroism," his indifference to his own well-being, his devotion to an idea, a great cause, a fatherland: without exception, misunderstandings. He flows out, he overflows, he uses himself up, he does not spare himself—and this is a calamitous involuntary fatality, no less than a river's flooding the land.[1]

Nietzsche Caesar

In early November or late October 1888 (the letter is undated), Nietzsche writes to August Strindberg expressing the hope that he might find a French translator: "As I am the most independent and maybe the strongest mind that today lives, sentenced to a great task, it is impossible for me to allow the absurd borders which an accursed dynastic national-politics has drawn between people, to prevent me from greeting those few who really have ears for me. I wish to be read in French. What is more, it is necessary."[2] Still pursuing French translators for *Beyond Good and Evil* and *The Twilight of the Idols*, Nietzsche writes a fourth letter to Strindberg on December 7: "But now a word or two between ourselves, very much between ourselves! When your letter reached me yesterday—the first letter in my life to reach me—I had just finished the last revision of the manuscript of *Ecce Homo*. Since there are no more coincidences in my life, you are consequently not a coincidence. Why do you write letters which arrive at such a moment!"[3]

Strindberg had written after reading *On the Genealogy of Morals*:

Without a doubt, you have given mankind the deepest book that it possesses, and not the least is that you have the courage, maybe also the necessity, to spew these magnificent words in the faces of this riff-raff—. I thank you for that!...I end all my letters to my friends: Read Nietzsche! That is my *Carthago est delenda*! At any rate your greatness, from the moment that you are known and understood, will be degraded, and the sweet rabble will start to address you as familiarly as one of themselves. It is better that you protect your noble solitude and 10,000 feet higher than we others, make a secret pilgrimage to your sanctuary, in order once there, to create to your heart's content. Let us guard the esoteric teaching, in order to preserve you clean and untouched, leaving you not without the mediation of devoted followers in general. I sign myself, August Strindberg.[4]

But this was exactly what Nietzsche was preparing to do! Strindberg's letter did two important things. He shared an uncanny impulse toward actions of a kind sympathetic with Nietzsche's temperament, that is, the suggesting that Nietzsche withdraw from the world for the benefit of his work and spirit, the pathos of distance. And he announced to Nietzsche that at the end of every letter he writes: Read Nietzsche! That he and others will stand good as his "devoted followers." This was the sign Nietzsche had been waiting for. Once he was sure that he would be read and read in a certain way the event could take place. Nietzsche was busy promoting translations of several of his works toward this very end. His world-historical tragedy would only be that if his predictions for his works were realized. In this letter of December 7 Nietzsche asks Strindberg if he would be willing to translate *Ecce Homo*: "Since it says unheard-of things and, sometimes, in all innocence, speaks the language of the rulers of the world, the number of editions will surpass even *Nana*....Consider it, *verehrter Herr*! It is a matter of the first importance. For I am strong enough to break the history of mankind in two."[5] Sometime after December 27, after having read Strindberg's play *The Father* and his short novella *Utopia in Reality: A Novelle of Freedom* (*Die Utopie in der Wirklichkeit: Eine Fiedensnovelle*), Nietzsche writes to Strindberg:

Dear Sir: You will soon have an answer about your novella—it sounds like a rifle shot. I have ordered a convocation of princes in Rome—I mean to have the young emperor shot. *Auf Wiedersehen!* For we shall see each other again. *Une seule condition: Divorçons...*

Nietzsche Caesar[6]

In response to this letter Strindberg writes on December 31:

Dearest Doctor!
I want, I want to be mad!
I received your letter not without agitation and I thank you for it.
"Better wilt thou live, Lucinius, by neither always pressing out to sea nor too closely hugging the dangerous shore in cautious fear of storms." (Horace)
Meanwhile it is a joy to be mad!
Live well and remain well disposed to your Strindberg (the best, the highest God)[7]

Nietzsche's last letter to Strindberg in answer to the above:

Herr Strindberg
*Eheu?...*not *Divorçons* after all?...   The Crucified.[8]

These last three letters were the bait for Ariadne. She was hooked! They commenced the path along the long thread of the riddle of Nietzsche's 'madness'. The announcement of madness! To say goodbye and announce the divorce of oneself—to pass through the gateway: 'madness.' *How do you announce madness?* Announcing means conscious premeditation, planning, at the least consciousness of 'madness.' This correspondence is the last and so deeply touching exchange with someone able to enter into aspects of the symbolic transformation and creation taking place with Nietzsche. And Nietzsche's confirmation in his later letter to Strindberg, that he has crossed over the Rubicon/'madness,' even if Strindberg could not follow him into that which he announces as his sole condition. He is now the Crucified.

The Decent Criminal

When one turns to the two works by Strindberg discussed in these letters, *The Father* (sent to Nietzsche in the middle of November) and

Utopia in Reality (sent December 27 and referred to in a letter from Strindberg as a story of the *bite of conscience*[9]) we find that in both works the protagonist goes mad. Laura, the wife of the captain in *The Father*, convinces the doctor to certify her husband as mad. It is necessary that he be removed, but that he not commit suicide, for then they would not receive his pension. There is a question as to whether the captain has really gone mad, or is only desperate about his position, but at the end he suffers a stroke from which he may recover consciousness, but what sort of consciousness it is not certain. The last lines of the play:

Laura: Help, Doctor, if it isn't too late. Look, he has stopped breathing.
Doctor: [feels the captain's pulse]: It is a stroke.
Pastor: Is he dead?
Doctor: No, he may yet come back to life, but to what an awakening we cannot tell.
Pastor: "First death, and then the judgment."
Doctor: No judgment, and no accusations. You who will believe that a God shapes man's destiny must go to him about this.
Nurse: Ah, Pastor, with his last breath he prayed to God.
Pastor: [to Laura]: Is that true?
Laura: It is.
Doctor: In that case, which I can understand as little as the cause of his illness, my skill is at an end. You try yours now, Pastor.
Laura: Is that all you have to say at this death-bed, Doctor?
Doctor: That is all! I know no more. Let him speak who knows more.[10]

Here there is the question of death and judgment. The doctor declines to judge the captain and leaves that to the priest.

In the last months before the event of his 'madness' Nietzsche talked constantly of criminals, trials, judgments, condemnations, and sentencing. In one of his letters to Strindberg he discussed the criminal type:

The hereditary criminal is *decadent*, even insane—no doubt about that! But the history of criminal families, for which the Englishman Galton (*Hereditary Genius*) has collected the largest body of material, points constantly back to an excessively strong person where a certain social level is the case. The latest great criminal case in Paris, that of Prado, presented the classic type: Prado was superior to his judges, even to his lawyers, in self-control, wit, and exuberance of spirit.

In the same letter Nietzsche writes that *Ecce Homo* is written in the "Prado" style.[11] Nietzsche further identifies himself with the trials of Prado, Lesseps, and Chambige as his last letter to Jacob Burckhardt shows: "Do not take the Prado case seriously, I am Prado, I am also Prado's father, I venture to say that I am also Lesseps....I wanted to give my Parisians, whom I love, a new idea—that of a decent criminal. I am also Chambige— also a decent criminal."[12]

Middleton informs us:

Prado was tried in Paris on November 5, 1888; on November 14 he was condemned to death. The story had been reported in the Gazette des Tribuneaux, 1888, on the following dates: June 29; July 4, 22, 23; August 5; September 10, 11; October 10, 18; November 1, 5, 6, 7, 8, 9, 10, 11, 12, 13, 14, 15 (and December 29 was to follow). Prado was a Spanish subject who claimed that his real name was Linska de Castilon. He had lived first in Peru, then in Spain, after exhausting his wife's fortune assessed at 1,200,000 francs. Heavily in debt, he came to France and lived with a girl named Eugenie Forestier; the couple had been without means since 1886. On November 28, 1887, Prado was arrested for theft in Paris. The investigation proved that he had also been involved in another theft outside Paris. During cross-examination, Eugenie asserted that Prado was the murderer of a prostitute named Marie Agrietant, who had been killed during the night of January 14, 1886, in the rue Caumartin. This assertion proved to be true.

Chambige was the subject of another 1888 murder trial. Henri Chambige was a law student who fancied himself a writer. He murdered the English wife of a Frenchman living near Constantine in Algeria. He was tried in Constantine on November 9, 1888, and was condemned to seven years of hard labor (it was a *crime passionel*).

Ferdinand Lesseps (1805–94) was the French diplomat responsible for building the Suez Canal and who initiated the earlier stages of the building of the Panama Canal....During the latter part of his life, he was involved in a scandal.[13]

Nietzsche repeats in his last letters that he is *sentenced* to a great task, a terrible task. One of the best examples of this is a draft of a letter, December 1888, in which he is obviously taking leave of his sister Elizabeth, saying goodbye:

> To put your mind at rest, I will say of myself only that I am extremely well, with a certainty and patience which in my earlier life I never enjoyed for a single hour; that the most difficult things are coming easily; that everything to which I put my hand is turning out well. The task which is imposed *upon* me is, all the same, my nature—so that only now do I comprehend what was my predestined good fortune. I play with the burden which would crush any other mortal....For what I have to do is *terrible*, in any sense of the word; I do not challenge individuals—*I am challenging humanity as a whole with my terrible accusation; whichever way the decision may go, for me or against me,* in any case there attaches to my name a quantity of doom that is beyond telling....In asking you, with all my heart, not to see any hardness in this letter, but the reverse—a real humanity, which is trying to prevent any necessary damage—I ask you, over and above this necessity, to keep on loving me.[14]

Nietzsche had also just written to his mother a last letter on December 21. After telling her how he is beginning to become famous he writes:

> Luckily, I am now ripe for everything that my task may require of me. My health is really excellent, the hardest tasks, for which no man was yet strong enough, are easy for me.
>
> *Meine alte Mutter*, receive, at the year's end, my most affectionate good wishes, and wish me a new year which will match in every way the great things that must come to pass in it.
>
>   Your old creature[15]

What he has to do is terrible; he challenges humanity with a terrible accusation—will the decision go for him or against him? He speaks as a criminal who will be judged, but also as a decent criminal, who accuses humanity and sentences himself. Prado and Chambige are murderers; Nietzsche will enter into a voluntary death out of decency with "wit and exuberance of spirit" as did Prado before his judges. On his way to his voluntary "self-hanging/crucifixion" Nietzsche is accompanied by criminals as was Christ.

In his last works and with the act of 'madness,' Nietzsche pulls down his whole decadent age. He pulls down Christianity with *The Antichrist*. He pulls down German culture with the *Case of Wagner* and *Nietzsche contra Wagner*. He pulls down ideals and idealism with *Twilight of the Idols*. He pulls down German Nationalism and makes a mockery of national politics in *Ecce Homo*, the two Wagner books, and his 'mad' notes to the major political houses of Europe whose purpose, he writes Overbeck at the end of December, is to "form an anti-German league": "I mean to sew up the Reich in an iron shirt and to provoke it to a war of desperation. I shall not have my hands free until I have the young emperor, and all his appurtenances, in my hands."[16] Lastly, and most important, he pulls *himself* down under cover of the mantel of 'madness' and the *Dionysus Dithyrambs*.

The destruction is catastrophic. The crime monstrous, the demolition ("I am no man, I am dynamite") of the values of two thousand years and the indictment of those who follow in these values. The immoralist, the criminal out of decency. The criminal that points the way to the new morals of the overhuman. The immolation in this is as spectacular as the conflagration at the end of Wagner's *Götterdämmerung*, the destruction of the gods. *The difference, however, is that Nietzsche acts in the flesh, with real gods and real human fate.* He sentences himself to death to create a promise for the future. The conflagration implicates humankind in sum. It is not a spectacle on a stage, with actors, costumes, lines, and the applause after the play is ended. The drama that Nietzsche stages is not one you can leave and go home from. It is the world you live and act in. It is you he is attempting to transform.

> To remain objective, hard, firm, severe in carrying through an idea—artists succeed best in this; but when one needs men for this (as teachers, statesmen, etc., do), then the repose and coldness and hardness soon vanish. With natures like Caesar and

Napoleon, one gets some notion of "disinterested" work on their
marble, whatever the cost in men. On this road lies the future of
the highest men: to bear the *greatest responsibility* and *not* collapse
under it.—[17]

This is what Bataille quoted from *Zarathustra*: "When a living thing,
Zarathustra said, takes charge of itself it is necessary that the living thing
expiate its authority and be judge, avenger and victim of its own laws."[18] If
Nietzsche indicts humanity to this point and he himself belongs to it, he
must be the first to be condemned. Thomas Mann expresses the before and
after of Nietzsche's self-condemnation:

> We who were born around 1870 are too close to Nietzsche, we
> participate too directly in his tragedy, his personal fate (perhaps
> the most terrible, most awe-inspiring fate in intellectual history).
> Our Nietzsche is Nietzsche militant. Nietzsche triumphant
> belongs to those born fifteen years after us. We have from him
> our psychological sensitivity, our lyrical criticism, the experience
> of Wagner, the experience of Christianity, the experience of
> "modernity"—experiences from which we shall never completely
> break free, any more than Nietzsche himself ever did. They are
> too precious for that, too profound, too fruitful. But the twenty-
> year-olds have from him what will remain in the future, his
> purified after effect. For them he is a prophet one does not know
> very exactly, whom one hardly needs to have read, and yet whose
> purified results one has instinctively in one. They have from him
> the affirmation of the earth, the affirmation of the body, the anti-
> Christian and anti-intellectual conception of nobility, which
> comprises health and serenity and beauty.[19]

Nietzsche sentences himself, becomes his 'self-hanger,' making it a
question of conscience. But it is the conscience of Nietzsche's sovereign
human, one who acts from "reality" and the "great health."[20] Whether the
judgment goes for him or against him, whether Ariadne comes to affirm his
'criminality' or adds her voice to the chorus condemning it as pure
madness, Nietzsche's teachings hang on this great chance.

Noel

These ideas of conscience, madness and a decadent society all come together in Strindberg's *Utopia in Reality* in a really uncanny coincidence of ideas.

In this novella a young German officer, Lieutenant Von Bleichroden, is forced to execute three French civilians as spies. He has the order carried out in his absence. He comes back, overhears a conversation about how bravely the men died, gets into bed, reads the following quote from Schopenhauer, and goes mad:

> Birth and death both belong to life; they constitute two opposites which condition each other; they are the two extreme poles in each manifestation of life. This is just what the deepest of all mythologies, the Hindu, has expressed by investing Siva the goddess of destruction with a necklace of skulls and the Lingam, the organ of reproduction. Death is the painful dissolution of a knot which was tied in pleasure, it is the forcible doing away with the fundamental mistake of our existence, it is deliverance from a delusion.[21]

Bleichroden lets the book fall from his hands and sees a body in his bed that is contorted and screaming and flailing about. He soon realizes that it is his own body. "Had he then been divided into two, that he heard and saw himself as though he were another person?"[22] Bleichroden is then visited by a priest who proceeds to explain what has happened to him: he is suffering from a bad conscience:

> It is now *you* who are condemned—to a worse lot than the—three!... I know the symptoms. You are on the edge of mad-ness....You have become two persons. You regard one part of yourself as though it were a second or a third person. How did that happen? It is the social falsehood, which makes us all double. When you wrote to your wife today you were a man—a true, simple, good man; but when you spoke with me you were another character altogether. Just as an actor loses his personality and becomes a mere conglomeration of the parts he performs, so an official becomes two persons at least. Now when there comes a spiritual shock, upheaval or earthquake, the soul splits, as it

were in two, and the two natures lie side by side, and contemplate each other.[23]

In *Ecce Homo* Nietzsche had already called himself a *döppleganger* with a
second face and perhaps also a third. The priest continues:

> Do you think I do not know the curse of the double life which I
> lead? Not that I feel any doubt of the holy things, which have
> passed into my blood and bones, so to speak, but I know, sir, that I
> do not speak in God's name when I speak. Falsehood passes into
> us from our mother's womb and breast, and he who would tell the
> whole truth is not possible under the present circumstances.
>
> You are naturally a good man, and I will not punish that
> side of you, but I punish you as a representative, as you called
> yourself, and your punishment will be a warning to others.[24]

Bleichroden stands and orders the priest to go: "Go, devil of a priest, or you
will make me do something desperate." The priest opens the door so that
the three dead spies can be seen and says: "Great victory! Three dead and
one mad! God be praised! It is not an occasion for writing odes, strewing
flowers in the streets, and singing Te Deums in the churches! It is not a
victory! it is murder, murder, you murderer!"[25]

Bleichroden, after hearing this, jumps out of bed and out of the
window. In the courtyard he tries to bite some of the men who take hold of
him. He is bound and placed in an ambulance to be taken to the asylum as
a complete maniac.

In the first pages of Chapter II of *Utopia in Reality* Bleichroden's wife
and her brother talk. She says: "to think that destiny can invent such
tragedies! I think I could have borne his death more easily than this living
burial." This is what Overbeck and other friends said of Nietzsche.
"Suddenly, there sounded from the hill above, a shrill, prolonged scream,
like the whistle of a locomotive, and then another...the scream was
repeated. But now it sounded as if someone were drowning."[26] The sister
and brother go up the hill to the hospital: "And so they ascended the long
hill to the hospital, though it was like a climb up Calvary." Bleichroden in
his madness becomes, as we will see, a victim and symbol of redemption
from a mad society. The madhouse is high on a hill, the hill of Calvary.

Nietzsche's 'madness' is *not* a Calvary, rather a Dionysian celebration, but of course, the Crucified is an intimate part of the play and Calvary is not far away. "As they got halfway up the hill, the mysterious screaming was repeated." An echo in advance of Nietzsche's screams in the night. At that moment, Bleichroden's pregnant wife goes into labor. "Now two cries were heard—the cries of two human creatures from the depths of sorrow."[27] The round of birth and death spoken of in the quote by Schopenhauer above, but this round is Dionysian.

In the asylum on the hill Bleichroden's madness has taken the form of bad conscience because he thinks he has murdered a wine grower (further shades of Dionysus?) "Now he thought himself condemned to death and sitting in prison awaiting the execution of the sentence."[28] He looks out the window at the extreme beauty of the landscape that slopes down to Lake Geneva and "he felt a wonderful joy and sensation of relief in his head: it was as though the convolutions of his brain, after having been hopelessly entangled, began to arrange and order themselves. He was so glad that he began to sing, as he thought, but he had never sung in his life and therefore he only uttered cries of joy. It was these which had issued from the window and filled his wife with grief and despair."[29] What had been screams of despair, rage, and madness to others were the song of joy to the madman! Later Bleichroden says to his doctor: "I feel as though I had been dead and come to life on another planet—so beautiful does it all seem. Never did I dream that the earth could be so wonderful." The doctor replies: "Yes, sir, the earth is still beautiful where civilisation has not spoilt it, and here nature is so strong that it resists the efforts of men. Do you think that your own country was always so ugly as it now is? No; where now there are waste sandy plains, which could not nourish a goat, there formerly rustled noble woods of oak, beech and fir, under whose shadow beasts of the chase fed, and where fat herds of the Norsemen's best kine fattened themselves on acorns."[30] The doctor goes on to talk of specific artists and thinkers and politicians who have labored to keep civilization healthy. "I believe in the inexhaustible power of nature to heal the sickness of civilisation." The doctor takes Bleichroden outside, and in response to the garden: "The lieutenant sought for familiar phrases with which to express his delight, but he felt that they were so inadequate that he resolved to be silent, listening to a wonderful soundless nerve music. He felt as though all the strings of his soul were being tuned again, and he experienced a calm such as he had not felt for a very long time."[31] "My soul, a stringed instrument, sang to itself, invisibly touched, a secret gondola song." The doctor tells a keeper that when Bleichroden asks for his wife, it will be the sign that he is saved.[32]

Bleichroden takes a walk and finds an unusual building into which he goes along with many of the other hospital patients. Bleichroden's eyes fall on a word. In the middle of a colossal wreath a single word was written in letters made out of pine tree branches. They spell the French word: Noel.

> What poet had arranged this hall? What knower of men, what deep mind had so understood how to awaken the most beautiful and purest of all recollections? Would not an overclouded mind feel an eager longing for light and clearness when it recollected the festival of light commemorating the end or, at any rate, the beginning of the end of the dark days at the turn of the year? Would not the recollection of childhood, when no religious strifes, no political hatred, no ambitious empty dreams had obscured the sense of right in a pure conscience—would it not stir a music in the soul louder than all those wildbeast howlings which one had heard in life in the struggle for bread, or more often for honour?
>
> How is it that man, so innocent as a child, afterwards becomes so evil as he grows older? Is it education and school, these lauded products of civilization, which teach us to be bad? What do our first school-books teach us? They teach us that God is an Avenger who punishes the sins of the fathers in the children unto the third and fourth generation; they teach us that those men are heroes who have roused nation against nation, and pillaged lands and kingdoms; that those are great men who have succeeded in obtaining honour the emptiness of which all see, but after which all strive; and that true statesmen are those who accomplish great and not high aims in a crafty manner, whose whole merit consists in want of conscience, and who will always conquer in the struggle against those who possess one. And in order that our children may learn all this, parents make sacrifices and renunciation and suffer the great pain of separation from their offspring. Surely the whole world must be a lunatic

asylum, if this place was the most reasonable one he had ever been in![33]

Nietzsche's whole philosophy has condemned these very 'ideals' of civilization in order to restore the innocence of becoming. He certainly considers, as he retires into 'madness,' that he is the sane one and his hopes for the future the reasonable and healthy ones.

Bleichroden looks again at the word *Noel* and it leads him to remember a specific Christmas and he remembers that he has a wife. "He was betrothed, he was married, he had a wife—his own wife who reunited him to life which he had previously despised and hated. But where was she? He must see and meet her now, at once! He must fly to her, otherwise he would die of impatience."[34] Bleichroden is reunited with his wife and learns that he also has a daughter. Nietzsche awaits his 'wife' Ariadne. The wedding of Dionysus and Ariadne will, like Bleichroden's realization of his need for his wife, signal Nietzsche's redemption. In the Jena hospital Nietzsche refers to his wife, Cosima Wagner, who, he says, brought him there. But Cosima represents Ariadne. Nietzsche considered her a fitting recipient of the Ariadne tidings.[35] Ariadne, we have seen, represents the death and rebirth principles in the eternal round of Dionysian joy; she represents the self-sacrifice into 'madness'—thus she does in a sense bring him there. She is the one who must lead him out again to joy.

Strindberg ends this part of the story by backing up and saying that Bleichroden is a product of his times. But as a doubled being he has seen into the lies of the society; he is thus like the only reasonable one in a madhouse. And to an uncanny degree, Strindberg describes Nietzsche's own struggles when he continues to say of Bleichroden that he threw himself into pessimism to moderate the pain. Bleichroden, like Nietzsche, chose Schopenhauer as friend and later found in Hartmann the most "brutal truthspeaker that the world had seen." Like Nietzsche, Strindberg represents Bleichroden as struggling to find meaning over against the cultural and nationalistic absurdities taking place around him. Bleichroden, like Nietzsche finally becomes "an optimist out of a feeling of duty."

At the head of the four pages of Nietzsche's crayon scrawl in red and blue that Ronald Hayman translates most of in his *A Critical Life of Nietzsche* and dates July 1892 is the word *Noel*.[36] Hayman does not translate this first page. This single word may tie Strindberg's novella to Nietzsche's act of 'madness.'

"Three shot and one mad!" from *Utopia in Reality*.[37] Nietzsche to Strindberg: "You will soon have an answer about your novella—it sounds like a rifleshot. I have ordered a convocation of princes in Rome—I mean to have the young emperor shot." To Overbeck, January 7: "I am having all anti-Semites shot."[38] Bleichroden orders three traitors shot. He suffers society's bite of conscience in the form of madness, but comes through it when he realizes that he is the sane one, the one who has a duty of hope for the future, and that it is the society that is the madhouse. Nietzsche's staged conflagration acts out in reality Strindberg's literary "bite of conscience." Nietzsche acting on the conscience of a sovereign human, condemns himself as a decadent representative of a mad society: "I am a *decadent* and a *beginning*."[39]

No Coincidence!

Has any other 'madman' had such a dramatic breakdown? As Thomas Mann says, perhaps the most awe-inspiring fate in intellectual history? Has any other madman spread his 'mad' writings on such a large scale? And why? To be sure that his 'madness' becomes a catastrophe impossible to miss? Is this true madness or is it historical method in acting? Isn't it the announcement of more than decline, rather of a historical resistance to the beliefs and governments of his day on the grandest scale, "great politics"? And why does Nietzsche write *Ecce Homo* just weeks before his 'breakdown'? And why quote Pontius Pilate's words just before Christ's crucifixion as its title? Doesn't the coincidence of an autobiography "written to say who I am before the event of confronting humanity with the most difficult demand ever made it," have to be read as more than a coincidence?

Nietzsche begins his "great politics" in *Nietzsche contra Wagner* and *Ecce Homo*, but announces it in connection with his specific task, the creation of an "event" for the first time in a letter of December 6 to Georg Brandes:

> Worthy friend,
> It is necessary, to communicate to you a couple of things of the first rank: give me your word of honor that this story will remain

between us. We are entering into great politics, even the greatest....I am readying an event, which it is highly likely will break history in two halves, to the point that we will have a new time reference: from 1888 as year one on. All that is at the forefront today, Triple Alliance, social questions will go completely over into an education of oppositional individuals (*eine Individuen-Gegensatz-Bildung*): we will have wars, as there have never been wars, but *not* between nations, *not* between states (*Ständen*): Everything is exploded,—I am the most terrible dynamite that there is.[40]

On December 11 Nietzsche writes to Carl Fuchs: "The most unheard of tasks easy as play; health and weather coming up daily with excessive brightness and stability. I cannot tell what all has become ready: *All is ready.* The world will be standing on its head for the next few years: since the old God has abdicated, *I* shall rule the world from now on."[41] In a letter to Peter Gast on December 16: "Occasionally nowadays I see no reason why I should accelerate too much the *tragic* catastrophe of my life, which begins with *Ecce Homo.*"[42] On December 27 he again writes to Carl Fuchs: "One should not worry about me from now on, but about the things for whose sake I am there—*Also in the next years a monstrous transformation in my outer situation could occur,* so that every individual question in fate and life-work of my friends would depend on it, not to mention that such ephemeral creations as 'the German Reich' in every reckoning of what is coming must be omitted."[43]

It is all too neat to be coincidence. Sometime during the days after December 25 Nietzsche writes to Strindberg: *Une seule condition: Divorçons,* signed Nietzsche-Caesar.[44] On New Years Eve he writes to Gast about the Rubicon, his decision to cross over as Caesar did. Exactly on January 1 Nietzsche begins to sign as Dionysus in his dedication of the *Dionysus Dithyrambs* to Catulle Mendès. On January 3 and 4 he sends approximately twenty "feuilletons" or "bad jokes," twelve to friends and acquaintances signed The Crucified or Dionysus, four (three unsigned and one signed Dionysus) to Cosima/Ariadne, and four to the royal houses of Europe and to Rome.[45] The haunting quality of these 'mad' communications is that each is grounded in autobiographical or political reality. They are not so much 'mad' as dripping with parodic irony. His last letter is sent to Burckhardt on January 6, the day of Epiphany, signed Nietzsche! All this while, until he leaves Turin with Overbeck on January 9 Nietzsche is correcting proofs and corresponding with his publisher Naumann perfectly lucidly and signing himself Nietzsche.

One can and will say, it is not the *act* of Nietzsche's 'madness' that is to bring about the moment of decision for humankind; he is referring to the works that he has just written and his projected work on the revaluation of all values when they are published. But, in a letter to Georg Brandes of November 20, 1888, Nietzsche writes: "*Ecce Homo*...is a prelude to the 'transvaluation of values,' the work that lies *finished* before me; I swear to you that in two years we shall have the whole earth in convulsions. I am a man of destiny."[46] Here Nietzsche refers to *The Antichrist* and later in the letter to Georg Brandes above, Nietzsche refers to "*The Antichrist. Revaluation of all Values*," which is to serve him as a "published agitation" (*Agitations-Ausgabe*). It seems clear to some scholars that Nietzsche had given up on writing four books of the revaluation and that *The Antichrist* and *Ecce Homo* were meant to be his final works. However, if Nietzsche staged his 'madness,' then he would also have to, in other letters, seem to plan for years ahead, or suggest that more books of the revaluation were to come. Yes, *Twilight of the Idols, Nietzsche contra Wagner, Ecce Homo*, and especially *The Antichrist* were all to create moral and philosophical catastrophe and carry the message of promise ("I having first tied the knot of morality into existence before I tied it so tight..."), but it is in his own 'madness' that the culmination was meant to come. It was his 'madness' that fueled interest in his works—it still is!

The writing of *Ecce Homo* presages the shattering resolve of the *act* of revaluation: "*Revaluation of all values*: that is my formula for an act of supreme self-examination on the part of humanity, *become flesh and genius in me*. It is my fate that I have to be the first *decent* human being; that I know myself to stand in opposition to the mendaciousness of millennia.—"[47] And Nietzsche writes to Peter Gast of *Ecce Homo* that "It concerns, with great audacity, myself and my writings. Not only did I want to present myself *before the uncannily solitary act of transvaluation*; I would also just like to *test* what risks I can take with the German ideas of freedom of speech."[48]

Nietzsche had conceived of his voluntary death since 1881, as we have seen, but as 1888 draws to a close he magnificently orchestrates and acts its realization: he puts *himself* into *play*. From this perspective, one cannot emphasize enough the importance of the content of Strindberg's novella and his correspondence with Nietzsche at precisely this moment.

Ariadne cannot digest all of this as simple coincidence.

"Oh, my Dionysus, is this madness? Or are you play acting on the grandest scale with language and flesh? Megalomania? Or calculated appearance of megalomania? Or prophecy? You, create and herald the revaluation of society, morality, and state values into an examination of individual conscience for humankind, and I, I herald you! You shout, and must shout 'mad' claims, 'loud' claims; they must sound 'mad,' for they resound with the din and pandemonium of Dionysus, but they are not thereby false claims! Beyond good and evil! These are not only words, they are translated, great one, into actions. You, Dionysus, my immoralist, dance into words and actions taken beyond good and evil! Don't these actions show a sublimity and an evil/criminality that transcends our common ability to understand it? And if we could, wouldn't we become stronger and more beautiful? Nietzsche: 'I am challenging humanity as a whole with my terrible accusation; whichever way the decision may go, for me or against me, in any case there attaches to my name a quantity of doom that is beyond telling...' I, Ariadne, declare you, my Dionysus, the most decent of criminals, who condemned yourself along with your pessimistic age in the hope that affirmation would take its place after the destruction. And the joy, the eternal joy of this affirmation, begins from this moment on my terrible, my divine one!"

"My dear readers, do not so calmly acquiesce in the label madness. Isn't there a supreme riddle here?"

He that is richest in the fullness of life, the Dionysian god and man, can afford not only the *sight* of the terrible and the questionable, but even the terrible deed and any luxury of destruction, decomposition, and negation: in his case, what is evil, senseless, and ugly seems, as it were permissible, as it seems permissible in nature, because of an excess of procreating, restoring powers which can yet turn every desert into luxurious farm land.[49]

Notes
1. Nietzsche, *Twilight of the Idols*, p. 549.
2. Karl Strecker, *Nietzsche und Strindberg* (München: Georg Müller Verlag, 1921), my trans., p. 31.
3. Middleton, *Selected Letters*, p. 78.
4. Strecker, *Nietzsche und Strindberg*, p. 35.
5. Ibid., pp. 80–81.
6. Ibid., pp. 90–91 and Middleton, *Selected Letters*, p. 344.
7. Ibid., p. 93 and Middleton, *Selected Letters*, pp. 344–45.
8. Ibid., and Middleton, Selected Letters, p. 345.
9. See Strecker, *Nietzsche und Strindberg*, p. 88.
10. Strindberg, *The Father*, trans. Edith and Warner Oland (Clinton, Mass: The Colonial Press, I1912), pp. 72–73.
11. Strecker, *Nietzsche und Strindberg*, pp. 78–80 and Middleton, *Selected Letters*, pp. 329–30.
12. Middleton, *Selected Letters*, p. 347.
13. Ibid., pp. 329 and 347. See also Appendix, Podach, *Madness of Nietzsche*.
14. Ibid., pp. 339–40; emphasis added.
15. Ibid.
16. Middleton, *Selected Letters*, p. 341.
17. Nietzsche, *Will to Power*, #975.
18. Nietzsche, *Zarathustra*, p. 175. See my page 57.
19. Stephen E. Aschheim, *The Nietzsche Legacy in Germany 1890–1990* (Berkeley: University of California Press, 1992), p. 37.
20. See Nietzsche, *On the Genealogy of Morals*, pp. 60 and 95–96.
21. August Strindberg, "Die Utopie in der Wirklichkeit: Eine Friedensnovella," in *Werke: Schweizer Novellen* (München: George Müller Verlag, 1920). English translation: *The German Lieutenant and Other Stories* (Chicago: A. C. McClurg, 1915), p. 26.
22. Ibid., p. 27.
23. Ibid., pp. 28–29.
24. Ibid., pp. 29–31.
25. Ibid., pp. 31–32.
26. Ibid., p. 35.
27. Ibid., pp. 35–36.
28. Ibid., p. 37.
29. Ibid., p. 41.

30. Ibid., p. 42.

31. Ibid., p. 46.

32. Ibid., p. 47.

33. Ibid., p. 52.

34. Ibid., p. 53.

35. The long-held thesis that Ariadne=Cosima Wagner is not discussed in this work because it is now realized by Nietzsche scholars that Ariadne's symbolic substance *far exceeds* Nietzsche's personal relationship to Cosima Wagner. See, for example, Adrian Del Caro, "Symbolizing Philosophy. Ariadne and the Labyrinth," in *Nietzsche Studien*, #17, 1988, for a very good review and discussion of this perspective.

36. Ronald Hayman, *A Critical Life of Nietzsche* (New York: Penguin Books, 1980), pp. 344–45. These notes by Nietzsche are not included in Sander Gilman's article which collects Nietzsche's writings and sayings from after the 'breakdown.' I think these four sheets of notes could have been written while Nietzsche was still in Jena because of their references to where his 'illness' comes from, his references to Neu Germania and Elizabeth, and other contents. I would be more comfortable in dating them sometime in 1890. I have copies of these writings from the Nietzsche archives in Weimar.

37. Strindberg, *German Lieutenant*, p. 31.

38. Middleton, *Selected Letters*, p. 346.

39. Nietzsche, *Ecce Homo*, p. 222.

40. NB, III, 5, p. 500.

41. Ibid., pp. 521–22.

42. Ibid., p. 334.

43. Ibid., p. 553; emphasis added.

44. Ibid., pp. 567–68.

45. Ibid., pp. 570–79.

46. Middleton, *Selected Letters*, p. 326.

47. Nietzsche, *Ecce Homo*, p. 326; emphasis added.

48. Middleton, *Selected Letters*, pp. 319–20; emphasis added.

49. Nietzsche, *Nietzsche contra Wagner*, p. 670.

Madness, Medical Discourse, or Script?

> All superior men who were irresistibly drawn to throw off the yoke of any kind of morality and to frame new laws had, *if they were not actually mad*, no alternative but to make themselves *or pretend to be mad*—[1]

Psychiatric and Medical Discourse

Karl Jaspers is Apollonian, scientific; his Dionysian possibilities are far away. Let us listen for a moment as he talks about Nietzsche's 'illness':

> A threefold approach to the relation of Nietzsche's sickness to his work is indispensable: first, that of the empirical investigation of the facts; second, after the criticism of his work, one that permits the removal from his work of those flaws which can be regarded as accidental disturbances resulting from illness, with a view to arriving at a pure conception of Nietzsche's way of philosophizing; third the increasingly mythical envisioning of a total reality in which the illness seems to become a moment of positive meaning, of consummate expression of being, of unmediated revelation of something that otherwise would remain inaccessible.

Empirical investigation of the facts and application of the facts to (surgically) remove flaws and accidental disturbances of illness. Facts to cut away the dirt of illness in order to arrive at a pure conception. And then a third approach, the mythical one. But let us see what Jaspers writes next:

163

Of primary importance for the first approach is the method of empirical science which never reaches the boundary of a knowledge that ultimately is all-encompassing. This is the condition for a self-restraining realization of the other two approaches; without it, the one—the critical one—would become an unmethodical and hence unrestrained criticism with the verdict "sick"; the other—the mythical view—would turn into unrealistic enthusiasm. An approach searching for the pure truth of Nietzsche will never be able to separate with finality from this truth everything that is not pertinent and should be eliminated for being *faux pas* or something meant to add color and tone for the sake of appeal. The mythical view of Nietzsche's total reality cannot be given communicable expression on our part. It is not possible to substitute, one for the other, the meaning of empirically ascertaining and critically cleansing utterances on the one hand and the mythical ones on the other; nor must they be confused.[2]

The critic of the event, the resentment cleanser, the one who wields the critically cleansing utterances, drawing lines that cannot be drawn between the pure truth of Nietzsche and unrealistic enthusiasm. Yet one senses that Jaspers draws these lines out of desperation; that he, like so many other Nietzsche admirers, wrestles with the 'madness' in the manner that Nietzsche says Christ's disciples wrestled with the death on the cross:

> The catastrophe of the evangel was decided with the death—it was attached to the "cross." Only the death, this unexpected, disgraceful death, only the cross which was generally reserved for the rabble—only this horrible paradox confronted the disciples with the real riddle: *"Who was this? What was this?"* Their profoundly upset and insulted feelings, and their suspicion that such a death might represent the refutation of their cause, the terrible question mark, "Why in this manner?"—this state is only too easy to understand.[3]

For Jaspers Nietzsche's 'madness' is disgraceful, madness, a disease of the rabble, a refutation of his passion for Nietzsche's philosophy. Yes, passion. But facts save Jaspers. The "biological factor" is what brought Nietzsche down.

Ariadne: "You see, one tends to think that the 'madness' brought Nietzsche down, ruined him, was the refutation of all that he thought and wrote. But no! The 'madness' was a culmination, a celebration, the supreme symbol of victory! Jaspers suspects this, but refuses to look at it."

Jaspers writes:

> The understanding of Nietzsche does not depend upon posses-
> sion of a medical diagnosis. But it is essential to know, first, that
> the mental illness at the end of 1888 is an organic brain disease,
> which derives from an external cause and not from an inner dis-
> position; second, that in the mid-1880s Nietzsche's entire
> spiritual constitution is probably transformed by a biological
> factor; and third, that the year 1888 immediately precedes the
> mental illness with its direct effect of profound disintegration
> and reveals changes in his mood and behavior that are unlike
> anything previously found.[4]

Jaspers enumerates many of the hypotheses of medical diagnosis attached to Nietzsche's 'breakdown.'

> So far as diagnoses are concerned, probability definitely favors
> the view that the mental disease at the end of 1888 was a
> paralysis. In addition, a severe "rheumatism" of 1865 extending
> to arms and teeth has been diagnosed as meningitis caused by
> infection; the attacks, as migraine (which doubtless they partly
> are, as a complex of symptoms; but the question is whether as a
> whole they are a symptom of another illness); the appearances of
> illness since 1873, as a psychoneurotic process occasioned by his
> inner separation from R. Wagner; the transformation from 1880
> to 1882 as the first indications of the later paralysis; the many
> sensations of intoxication of the later period and even the col-
> lapse itself as the consequence of toxins (particularly hashish). If
> we were to accept the principle of explaining, as far as possible,
> symptoms of illness from a single cause, we would conclude that
> all illnesses after 1866 were stages on the path to paralysis. *This is
> however entirely open to question.* Medical categories are of sig-
> nificance to a philosophically relevant conception of Nietzsche
> only if they need not be doubted. Except for the fact that the

concluding mental disease was almost certainly a paralysis, these diagnoses are dubious.[5]

These are only a small part of all of the proffered hypotheses regarding the cause of Nietzsche's breakdown. The literature on this is quite vast and I leave the reader who is interested to pursue it on his or her own.[6] The sheer variety of hypotheses themselves lead one to conclude that there never was any clear medical foundation for Nietzsche's 'madness' and to wonder at the fascination that Nietzsche's 'madness' exercised on the medical world, Nietzsche scholars, and the public. Jaspers has taken the 'evidence'—Nietzsche's life-long illnesses, their ups and downs, and various diagnoses after the 'breakdown'—and has concluded that Nietzsche's illness is the result of progressive paralysis. This, of course, is the most accepted and parroted, yet inconclusive, agreement among Nietzsche scholars. And, of course, the cause of the paralysis is attributed to a syphilitic infection— again, not conclusive. After sending all available medical records of Nietzsche's illness (which are relatively scanty) to several eminent doctors, Podach writes:

> The entry in the Jena record "syphilit. infection" has raised rather more dust than was necessary. There is no certain evidence of such an infection. Nor is there any sure evidence of Nietzsche's "paralysis." In all probability there can be no definite verdict on the matter because of the inadequacy of the data.
>
> The author has submitted the available evidence to several experts. They have replied as follows:
>
> Dr. Gustav Emanuel, a neurological psychiatrist of high standing, writes: "The available medical evidence is not sufficient to allow us to be sure in concluding that paralysis progressiva is the correct diagnosis. We must admit that, speaking purely neurologically, the evidence (especially relating to pupillar condition) indicates the possibility of a nervous disorder of syphilitic origin, but there can be no certainty about this."
>
> The psychiatrist, Dr. Michaelis, writes: "The psychological data contained in the records are, in my opinion, too fragmentary to allow any deep insight into its nature....We cannot conclude that 'dementia paralytica' is typical. The absence of any disturbances in the patient's speech is noteworthy. The

repeatedly occurring 'physical persecution mania' is also remarkable, especially if the scantiness of the entries is taken into consideration. The patient's peculiar psychomotor behavior might suggest that his psychosis was of 'schizophrene' character. But considering the general uncertainty with regard to the process covered by this term, little value can be attached to such a classification."

On the other hand, Dr. Stutz, the head doctor at the Basle clinic, expresses the opinion that "the data confirm progressive paralysis as being the correct diagnosis. There can hardly be any doubt on the subject."

Podach concludes:

If the problem of the diagnosis of Nietzsche's illness were to be re-opened once more, it would be necessary to investigate the accuracy of the entries relating to cases of paralysis in general in the Jena records round about the year 1889. Dr. Stutz found many cases of "paralysis" entered in the Basle records of the period which would certainly be diagnosed as schizophrene today. Dr. A. Kronfeld has also pointed out that the Jena records were obviously made by persons who had paralysis in mind all the time.[7]

Jaspers writes: "Nietzsche did not recognize his mental illness (scarcely ever does a person afflicted with paralysis have insight into his illness) and did not expect it. In the year 1888, when the changes in his emotional life and extreme tension already appeared as harbingers of the insanity that would soon overwhelm him, he possessed an unshakable confidence concerning his health."[8]

"Yes," says Ariadne, "because he was healthy! Nietzsche was not ill and was jubilantly preparing to take on the mantle of 'madness,' while emphasizing his extraordinarily good health as an opposition to the role he was about to play. Indeed playing such a demanding role would require that Nietzsche be in unusually good health."

Nietzsche writes in *Ecce Homo*: "Whoever saw me during the seventy days this fall when, without interruption, I did several things of the first rank the like of which nobody will do after me—or impose on me—with a responsibility for all millennia after me, will not have noticed any trace of tension in me; but rather an overflowing freshness and cheerfulness. I never ate with more pleasant feelings; I never slept better."[9] Nietzsche describes his euphoria as health. Are we to disbelieve him?

Jaspers presents the events of the last year very well, but interprets them as a path to the disintegration and ruin of madness. But the same events can be seen as steps on the way to a voluntary and celebratory 'madness.'

A final decisive change clearly begins toward the end of 1887. It in turn leads to new phenomena which totally dominate everything after September, 1888. He now becomes for the first time confident that his activity will determine the entire course of world-history—so confident that in the end his insanity assumes the appearance of a meaningful leap into the actualization of an illusion that takes the place of reality. Next he undertakes to secure his own immediate success (an enterprise to which he was unaccustomed), then a new polemical style appears, and finally he yields to an all-absorbing euphoria.

The *new note* expressing an extreme further intensified is heard in these strange but perhaps true statements: "It is not impossible that I am the foremost philosopher of this age, indeed perhaps even a little more, something decisive and fateful that stands between two millennium" (to Seydlitz, Feb. 12, '88). This runs through the whole year. He speaks of his "decisive task which...splits the history of mankind into two halves" (to Fuchs, Sept. 14, '88) and says: "Concerning the *consequences*, I now occasionally look at my hand with some distrust because it seems to me that I hold the destiny of mankind 'in my hand'" (to Gast, Oct. 30, '88).

These kinds of statements in the last months are usually dismissed as megalomania. Why? Only society determines the limits of what it is 'permissible' to say, and did not Nietzsche write to Gast, that in *Ecce Homo* he is consciously testing the limits of what is permissible? Why not in letters and speech as well? In the mouth of Tom off the street these words may seem mad, but in Nietzsche who had indeed created one of the weightiest critiques of history to date they are more at home than anywhere else. Nietzsche, who understood the language of catastrophe, phantasm, and seduction, who was able to wield them more powerfully than most!

> While his self-confidence, especially with respect to its theme, remains understandable throughout, since it is part of his mode of thinking and has been repeatedly expressed during the years since 1880, Nietzsche now undertakes a *new activity* which is foreign to his former nature. Although he has repeatedly rejected, during previous years, the idea of someone writing about him...he now engages in *enterprises*: he promotes translations and establishes connections with the *Kunstwart*, with Spitteler, with Brandes, and with Strindberg....Furthermore, he induces Gast to write in the *Kunstwart* about *The Case of Wagner* (to Gast, June 14, '88) and, after this has been done, insists on issuing a special publication in which Gast's article is to be combined with one by Fuchs ("The Nietzsche Case, Marginal Notes by Two Musicians." [To Gast, Dec. 27, '88]). Nietzsche's last writings are meant to be effective immediately—at this very moment—and consequently are written according to plan and designed for publication in a definite sequence.

If Nietzsche was planning to withdraw into 'madness,' this activity seems perfectly understandable. He wanted his works ready for publication, and he wanted to broaden his reading public.

> Another indication is provided in the *blunt letters* through which he breaks with people close to him or venerated by him: a still somewhat restrained harbinger of this is the letter to Rohde of May 21, '87. Then comes the break with Bulow on Oct. 9, '88: "Honored Sir, you did not reply to my letter. I shall never again molest you, that I promise you. I am sure you have an idea that *the foremost spirit of this age* expressed a wish to you. Friedrich Nietzsche." This is followed by the break with Malvida von Meysenbug on Oct. 18, '88, and the farewell letter to his sister in Dec. '88.

Jaspers continues:

If one compares the excited years of the Zarathustra period with the excitement of 1888, the later shows an increase in aggressiveness, drastic harshness, and extravagance of rational utterance, in the absence of vision and serenity. The will to action dominates.

But the decisive symptom of the new condition is a *euphoria* which appears only occasionally in the course of the year but is constant during the last months....The tone of happiness is never again interrupted.[10]

To Ariadne, this does not sound like a man falling into ruin, rather a man with a purpose, actively pursuing a course to see that his works are known, pursuing a process of leavetaking as he heads happily, euphorically toward a task that is his necessity, his voluntary 'madness', which may indeed have the possibility of breaking the course of history in two.

Ariadne: "Are we so poor in spirit, exuberance, and health that we call Nietzsche's descriptions of his happiness in the last days illness? Haven't we ever been in love? Don't we know states of power and pleasure when the world seems to be ours, when we command it, when we feel as gods on earth? And in Nietzsche!—who had spent his whole life cultivating these states in himself!"

To Gast he writes (Sept. 27, '88): "*Marvelous* clarity, autumnal colors, an exquisite feeling of well-being on all things." Later on: "I am now the most grateful person in the world—of an *autumnal* mood in every good sense of the word: this is my great *harvest time*. Everything is easy for me, everything turns out well for me..." (to Overbeck, Oct. 18, '88). "I looked at myself in the mirror. Never before have I looked like that: in exemplarily fine spirits, well-nourished, and ten years younger than permissible.... I rejoice in having an excellent tailor and value being considered everywhere as a distinguished foreigner. I am convinced that in my *trattoria* I am served the best food they have to offer.... Between the two of us, I have never known, until this day, what it means to eat with appetite....Here day comes after day with the same unrestrained perfection and flood of sunlight" (Gast, Oct. 30, '88). "On and on it goes, in a *tempo fortissimo* of work and good mood. Exuberantly beautiful autumn day. Just came back from a great concert which, in the last analysis, is the most

powerful concert-impression of my life; my spirit continually
made grimaces in order to cope with an extreme pleasure..."
(Gast, Dec. 2, '88). "Four weeks ago, I began to understand my
own writings, and what is more, I treasure them....I am now of
the absolute conviction that all has turned out well, from the
very beginning; all is one and has one purpose" (to Gast, Dec.
22, '88).[11]

In these matters, one cannot forget Nietzsche's ideas about illness and
health, "great health." The great health is a squandering of power.
Resentment and decadence must be continually overcome through great
health, the Yes to life even in its hardest and most questionable moments.
But this, once again, is the Dionysian round of life, death, and rebirth! The
great health Nietzsche displays during the last months of 1888, his
autumnal time, his harvest time, the time when all has "turned out well,"
including himself, is the time, according to Zarathustra, when the
voluntary death has its greatest effect. Zarathustra: "He who has a goal and
an heir will want death at the right time for his goal and heir."[12]
Nietzsche writes:

Decline
"He sinks, he falls, he's done"—says who?
The truth is: he climbs down to you.
His over-bliss became too stark,
His over-light pursues your dark.[13]

Nietzsche's Ode to and Invocation of Madness

Significance of Madness in the history of morality.—When in spite of
that fearful pressure of 'morality of custom' under which all the
communities of mankind have lived, many millennia before the
beginnings of our calendar and also on the whole during the
course of it up to the present day (we ourselves dwell in the little
world of the exceptions and, so to speak, in the evil zone);—
when, I say, in spite of this, new and deviate ideas, evaluations,
drives again and again broke out, they did so accompanied by a
dreadful attendance: almost everywhere it was madness which

prepared the way for the new idea, which broke the spell of a venerated usage and superstition.

Do you understand why it had to be madness which did this? Something in voice and bearing as uncanny and incalculable as the demonic moods of the weather and the sea and therefore worthy of a similar awe and observation? Something that bore so visibly the sign of total unfreedom as the convulsions and froth of the epileptic, that seemed to mark the madman as the mask and speaking-trumpet of a divinity? Something that awoke in the bearer of a new idea himself reverence for and dread of himself and no longer pangs of conscience and drove him to become the prophet and martyr of his idea?—

While it is constantly suggested to us today that, instead of a grain of salt, a grain of the spice of madness is joined to genius, all earlier people found it much more likely that wherever there is madness there is also a grain of genius and wisdom—something 'divine,' as one whispered to oneself. Or rather: as one said aloud forcefully enough. 'It is through madness that the greatest good things have come to Greece,' Plato said, in concert with all ancient mankind.

Let us go a step further: all superior men who were irresistibly drawn to throw off the yoke of any kind of morality and to frame new laws had, *if they were not actually mad, no alternative but to make themselves or pretend to be mad*—and this indeed applies to innovators in every domain and not only in the domain of priestly and political dogma:—even the innovator of poetical metre had to establish his credentials by madness. (A certain convention that they were mad continued to adhere to poets even into much gentler ages: a convention of which Solon, for example, availed himself when he incited the Athenians to reconquer Salamis.)—

'How can one make oneself mad when one is not mad and does not dare to appear so?'—almost all the significant men of ancient civilisation have pursued this train of thought; a secret teaching of artifices and dietetic hints was propagated on this subject, together with the feeling that such reflections and purposes were innocent, indeed holy. The recipes for becoming a medicine-man among the Indians, a saint among the Christians of the Middle Ages, an angekok among Greenlanders, a pajee among Brazilians are essentially the same: senseless fasting, perpetual sexual abstinence, going into the desert or ascending a mountain or a pillar, or 'sitting in an aged willow tree which looks upon a lake' and thinking of nothing at all except what might bring on an ecstasy and mental disorder.

Who would venture to take a look into the wilderness of bitterest and most superfluous agonies of soul in which probably the most fruitful men of all times have languished! To listen to the sighs of these solitary and agitated minds: 'Ah, give me madness, you heavenly powers! Madness, that I may at last believe in myself! Give deliriums and convulsions, sudden lights and darkness, terrify me with frost and fire such as no mortal has ever felt, with deafening din and prowling figures, make me howl and whine and crawl like a beast: so that I may only come to believe in myself! I am consumed by doubt, I have killed the law, the law anguishes me as a corpse does a living man: if I am not *more* than the law I am the vilest of all men. The new spirit which is in me, whence is it if it is not from you? Prove to me that I am yours; madness alone can prove it.'

And only too often this fervour achieved its goal all too well: in that age in which Christianity proved most fruitful in saints and desert solitaries, and thought it was proving itself by this fruitfulness, there were in Jerusalem vast madhouses for abortive saints, for those who had surrendered to it their last grain of salt.[14]

Script for 'Madness'?

In *Ecce Homo* Nietzsche writes: "All pathological disturbances of the intellect, even that half-numb state that follows fever, have remained entirely foreign to me to this day: and *I had to do research to find out about their nature and frequency*."[15]

"Well," thought Ariadne, "what a strange statement to find at the beginning of Ecce Homo *and especially in a passage in which Nietzsche claims to be the most experienced in matters of health and decadence."*

Nietzsche also writes in *Ecce Homo*: "There is no pathological trait in me; even in periods of severe sickness I never became pathological; in vain would one seek for a trait of fanaticism in my character."[16] Ariadne looked into Nietzsche's library and found Henry Maudsley, *Responsibility in Mental Disease* (1874); Nietzsche had an 1875 German translation. Nietzsche's aphorism on madness above, published in *Daybreak* in 1881 during the time of "Sanctus Januarius," was directly inspired by Maudsley's book. Thus, Nietzsche owned this book for seven or more years. Maudsley discusses all of the aspects of madness and divine inspiration that Nietzsche touches on in his aphorism, including the quote from Plato, the necessity of simulating madness, epilepsy and its connection to divine inspiration, the distinction between the inspired madman who brings new moralities and the aborted madman who, because he does not speak for his times, ends up in the madhouse.[17]

Did Nietzsche find in this book not only the suggestion of simulated madness, but also the script of specific symptoms and case histories given as examples of madness? Maudsley says that the general tendency of the public is to "look upon the disease (of insanity) as a calamity of quite special kind, conceal it as a disgrace, and sometimes treat it as a crime."[18] And didn't Nietzsche know this? The whole literature on Nietzsche's 'madness' bears this out. It is only very recently that madness has begun to lose some of this moral stigma.

In addition to its usefulness as a possible script for 'madness', Nietzsche would have felt himself in good company with Maudsley. Maudsley reviews the suffering inflicted in the treatment of mental illness that arose from theological and metaphysical views.

> Monastic teaching and monastic practice taught a harsh asceticism, through which the body was looked down upon with contempt, as vile and despicable, the temple of Satan, the home of the fleshly lusts which war against the soul, and as needing to be vigilantly kept in subjection, to be crucified daily with its affections and lusts....Now it is a fact, abundantly exemplified in human history, that a practice often lasts for a long time after the theory which inspired it has lost its hold on the belief of mankind. No wonder, then, that the cruel treatment of the insane

survived the belief in diabolical possession, though it is justly a wonder that it should have lasted into this century.

Theology and metaphysics, having common interests, were naturally drawn into close alliance, in order to keep entire possession of the domain of mind, and to withstand the progress of inductive inquiry. To have supposed that the innermost sanctuary of nature could be so entered through the humble portals of bodily functions, would have been regarded as an unwarrantable and unholy exaltation of the body....Metaphysical speculation on madness applied itself to the observation of mental phenomena....When all knowledge of mental action was gained in this way by observation of self-consciousness, men naturally formed opinions from their own experience which they applied to the mental states of insane persons; feeling that they themselves had a consciousness of right and wrong and a power of will to do the right and forbear the wrong, they never doubted that madmen had a like clearness of consciousness and a like power of will—that they could, if they would, control their disorderly thoughts and acts....It was when men recognized insanity as a disease, which, like other diseases, might be alleviated or cured by medical and moral means—that they began to struggle to free themselves in this matter from the bondage of false theology and mischievous metaphysics.[19]

These are the very maladies of civilization that Nietzsche wishes to overturn in his revaluation of values, privileging of mind and consciousness over body, rationality over physiology, Christian and metaphysical judgments, condemnations, and punishments. Maudsley writes:

No one now-a-days who is engaged in the treatment of mental disease doubts that he has to do with the disordered function of a bodily organ—the brain. Whatever opinion may be held concerning the essential nature of mind, and its independence of matter, it is admitted on all sides, that its manifestations take place through the nervous system, and are affected by the condition of the nervous parts which minister to them. If these are healthy, they are sound; if these are diseased, they are unsound. Insanity is, in fact, disorder of brain producing disorder of mind; or, to define its nature in greater detail, it is a disorder of the supreme nerve-centers of the brain—the special organs of mind—producing derangement of thought, feeling, and action, together or separately, of such degree or kind as to incapacitate the individual for the relations of life.[20]

This physiological basis was the latest interpretation of madness in a history of varying interpretations as Maudsley demonstrates. Today the physiological explanation as the basis for *most* cases of mental illness is still held by some and strongly disputed by others. But what is important for our purposes is that this is what was believed by doctors, laymen and Nietzsche at the time of his 'madness.' Following Nietzsche's statement above from *Ecce Homo* he writes:

> A physician who treated me for some time as if my nerves were sick finally said: 'It's not your nerves, it is rather I that am nervous.' There is altogether no sign of any local degeneration; no organically conditioned stomach complaint, however profound the weakness of my gastric system may be as a consequence of over-all exhaustion. My eye trouble, too, though at times dangerously close to blindness, is only a consequence and not a cause: with every increase in vitality my ability to see has also increased again.[21]

Thus, Nietzsche takes pains to tell us that there is nothing mentally or organically wrong with him!

Maudsley also emphasizes that "fate is made for a man by his inheritance, there is a destiny made for a man by his ancestry, and no one can elude, were he able to attempt it, the tyranny of his organization." We know that one of Nietzsche's major contentions, and one he and Maudsley share with their Darwinian age, is that one's physiology, one's biological inheritance is a fundamental factor in whether or not one affirms or negates life. Nietzsche would probably agree with Maudsley that "inheritance and education form the madman and the criminal as well as the healthy," as we saw in his letter to Strindberg in which he discusses the criminal family.[22] Nietzsche knew that his father's illness of the brain and a couple of other ill family members would bring up the question of inherited madness.

Maudsley spends much effort on connecting the loss of moral restraint with insanity. But he argues against holding the madman responsible for moral decay by the fact that madness is an empirical disease devoid of moral or responsibility questions.

> There is a borderland between crime and insanity, near one boundary of which we meet with something of madness but more of sin, and near the other boundary of which something of sin but more of madness. A just estimate of the moral responsibility of the unhappy people inhabiting this borderland will assuredly not be made until we get rid of the metaphysical measure of responsibility as well as of the theological notion that vices and crimes are due to the instigation of the devil.[23]

Maudsley gives the example of a man who hitherto perfectly normal suddenly turns to reckless and criminal behavior, neglects his family and obligations: "his surprised friends see only the effects of vice, and grieve over his sad fall from virtue: after a time they hear that he is in the police court accused of assault or of stealing money or jewelry, and are not greatly astonished that his vices have brought him to such a pass."[24] Maudsley continues:

> Not only may moral derangement thus go before intellectual derangement for some time and itself constitute the disease, but it constantly accompanies the latter; so much so that Esquirol declared "moral alienation," not delusion, "to be the proper characteristic of mental derangement." "There are," he says, "madmen in whom it is difficult to find any trace of hallucination, but there are none in whom the passions and moral affections are not disordered, perverted, or destroyed. I have in this particular met with no exceptions."[25]

Nietzsche learns in his researches on pathology, assuming Maudsley's book was a major source, that a moral degeneration and criminal aspect have to be played out and that they can be sudden. Yet Maudsley writes: "As a rule certainly a person does not go mad in a few hours or days; on the contrary, he may take several weeks or months, before he is clearly deranged."[26] As we have seen, Nietzsche spent several months building up to the final point of 'sudden madness' by displaying a manic and megalo-manic mask in letters and works, and by building over a period of time his role as criminal. And it follows quite naturally upon his definitions of 'evil' and the values of the immoralist. If there are acts of violence on the part of the mad person, Maudsley writes, "There can be no doubt that the act of violence, whatever it be, in these cases is sometimes suggested by the sensational reports of similar deeds in the newspapers."[27] Nietzsche's identification with the cases of Prado, Chambige, and Lesseps in the newspapers, his 'mad letters' to friends suggesting that he will have the young emperor shot, all anti-Semites shot, plays out this characteristic perfectly. He writes admiringly of murderers and styles himself as an executioner and murderer of himself, a "self-hanger." In a letter to Georg Brandes on September 13 announcing the revaluation, Nietzsche writes: "Europe will need to discover a new Siberia where it can exile the origi-nator of these experiments in valuation."[28]

There is no doubt that Nietzsche considers himself an immoralist, 'evil', a criminal because the demand he will make of humanity will lead to a period of wars and catastrophe, but this is all staged with irony and for rhetorical purposes, for he also means it. And we must remember that Nietzsche styles himself as the *decent* criminal. This play and identification with criminality, intensified at the end of 1888 and tied in with specific reports in the newspapers, enacts this symptom perfectly. Maudsley specifically writes that "Perhaps the strongest evidence of the nature of moral insanity as a disease of brain is furnished by the fact that its symptoms sometimes precede for a time the symptoms of intellectual derangement in cases of acute mania, or of general paralysis, or of senile dementia."[29]

Another symptom Nietzsche read about in Maudsley states that "A person may appear completely sane and then suddenly have an uncontrollable outburst."[30] He continues that "most frequently the attack is made upon a near relative who happens to be at hand when the paroxym occurs."[31] On the train from the Basle clinic to the Jena clinic Nietzsche flew into a rage against his mother. She wrote to Overbeck: "I did not travel in the same compartment with him after Frankfort because he had a fit of rage against me. It only lasted about a minute, but it was dreadful to see and hear."[32] Maudsley further describes impulsive and violent behavior as the very essence of insanity: "for in all forms of the disease paroxysms of impulsive violence are common features; without assignable motive insane patients suddenly tear their clothes, break windows or crockery, attack other patients, do great injury to themselves; they exhibit unaccountable impulses to walk, to run, to set fire to buildings, to steal, to utter blasphemous or obscene words."[33] The Jena record shows that Nietzsche was often loud and very noisy with frequent, unprovoked displays of rage and unarticulated screaming. He frequently had to be isolated or put under surveillance. He often sang and stamped his feet. On April 25 and 27 he displayed frequent fits of rage. He always had to be isolated at night. On May 18 the record reads: screams inarticulately fairly often. August 14: again very noisy. December 1: when patient was allowed to sleep in a bed, second-class, with an attendant, instead of in the cell, he was so noisy that he had to be isolated again.

On June 10 Nietzsche suddenly smashed a window. July 4: he breaks a tumbler "to protect his approaches with splinters of glass." The entry for November 1 says he steals books. January 1, 1890: is collecting things again, and for the most part quite useless objects: scraps of paper, rags, etc.[34] These reports from Jena show that Nietzsche does *the exact things* Maudsley offers as examples: sudden outbursts of violent behavior, breaks windows and crockery, steals things.

"Delusions of persecution are typical characteristics of insanity," writes Maudsley.[35] August 16: Nietzsche suddenly smashed several windowpanes and declared he saw the barrel of a rifle behind the window. On April 17 Nietzsche is quoted as saying: "They cursed me in the night, they have used the most terrible contrivances against me." On April 19: "I want a revolver if the suspicion is true that the Grand Duchess herself is the author of these dirty doings and of these attempts against my life." May 16: "I was poisoned again and again."[36] If Nietzsche had progressive paralysis as Dr. Michaelis, in offering his diagnosis of Nietzsche's illness for Podach, said, "the repeatedly occurring physical persecution mania is also remarkable," that is, it is not a typical symptom. *Nietzsche displays a hodge-podge of symptoms that Maudsley describes as belonging to different disorders!*

Maudsley offers further symptoms of insanity:

Where there is disease of the brain which produces derangement of mind, it is of the nature of the disorder to express itself in all sorts of perverted appetites, instincts, and desires, as well as in perverted ideas. In all large asylums there are inmates who display the most depraved appetites; some who, if not carefully watched, eat with apparent relish grass, frogs, worms and even garbage of the most offensive kind; others who exhibit depraved and exaggerated manifestations of the sexual instinct.[37]

Nietzsche reported nightmares or delusions about women, smeared excrement on himself, drank his own urine. Dr. Baumann, who wrote a brief report on Nietzsche in Turin, writes: Maintains he is a famous man and asks for women all the time.[38] The Jena entry for April 1: (Smeared with excrement) "I want a nightgown to save me. There were 24 whores with me in the night." December 2: Maintains that he saw completely crazy women in the night.[39] Podach, in his summary of the Jena medical report in *The Madness of Nietzsche*, left out entries like these because he felt they were too offensive. He later published the entire Jena record in *Medizinische Welt* in 1930.[40]

Mausdley ties neuralgia and chorea to insanity.[41] Chorea is uncontrollable movements of arms, legs, face—both are diseases of the nervous center. "Thus, a severe neuralgia disappears and the patient is attacked with some form of madness, the morbid conditions of perverted function having been transferred from the sensory centers to the mind centers; when the madness has passed away the neuralgia may return."[42] Jena report of March 28: often complains of supraorbital neuralgia on the right side. Nietzsche writes to Gast a couple of times in November and December about uncontrollable grimaces of happiness in the days before January 1889. The Jena record of January 19: While he talks he pulls grimaces almost all the time. July 9: Jumps about, makes faces, screws up his left shoulder.[43]

Maudsley writes that "senile dementia is synonymous with the loss of consciousness of identity....individuality is altogether extinguished, and that which was an individual blends with external nature."[44] This is a prominent part of Nietzsche's play. In his last letter to Burckhardt: "I am Prado, I am also Prado's father, I venture to say that I am also Lesseps....I was twice a spectator at my own funeral, the first time as Count Robilant (no, he is my son, in so far as I am Carlo Alberto...), but I myself was Antonelli."[45] In Jena June 17: "I was Frederick William IV." Calls himself Duke of Cumberland, Kaiser, and so on. He implies he is Wagner when on March 27 he says: "My wife Cosima Wagner brought me here."[46] And, of course, Nietzsche signs himself as Dionysus, the Crucified, and Caesar and in his last letter to Burckhardt he writes: "I am all names in history."

Maudsley spends several pages connecting epilepsy to insanity. In Jena on September 5 Nietzsche declares he suffered from epileptic seizures without loss of consciousness until his seventeenth year. The symptoms of epilepsy Maudsley offers are so similar to those discussed so far as to be almost indistinguishable: the persecution mania and paranoia, theft, patients who destroy inanimate objects to get rid of their anxieties and fears, convulsive movements of face or limbs, irritability and excitement, violence and incoherent words, and moral imbecility.[47]

Maudsley describes several forms of insanity, all of which usually take place one after another in general paralysis of the insane:

> the received classification is founded on the recognition of a few of the most prominent mental symptoms only—....It amounts simply to this: when a person is excited, and raves more or less incoherently, he has *acute mania*; when, after subsiding into a more quiet state, he continues to have delusions and to be incoherent, he has *chronic mania*; when he exhibits insane delusions on one subject or in regard to certain trains of thought, and talks sensibly in other respects, he is said to have *monomania*; when he is gloomy, wretched, and fancies himself ruined or damned, he has *melancholia*; and when his memory is impaired, his feelings quenched, his intelligence enfeebled or extinct, he is said to be suffering from *dementia*.[48]

Maudsley gives another definition of monomania: when the person is elated, confident, self-complacent, and has deranged ideas in conformity with these feelings. Nietzsche displays all of these at one time or another almost in a textbook way. Maudsley goes on to write, however:

> much dissatisfaction has been felt with this classification, and many fruitless attempts have been made to supersede it by a better one. It is extremely vague, and obviously teaches us very

little concerning the disease; it is in fact a rough classification of certain marked symptoms, not an exact classification of the different varieties of disease which are included under the general term insanity; we learn nothing from it concerning the cause of the particular form of disease, its course and duration, its probable termination, its most suitable treatment.

Describing some of the specific physiological symptoms of general paralysis Maudsley writes:

> When a competent physician examines [the patient] he is dis-
> covered to have a slight peculiarity of articulation and perhaps
> an inequality of size of the pupils, symptoms which, in conjunc-
> tion with the previous history, enable the physician to say with
> positive certainty that he is struck with a disease which, sapping
> by degrees his intellect and strength, will within no long time
> destroy his mental and bodily powers, and finally his life.[49]

Nietzsche was found to have an inequality of size of pupils and this was taken without question as a symptom of paralysis. Basle record: Pupillar disparity, right larger than the left, reaction sluggish.[50] But Nietzsche had suffered from chronic eye trouble since childhood, which could account for pupil irregularity. The fact that there was no peculiarity of articulation (Basle record, January 17, 1889: No obvious disturbance of his speech—[51]) in Nietzsche was already noted by one of the physicians Podach quotes as atypical of progressive paralysis. Despite this, Dr. Wille of Basel entered the diagnosis "progressive paralysis," which echoed Dr. Baumann of Turin's diagnosis "mental degeneration."

The question of Nietzsche's 'previous history' as recorded by doctors after his 'breakdown' is interesting to follow. Medical entries in Dr. Baumann's brief report on Nietzsche in Turin, which was sent along with Nietzsche to the Basle clinic, read: "Symptoms were preceded by severe headaches accompanied by vomiting. These sometimes lasted for months. Between 1873 and 1877 frequent interruptions of his professorial work on account of excessive headaches."[52] Later in Basle Nietzsche's mother adds to this for the Basle record: "Father died at the age of thirty-five and a half of softening of the brain...after falling downstairs....One of the mother's brothers died in a nerve sanatorium. The father's sisters were hysterical and somewhat eccentric....Suffered considerably from headaches and eye pains, and had to give up his position in order to recuperate."[53] It is interesting to note that the Basle record reads: "States that he had infected himself on two specific occasions."[54] First, it is interesting that Nietzsche himself is the source of this information. What Nietzsche meant by this cannot be clear. These two medical histories are rewritten in the Jena clinic record in the following:

2. Heredity: father died softening of the brain—Some of father's brothers and sisters suffering from rickets, very talented—Mother living, untalented...
3. Life history: always rather peculiar. Very gifted...syphilit.infect.
4. History of disease: 1878[!] Gave up Professorship because of nervousness and eye trouble."[55]

What is interesting is the brevity of the histories concerning medical information. The later entries only recopy earlier information with the entry of "syphilit. infect." appearing suddenly, perhaps based on Nietzsche's having said he was infected two times. Because Nietzsche was displaying the "symptoms" of paralysis did this cause the writers of the histories to go from some unspecified "infection" to syphilitic infection? And because he was displaying these "symptoms," Overbeck and Nietzsche's mother offered information about his illnesses and family members that "confirmed" what was already taken for granted, that he was mad. After looking at this history and the Basle records, and after a physical examination in which it is again noted that there are "no defects of speech, rarely hesitates over initial consonants," the medical diagnosis is recorded in the Jena record as "a paralytic psychic disturbance."[56]

That Nietzsche exhibited no defects of speech or articulation is consistently maintained; however, *what* Nietzsche says is repeatedly recorded as nonsensical. It is significant that as early as the Basle record it is recorded: "In the afternoon the patient kept up continual confused talk, breaking occasionally into singing and screaming. The content of his conversation is a jumble of previous experiences, each thought following the next without any logical connection."[57] The Jena clinic concurs: January 19: "As for what he actually says, the disconnection of the ideas is noticeable....While he talks he pulls grimaces almost all the time."[58] This sort of nonsensical talk, singing and screaming are recorded throughout the entire period of Nietzsche's 'illness.'[59]

But Nietzsche appears to have 'practiced' this sort of disconnected talk. One of the best published examples is his last letter to Burckhardt, which seems mad and disjointed, making outrageous and nonsensical statements and claims. However, on December 30, 1888, Nietzsche wrote the draft of a letter to Peter Gast that he never sent, and which can in many respects be understood to be a *draft* of his letter to Burckhardt. How do you *draft* a mad letter?

(Turin) Sunday—Sunday (December 30, 1888) par excellence (although it is overcast—)

Old Friend,

Under my window with great power the municipal orchestra of Turin plays, completely as if I were already princeps Taurinorum, Caesar Caesarum and the like, for example, among other hungarian rhapsodies I recognized the grandiose Cleopatra-work of Mancinelli. Before that I went past the Antonelliana breakwater, the most ingenious ediface ever built—interestingly, it has no name—outside of an absolute instinct for heights—reminds me of nothing more than of my Zarathustra. I have baptised it *Ecce Homo* and have sent it around in the spirit of a monstrously free space.—Then I went to my palace, now the palace Madama— the madama too let's say—: can completely *stay* what it is, far in a way the most picturesque kind of greatly conceived castle— namely a staircase well. Then I received an oath of allegiance to the honor of my "grandiosissime Genealogie de la Morale," from my poet Auguste Strindberg, a veritable genius, with the new impression of his profound admiration. Then I wrote in a heroic-aristophanic bravado to the European courts about a *destruction* of the houses of Hohenzollern, these scarlet idiots and criminal race for more than 100 years, arranged in addition the throne of France, also of Elsass, in that I Victor Buonaparte, the brother of our Laetitia was made Kaiser and my excellent Msr. Bourdeau, chief editior of the *Journal de Debats* and *Revue des Deux Mondes* was named ambassador of my court,—ate after that with my cook at noon (—he is called de la Pace not without reason—) and write in addition to my friend and highest consumate maestro a letter, to hold out a prospect to him of Theater, Orchestra and all kinds of camera....Also I have already written, out of love for him, the most beautiful page about music that has ever been written—and in the end not out of love of him, much more someone—der, die das—out of love, der—die—das that should once read the page.

Friedrich Nietzsche

N

—I was just present at the funeral of the ancient Antonelli this November.—He lived exactly as long as it took until the book *Ecce Homo* was finished.—the book and the man also...

—Yesterday I sent my non plus ultra to the printer, entitled "Fame and Eternity" poetized beyond all seven heavens. It goes at the end of *Ecce Homo.*—One dies of reading it, if one is unprepared...

One will speak german at my court: because the highest works of mankind are written in german...

Gymnastics and Pastilles Geraudel will be taken...

At the head of the draft and on the left border of the first page the following is directed to Jean Bourdeau:

So that I do not bring forward my ultimate motives, I send you a letter which I wrote yesterday for my maestro Herr Pietro Gasti—and which may be allowed to wait still a couple of days— I bequeath this letter to any use you wish.

If you ask, you will also get the proclamation for the *Journal des Debats*: it suffices...Triple alliance—but that is only a politeness for misalliance...[60]

Perhaps it was Nietzsche's first intention to send his Epiphany letter to Peter Gast and then to Bourdeau hoping that he would make it public, but later changed his mind and sent it to Burckhardt realizing that Burckhardt would probably go to Overbeck with it. The point is that these two letters, the draft and the actual letter to Burckhardt, were aimed to reach friends who he knew would come to him in Turin if they thought they were needed. Nietzsche tells Gast already on December 30 that he has written the notes to the European Houses although they are dated January 4!

Nietzsche's handwriting has also been taken as evidence of a neurological disease. Sander Gilman writes in "Friedrich Nietzsche's 'Niederschriften aus der Spätesten Zeit' and The Conversation Notebooks, 1889–1895":

> The written texts preserved from the period following his breakdown illustrate two types of the reproduction of linguistic patterns. The first group are those texts which copy existing texts, often in a confused and unclear hand; the second group consists of those inchoate texts which were the product of Nietzsche's attempt at free composition. The disjunctive nature of these texts, coupled with the confused handwriting, are indications of a major disruption of the language and muscle-control centers of the brain.[61]

Thus, Nietzsche's handwriting in 'madness' is shaky and uncontrolled, but very controlled when he writes his 'mad' notes that are copied out in a beautiful script. He clearly copies out *Ecce Homo* for the printer and is correcting proofs of *Nietzsche contra Wagner* on January 7 when Overbeck arrives in Turin. Most any time he was asked to write after his 'breakdown,' usually by his mother or sister in letters to friends or relatives, his handwriting is uncontrolled. The four pages of crayon scrawl that Hayman translates are a combination of Nietzsche's normal writing (already very difficult to read for years before the 'breakdown') with sections that seem to exhibit loss of muscle control. What he writes echoes the disconnection and jumble of experiences and ideas in which he speaks. A damning piece of evidence of physiological deterioration, or conscious effort to give damning evidence in playing out the symptoms of 'madness'? That Nietzsche is capable of taking on masks in this area too cannot be discounted. Nietzsche knew, after reading Maudsley, that his eyes, speech, gestures, and writing must show loss of control, and except for speech, which would be very difficult to simulate, he exhibits these to some degree.

Maudsley offers the stages on the way to dementia (senile dementia, last stage of insanity). Nietzsche plays them out perfectly.

1. the first marked symptom of the mental decay of senile dementia is an impairment of memory, especially of recent events. The past may be recalled with exactness; but recent impressions make no mark, soon pass away, and are forgotten. It is not that they are not rightly apprehended at the time, for at this early stage perception takes place properly, but they are not retained. So it happens that the visit of a friend, or some similar event, which caused interest at the time, is clean forgotten after a few days, while a similar event of former years is remembered accurately.[62]

Overbeck came to visit Nietzsche at Jena on February 24, 1890, and wrote of him:

Nietzsche had greeted me at once on our first meeting...as though nothing had undermined our old friendship and so it remained till my departure from Jena. Nietzsche's loquacity almost grew during our conversations, but these talks were based almost entirely on events that occurred before insanity befell him. There was no lack of attempts on my part to direct his thoughts to things that had occurred lately, such as his association with Dr. Langbehn....In vain....*On the whole he appeared to have no memory of his immediate past and sometimes indeed to avoid it deliberately*—....We could only talk about matters that had occurred during the earlier period and even of these Nietzsche had nothing but fragmentary memories....Then it struck me as noticeable he referred chiefly to outer events in his life, particularly to persons with whom he had been associated (Wagner, etc.), whereas he seldom referred to his literary work and to the plans still unrealized which had been the absorbing interest of his last lucid days.[63]

The record in Jena also bears out the fact that Nietzsche did not "remember" much of his own work: February 20, 1889: No longer knows the beginning of his last book. March 1: Understands or remembers thoughts and passages in his works to a very small extent.[64]

Maudsley describes the next stage in dementia:

2. the impairment of the power of perception, so that the person fails ordinarily to apprehend all the qualities of an object, and so makes mistakes as to the identities of persons or places. The activity of his mind being mainly in the past, his memory of the lapse of time lost, and his perception of present circumstances blunted, trains of ideas are mistaken for realities, and he talks as if he were now in a place where he was formerly, or supposes a person whom he sees for the first time to be someone whom he knew years ago....He may not recognise one whom he had previously known well, inquire after the health of some one who has been dead for some time, or ask after the health of the person with whom he is talking as if he were asking after it from someone else....It will happen that he one day remembers an event of which he evinces no remembrance on another day, or that on one occasion he makes a mistake as to the identity of a person whom he recognises perfectly on another occasion.[65]

When Nietzsche's friend Deussen visits him in the autumn of 1891 at his mother's home he writes:

On the way home I took his arm in a friendly fashion and he did not resist, but he did not recognize me. I turned the conversation to Schopenhauer, and all he could say, as if he were speaking the most important truth, was: "Arthur Schopenhauer was born in Danzig." I told of Spain where I had travelled the year before with my wife. "Spain!" he cried and became lively. "Deussen was there too!"—"But I am Deussen," I answered. Then he stared at me and could not gather his thoughts. So he still had the concept of me, and mentally he recognized his friend, but the power to subsume this image under the proper concept was no longer present.[66]

Maudsley continues:

3. Matters becoming worse, as the effacing action of decay proceeds, the impairment of memory and the loss of power of perception increase. The individual fails to recognise those who are about him while constantly receiving their attentions, and

forgets everything that occurs directly it has occurred. Even the past is not remembered coherently; incidents and persons are jumbled together in a confused way, and the conversation is a fragmentary and incoherent rambling. He does not recognise where he is, has no notion of the day of the week, or of the time of day, and will get up in the night insisting that it is daylight, etc.[67]

Erwin Rohde visited Nietzsche at Easter 1894:

He is completely apathetic, recognizes no one but his mother and sister, speaks scarcely a single sentence for a month at a stretch. His body is shrivelled and weak, though his complexion is healthy....But obviously he no longer feels anything—neither happiness nor unhappiness.[68]

Deussen visited Nietzsche again on his fiftieth birthday, October 15, 1894.

I showed up early in the morning since I had to leave soon. His mother led him in; I wished him happiness, told him that he was turning fifty that day, and handed him a bouquet. He understood nothing of all this. Only the flowers seemed for a moment to arouse his interest, then they too lay there ignored.[69]

Maudsley describes the final stages of senile dementia:

Feeling is involved with intelligence in the common "ruin of oblivion"; by the ravages of decay he is brought to the philosopher's ideal of freedom from passion....Finally, he cannot comprehend a simple question, does not understand at all; and his reply, if he makes one, is utterly irrelevant and incoherent. His habits are often uncleanly; he has lost even the animal instincts and propensities; and so he lingers superfluous on the stage until exhaustion or apoplexy carries him off.

Before this last stage of decay, however, Maudsley writes,

there are sometimes delusions with periods of excitement: he has fears that some injury is to be done to him—that he is to be robbed, ruined, or killed, does not sleep, complains and cries out, and is at times maniacal. Paroxysms of noisy excitement, with delusions and apprehensions of the character described, are, indeed not uncommon features of senile dementia at one stage or other of its course.[70]

Overbeck visits Nietzsche in September 1895:

I saw him only in his room, half-crouching like a wild animal mortally wounded and wanting only to be left in peace. He made literally not one sound while I was there. He did not appear to be suffering or in pain, except perhaps for the expression of profound distaste visible in his lifeless eyes....He had been living for weeks in a state of alternation between days of dreadful excitability, rising to a pitch of roaring and shouting, and days of complete prostration.[71]

In the summer of 1898 Nietzsche suffered a minor stroke and a more serious one in May 1899. On August 25, 1900, he had a final stroke that killed him.

After detailing these stages of dementia and their similarity and dissimilarity to the senile dementia of old age Maudsley writes: "and whosoever would realize what his probable mental state will be in that last scene of all [in the act of dying], when he has the stage all to himself, and easily excites interest, *however poorly he plays his part, may help himself to do so by a study of these successive stages of mental decay.*"[72] Is this just what Nietzsche did? Did he study all of the symptoms of progressive paralysis, epilepsy, and senile dementia that Maudsley's book offered and use them as a script for 'madness'? If one examines the records, Nietzsche's behaviors are a mixture of symptoms from different mental diseases. He exhibits symptoms from the beginning of a disease that often do not appear until later in the progression of paralysis or dementia, and his actions often seem to those around him to be deliberate, swinging from complete lucidity to incomprehensibility, and to Gast and Overbeck at least arousing the occasional suspicion that it was all simulated.

In two notes relating to specific cases of insanity Maudsley writes about the case of a man who had struck a cab-horse on the head with an axe as he drove past it.

He was acquitted at his trial on the ground of insanity....And yet this gentleman, as it appeared afterwards, believed all the while that he was Jesus Christ, and had made the attack on the cab-horse in consequence of that delusion: he wished by the publicity which he would thus gain to attract attention to his mission. Insane enough to conceive and act upon such a motive he was still intelligent enough to appear so sane as to deceive two physicians, who were informed what had been his delusion and what he had done.[73]

In another note Maudsley reports the account of a learned Divine and Professor of Divinity from Peru in the fifteenth or sixteenth century who upon the influence of a female charlatan goes mad.

He appoints himself Redeemer of the world, as to matter of efficacy: which Christ, he said, had been no further than to sufficiency only. That all ecclesiastical estate was to be abrogated; and that he would make new laws....He told his examiners that by revelation it was come to his knowledge that the Serenissimus John of Austria was vanquished by the Turks upon the seas: that Philip the most puissant king of Spain, had lost most part of his kingdom: that a Council was held at Rome, about the deposition of Pope Gregory, and another to be chosen in his place.[74]

Can we still call all of this coincidence? Nietzsche does not hit the cab-horse over the head, but embraces it because it is being mistreated by its master and it does call attention to him. And at this time Nietzsche is signing himself The Crucified after having written *The Antichrist*, which clearly details the insufficiencies of Christianity. Nietzsche does appoint himself redeemer of the world as Dionysus, a new lawmaker ushering in a revaluation of all values. Nietzsche calls a convocation in Rome by writing 'mad' notes to major political houses where he plans to greet the pope and as he writes to Strindberg and Gast, to have the young emperor shot. To Umberto, king of Italy, Nietzsche writes:

To my beloved son, Umberto.—
My peace be with you! I shall come to Rome on Tuesday and shall see you next to his Holiness, the Pope.
                                                                    —The Crucified

To Mariani, the Vatican secretary, Nietzsche writes:

> To my beloved Mariani.—
> My peace be with you! I shall come to Rome on Tuesday to do
> reverence to his Holiness....   The Crucified

To the House of Baden, Nietzsche wrote:

> Children it is not good to have anything to do with the mad
> Hohenzollerns....I gave Bavaria the same advice....
>   The Crucified[75]

One thing becomes clear in going over Maudsley's descriptions of
paralysis, epilepsy, and senile dementia. Generally they all share common
symptoms. If Nietzsche wished to simulate madness, this book provided
him with the perfect script for an incredible role. And the case histories
Maudsley presented provided some of the scenes for the play!

At the end of his book, Maudsley gives out with his own brand of
morality, one unambiguously similar to that of Nietzsche's!

> The life of an individual in this age of civilisation is assuredly not
> a life in which the best use is made of his physical, moral, and
> intellectual capacitites.[76]

> There is hardly any one who sets self-development before himself
> as an aim in life. The aims which chiefly predominate—riches,
> position, power, applause of men inevitably breed bad passions in
> the eager competition to attain them. One comes to grief over
> them—some to insanity.
>
> Thus, their nature is an inconsistency: it is a house divided
> against itself, and how can it stand when trouble comes? How
> can a nature be strong which is at war with itself, whose faith and
> works are in discord?

This is exactly what Strindberg diagnosed as the malady of Bleichroden
and it is the malady that Nietzsche diagnoses as well. Maudsley continues:

> A decrease in the amount of insanity in the world would
> probably take place in a generation or two, if men were to cease
> to deceive themselves, and were to make their natures strong by
> making a real harmony of them.[77]

The happiness of the race, the exaltation of humanity, is its real end, in ministering to which a right-minded person is to find inward satisfaction, even though the way be through self-denial and suffering: if this be selfishness it is so only in so far as it is selfish for mankind to desire and strive to progress in evolution. The development of the mental organisation being part of the order of nature, and taking place in accordance with the laws of the nature which surround it and of which it is part and product, the moral law in man is the conscious reflection of the moral law in the universe—a result among other results of nature having become selfconscious in man.[78]

At one point in his book Maudsley writes: "If a sane mind takes on the task of diving into the troubled depths of a lunatic's mind, if a sane person could succeed in doing this it could be only on one condition—namely, that he should become as insane as the person whose mind he was studying: in that way only could he follow and appreciate its insane reasons."[79]

Ariadne: "No, I am not mad. These stories and fables must stand as the greatest enigma. Which side do we stand on? Is Nietzsche acting out the labyrinthian symptoms of insanity offered in Maudsley's book or are the symptoms confirmation of actual insanity? How deep into decadence and terror is one able to dance, how clearly look the forbidden in the face, how much turn leaden gravity into moving joy? Can one enter the labyrinth and come out again, or become sacrifice and meal of the Minotaur? Daedalus once built me a dancing floor upon which he copied the pattern of the Egyptian Labyrinth in marble relief. Here I dance the labyrinthian evolutions in measured steps with Dionysus to the music of the harp.[80] Yes, Dionysus and I play with the labyrinth and dance upon the Minotaur's head!"

Notes

1. Nietzsche, *Daybreak*, trans. R. J. Hollingdale (Ithaca, N.Y.: Cornell University Press, 1982), #14; partly my emphasis.
2. Karl Jaspers, *Nietzsche* (Chicago: Henry Regnery, 1965), p. 108.
3. Nietzsche, *Antichrist*, p. 614.

4. Jaspers, *Nietzsche*, p. 100.

5. Ibid., pp. 100–01; emphasis added.

6. Many books and articles have been written since Nietzsche's 'madness' and eventual death in 1900 concerning themselves solely with claiming to have come upon the true cause of Nietzsche's madness. Out of these writings four main hypotheses emerged as to the origins of Nietzsche's illness. His sister, Frau Elizabeth Förster-Nietzsche, maintains both in her biography of Nietzsche and in articles written primarily in *Zukunft* (for example, "Die Krankheit Friedrich Nietzsches," *Zukunft*, 8, 1900, No. 14, pp. 9–27) that Nietzsche's illness stemmed from the merging of several factors: overwork, loneliness, and the misuse of medicaments, especially chlorohydrate and a mysterious Japanese medicine. Elizabeth proposes this hypothesis as a relatively harmless alternative to the most widely held hypothesis that Nietzsche contracted in 1866 or 1867 or both, a case of syphilis through whose various stages of physical degeneration he lived until finally in 1889 the disease robbed him of his reason and reduced him to idiocy. Alongside this hypothesis, one that Elizabeth also contested, is the one that claims that Nietzsche's madness was inherited. This thesis is held by its foremost proponent, Dr. Paul Möbius, *Über das Pathologische bei Nietzsche* (Wiesbaden: J. F. Bergmann, 1902), to be the cause of Nietzsche's collapse in 1889. The fourth most widely held hypothesis implies that Nietzsche's status as genius, as self-overcomer, and his philosophy could lead him at the last nowhere else than into madness. This is the thesis that led people to mythologize Nietzsche for various purposes. Add to these four hypothesis a score of others, for example, Paul Cohen, *Um Nietzsches Untergang* (Hannover: Morris-Verlag, 1931), who attributes it to hashish poisoning and the Freudian Steckel who claims Nietzsche was a homosexual who loved and hated Wagner to the point of hysteria and paranoia. Other references: Dr. Ernst Benda, "Nietzsche's Krankheit," *Monatsschrift für Psychiatrie und Neurologie*, ed. L. X., Heft 1, pp. 65–80; H. W. Brann, *Nietzsche und die Frauen*, 1931; Joachim Wecker, "Der Allzumenschliche Nietzsche," *Der Vorstoss*, I, 1931, No. 24, pp. 929–36; Friedrich von Oppeln-Bronikowski, "Gedanken Über das Pathologische bei Nietzsche," *Das Magazine für Literature*, Berlin, No. 68, 1899, pp. 681–86. Dr. Kurt Hildebrandt, "Der Beginn von Nietzsches Geisteskrankheit," *Zeitschrift für die gesamte Neurologie und Psychiatrie*, No. 89, Berlin, pp. 283–309; Max Kesselring, "Nietzsches Kranken-Optik," *Deutsche Rundschau*, February 1953; Johannes Grosse, "Nietzsches Geisteskrankheit," *Zukunft* 17, 1899,

Vol. 28, pp. 208–14; Dr. L. Pratteln, "Versuch einer Ehrenrettung Friedrich Nietzsches," Sonderabdruck aus "Gesundheit und Wohlfahrt," 1941, Heft 2, Zürick: Art. Institut Orell Füssll; A.-G. Ottokar Fischer, "Eine psychologische Grundlage des Wiederkunftsgedankens," *Zeitschrift für angew. Psychologie*, 5, 1911, p. 487; all of Erich Podach's work on Nietzsche's madness which I have referred to in this work. This still does not cover all the resources, but offers the major discussions surrounding the probable cause of Nietzsche's 'illness.'

7. Podach, *Madness of Nietzsche*, pp. 235–36.

8. Jaspers, *Nietzsche*, p. 110.

9. Nietzsche, *Ecce Homo*, pp. 257–58.

10. Jaspers, *Nietzsche*, pp. 98–99.

11. Ibid., pp. 99–100.

12. Nietzsche, "On Free Death," *Zarathustra*, p. 184.

13. Nietzsche, *Gay Science*, p. 61.

14. Nietzsche, Daybreak, trans. R. J. Hollingdale (Ithaca, N.Y.: Cornell University Press, 1982) #14; emphasis added. Reprinted with permission of Cambridge University Press.

15. Nietzsche, *Ecce Homo*, p. 223; emphasis added.

16. Ibid., p. 257.

17. Henry Maudsley, *Responsibility in Mental Disease* (New York: D. Appleton, 1874). I am using the 1892 edition; see pages 47–55. Nietzsche owned a German translation: Henry Maudsley, *Die Zurechnungsfahigkeit der Geisteskranken* (Leipzig: Brockhaus, 1875.)

18. Ibid., pp. 4–5.

19. Ibid., pp. 8–12.

20. Ibid., p. 15.

21. Nietzsche, *Ecce Homo*, p. 223.

22. Maudsley, *Responsibility in Mental Disease*, pp. 21–22.

23. Ibid., p. 34.

24. Ibid., pp. 74–75.

25. Ibid., p. 175.

26. Ibid., p. 25.

27. Ibid., p. 161.

28. Hayman, *Nietzsche*, p. 326.

29. Maudsley, *Responsibility in Mental Disease*, p. 174.

30. Ibid., pp. 207–8.

31. Ibid., p. 209.

32. Podach, *Madness of Nietzsche*, p. 178.

33. Maudsley, *Responsibility in Mental Disease*, p. 153.

34. Podach, Jena medical records, in *Madness of Nietzsche*, pp. 182–225.

35. Maudsley, *Responsibility in Mental Disease*, pp. 202–3.

36. Podach, Jena medical records, in *Madness of Nietzsche*, pp. 182–225.

37. Maudsley, *Responsibility in Mental Disease*, p. 153.

38. Podach, *Madness of Nietzsche*, p. 168.

39. Ibid., pp. 182–225.

40. Erich Podach, "Grenzgebiete: Nietzsches Krankengeschichte," *Medizinische Welt*, 4, No. 40, pp. 1452–54.

41. Maudsley, *Responsibility in Mental Disease*, pp. 41–42.

42. Ibid., pp. 44–45.

43. Podach, Jena medical records, in *Madness of Nietzsche*, pp. 182–225. Also see NB, III, 5, pp. 498–89.

44. Maudsley, *Responsibility in Mental Disease*, p. 263.

45. Middleton, *Selected Letters*, p. 348.

46. Podach, *Madness of Nietzsche*, pp. 182–225.

47. See Maudsley, *Responsibility in Mental Disease*, pp. 239–42.

48. Ibid., p. 73.

49. Ibid., pp. 73–75.

50. Podach, *Madness of Nietzsche*, p. 170.

51. Ibid., p. 176.

52. Ibid., p. 167. For Baumann's complete report see Curt Paul Janz *Nietzsche*, Vol. 3 (Müchen: Carl Hanser Verlag, 1979), p. 308.

53. Ibid., pp. 173–74.

54. Ibid., p. 171.

55. Ibid., pp. 182–83.

56. Ibid., p. 185.

57. Ibid., p. 171.

58. Ibid., p. 185.

59. See *Conversations with Nietzsche*, ed. Sander L. Gilman, trans. David Parent (New York: Oxford University Press, 1987), pp. 227–36.

60. Nietzsche, NB, III, 5, pp. 565–66.

61. Sander Gilman, "Niederschriften aus der Spätesten Zeit," in *Psychoanalytische und Psychopathologische Literaturinterpretation*, Herausgegeben von Bernd Urban und Winfried Kudszus (Darmstadt: Wissenschaftliche Buchgesellschaft, 1981), p. 339.

62. Maudsley, *Responsibility in Mental Disease*, p. 255.
63. Podach, *Madness of Nietzsche*, pp. 219–20; emphasis added.
64. Ibid., p. 192.
65. Maudsley, *Responsibility in Mental Disease*, pp. 256–57.
66. Gilman, *Conversations*, p. 226.
67. Maudsley, *Responsibility in Mental Disease*, pp. 257–58.
68. Hayman, *Nietzsche*, p. 347.
69. Gilman, *Conversations*, p. 226.
70. Maudsley, *Responsibility in Mental Disease*, pp. 258–59
71. Hayman, *Nietzsche*, p. 349.
72. Maudsley, *Responsibility in Mental Disease*, p. 262; emphasis added.
73. Ibid., p. 218.
74. Ibid., pp. 35–37.
75. Podach, *Madness of Nietzsche*, p. 229.
76. Maudsley, *Responsibility in Mental Disease*, p. 290.
77. Ibid., p. 291.
78. Ibid., pp. 306–7.
79. Ibid., pp. 219–20.
80. Graves, *Greek Myths: 1*, p. 342.

The Glad Tidings

> Noble morality, master morality,...is rooted in a triumphant Yes
> said to *oneself*—it is self-affirmation, self-glorification of life; it
> also requires sublime symbols and practices, but only because "its
> heart is too full."[1]

In one of his 'mad' notes to Ariadne—Cosima Wagner—Nietzsche writes:
"*You* shall announce this brief to humankind from Bayreuth with the title
THE GLAD TIDINGS." The same day Nietzsche writes in one of his other
notes to Ariadne that he "has also hung on the cross," and we know that he
is signing his 'mad' notes with the Crucified and Dionysus.[2] In *Ecce Homo*
Nietzsche writes: "I am the bringer of glad tidings like no one before me."[3]

The Antichrist is the dramatic setting against which Nietzsche's
Dionysian drama is played out. There is convincing evidence that
Nietzsche gave up the idea of completing four books of the revaluation and
that *The Antichrist* and *Ecce Homo* take the place of this plan and complete
what Nietzsche wished to accomplish. The drama, the 'act' of madness,
long contemplated by Nietzsche, the dismantling of the gods ("I myself
have slain all gods in the fourth act,"[4]) the voluntary death—*is* the task,
the deed, which consummates Nietzsche's life and ideas, and when seen is
to be understood as the great *symbol of the revaluation* and a great promise to
the living. In *Zarathustra* in "The Gift Giving Virtue": "Dead are all gods:
now we want the overman to live."[5] Nietzsche's 'act' of madness seals the
doom of Christianity and all like thinking. Nietzsche enacts his divine
drama to announce *his* glad tidings; therefore, it is essential to determine
what his glad tidings are.

In *The Antichrist* Nietzsche gives a detailed description of Christ's glad tidings; they are *in part* Nietzsche's glad tidings, too. Nietzsche describes Jesus' glad tidings as a state of the heart:

> not something which is to come "above the earth" or "after death." The whole concept of natural death is lacking in the evangel: death is no bridge, no transition; it is lacking because it belongs to a wholly different, merely apparent world, useful only insofar as it furnishes signs. The "hour of death" is *no* Christian concept—an hour, time, physical life and its crises do not even exist for the teacher of the "glad tidings." The "kingdom of God" is nothing that one expects; it has no yesterday and no day after tomorrow, it will not come in "a thousand years"—it is an experience of the heart; it is everywhere, it is nowhere.[6]

> *Precisely this* is the "glad tidings:" blessedness is not promised, it is not tied to conditions: it is the only reality—the rest is a sign with which to speak of it.[7]

One recognizes here, of course, a mystical state of the heart: oneness with all things that precludes a sense of time or transition from life to death, which knows nothing of space and time or human signs, but simply is. These glad tidings are those of Dionysus as well:

> The word *Dionysian* means: an urge to unity, a reaching out beyond personality, the everyday, society, reality, across the abyss of transitoriness: a passionate-painful overflowing into darker, fuller, more floating states; an ecstatic affirmation of the total character of life as that which remains the same, just as powerful, just as blissful, through all change; the great pantheistic sharing of joy and sorrow that sanctifies and calls good even the most terrible and questionable qualities of life; the eternal will to procreation, to fruitfulness, to recurrence; the feeling of the necessary unity of creation and destruction.[8]

Whether the glad tidings of Christ or of Dionysus, what is alluded to is the feeling of unity with what is, that one finds one's bliss in the reality of salvation in each moment. This is Nietzsche's Dionysian world, which is a world of will to power, the energy force of a totally necessary whole. The world that is and is becoming. The world in which Nietzsche's *amor fati* speaks, where nothing needs to be different, indeed, where nothing can be different than it is. A world where truth is not knowing with human intellectual signs, but where the power of instinctual imperatives and physiology become truth. A world where affirmation even of destruction reigns. This is the world of nature; it is life. A world where what one ought to be is what one already is and is becoming.

The best way to describe this world is that it is nonteleological. If one *is* what one ought to be in each moment, it precludes the idea of striving, of cause and consequence, of purpose or goal. One *is* "the best" one can be *right now*; the world is all it can be *right now*.[9] Joy and affirmation in one's self in this present moment, and in the next, and the next. "Becoming must be explained without recourse to final intentions; becoming must appear justified at every moment...the present must absolutely not be justified with reference to a future, nor the past by reference to the present."[10] This ends moral thinking; it does away with the idea of progress or the idea that people or cultures can be or ought to be better than they are now for this comes from a position of lack rather than what is—fullness and overfullness! This does not lead to new moralities with new oughts, but to great health—affirmation and power from what *is* real: *Ecce Homo*: How One Becomes What One Is—this is the glad tidings.

From this perspective understanding what the "glad tidings" are can only be manifested in a way of life, in the living or practice of a life in this unity, and not through intellectual or moral means.

> It is only in the *practice* of life that one feels "divine," "blessed," "evangelical," at all times a "child of God." Not "repentance," not "prayer for forgiveness," are the ways to God: *only the evangelical practice* leads to God, indeed, it *is* "God"!...The deep instinct for how one must *live*, in order to feel oneself "in heaven," to feel "eternal," while in all other behavior one decidedly does *not* feel oneself in heaven—this alone is the psychological reality of "redemption." A new way of life, *not* a new faith.[11]

For Nietzsche the thinking in signs belongs to the "true world" where the conventional understanding of humans through language operates only as a teleological semiotics of the amoral movement of life and the will to power.[12] Nietzsche speaks of Jesus on these two levels, that of the Dionysian world and that of the semiotic world of the intellect. Nietzsche refers to Christ's relationship with the world and signs:

> For this anti-realist, that not a word is taken literally is precisely the presupposition of being able to speak at all. Among Indians he would have availed himself of Sankhya concepts; among the Chinese, of those of Lao-tse—without having felt any difference. Using the expression somewhat tolerantly, one could call Jesus a "free spirit"—he does not care for anything solid: the word kills, all that is solid kills. The concept, the *experience* of "life" in the only way he knows it, resists any kind of word, formula, law, faith, dogma. He speaks only of the innermost: "life" or "truth" or "light" is his word for the innermost—all the rest, the whole of reality, the whole of nature, language itself, has for him only the value of a sign, a simile.[13]

Nietzsche emphasizes that for someone who lives in this manner the need for signs is unnecessary and yet signs always accompany such a one. One of the most significant signs is that of death.

> This "bringer of glad tidings" died as he had lived, as he had taught—*not* to "redeem men" but to show how one must live. This practice is his legacy to mankind: his behavior before the judges, before the catchpoles, before the accusers and all kinds of slander and scorn—his behavior on the *cross*. He does not resist, he does not defend his right, he takes no step which might ward off the worst, on the contrary, he *provokes* it. And he begs, he suffers, he loves *with* those, *in* those, who do him evil. *Not* to resist, *not* to be angry, *not* to hold responsible—but to resist not even the evil one—to *love* him.[14]

Again, the Dionysian embracing of death echoes this:

> Man's experience tells him that wherever there are signs of life, death is in the offing. The more alive this life becomes, the nearer death draws, until the supreme moment—the enchanted moment when something new is created—when death and life meet in an embrace of mad ecstasy. The rapture and terror of life

are so profound because they are intoxicated with death. As often as life engenders itself anew, the wall which separates it from death is momentarily destroyed. Death comes to the old and the sick from the outside, bringing fear or comfort. They think of it because they feel that life is waning. But for the young the intimation of death rises up out of the full maturity of each individual life and intoxicates them so that their ecstasy becomes infinite. Life which has become sterile totters to meet its end, but love and death have welcomed and clung to one another passionately from the beginning.[15]

In *The Antichrist* Nietzsche blames the Pauline interpretation of the signs that were the life and death of Christ.

Evidently the small community [of disciples] did *not* understand the main point, the exemplary character of this kind of death, the freedom, the superiority over any feeling of *ressentiment*: a token of how little they understood him altogether! After all, Jesus could not intend anything with his death except to give publicly the strongest exhibition, the *proof* of his doctrine. But his disciples were far from *forgiving* this death—which would have been evangelic in the highest sense—or even from offering themselves for a like death in gentle and lovely repose of the heart....After all the evangel had been precisely the presence, the fulfillment, the *reality* of this "kingdom." Just such a death was this very "kingdom of God."[16]

Thus, Jesus' death was the proof and culmination of a life as Nietzsche believed it should be. And Nietzsche refers to a certain type of onlooker who finds some good in the Christian misinterpretation, gods who look at it from the height of Naxos:

Christianity as a religion, based on the misinterpretation of the "glad tidings" is not only dependent on errors but which has its inventiveness and even its genius *only* in harmful errors, *only* in errors which poison life and the heart—is really a *spectacle for gods*, for those gods who are at the same time philosophers and whom I have encountered, for example, at those famous dialogues on Naxos. The moment *nausea* leaves them (*and* us!), they become grateful for the spectacle of the Christian.[17]

And these gods and philosophers (Dionysus and Ariadne) understand that great health needs great sickness, and thus are grateful to the Christian sickness:

> That faith makes blessed under certain circumstances, that blessedness does not make of a fixed idea a *true* idea, that faith moves no mountains but *puts* mountains where there are none—a quick walk through a madhouse enlightens one sufficiently about this. *Not* to be sure, a priest: for he denies instinctively that sickness is sickness, that madhouse is madhouse. Christianity *needs* sickness just as Greek culture needs a superabundance of health—to *make* sick is the true, secret purpose of the whole system of redemptive procedures constructed by the church. And the church itself—is it not the catholic madhouse as the ultimate ideal? The earth altogether as a madhouse?[18]

Both Strindberg and Nietzsche used the symbol of the earth as a madhouse and 'madness' of the individual as a certain health in opposition to the common madness. Because this symbolic of sickness has dominated, the gods on Naxos realize that by contrast the spectacle of great health *must* become attractive, Dionysian health: "The madness which is called Dionysus is no sickness, no disability in life, but a companion of life at its healthiest. It is the tumult which erupts from its innermost recesses when they mature and force their way to the surface. It is the madness inherent in the womb of the mother. This attends all moments of creation, constantly changes ordered existence into chaos, and ushers in primal salvation and primal pain—and in both, the primal wildness of being."[19] The idea that blessedness is here now *is* Dionysian too. It is Zarathustra's belief, which the world has tried its hardest to destroy. "My eternal bliss is: all beings shall be divine to me, all days shall be holy to me, I look for happy omens from the birds, I renounce nausea, I walk as a blind man on blessed paths, I celebrate my overcomings of the hardest, I dance over all heavens."[20]

Christ and Nietzsche/Dionysus share a vision of the glad tidings, *but from different motives*. Jesus and Dionysus are among the many gods who are born, die, and are resurrected. They are connected with what it means to live, die, and be regenerated in the plant and animal world. Dionysus dismembered, torn to pieces, and devoured, is Christ crucified whose body and blood are shared by the communicants. But it is a *life-denying weakness and protection* that Nietzsche sees as Christ's motivation for seeking and finding the world of the glad tidings. And it is this life-denying, weakened side of Christ that Paul magnifies sevenfold. While Christ lived the glad tidings, he lived them for the wrong reasons. Nietzsche writes of the person of Jesus:

> Just the opposite of all wrestling, of all feeling-oneself-in-a-struggle, has here become instinct: the incapacity for resistance becomes morality here ("resist not evil"—the most profound word of the Gospels, their key in a certain sense), blessedness in peace, in gentleness, in not *being able* to be an enemy. What are the "glad tidings"? True life eternal life, has been found—it is not promised, it is here, it is *in you*: as a living in love, in love without subtraction and exclusion, without regard for station. Everyone is the child of God—Jesus definitely presumes nothing for himself alone—and as a child of God everyone is equal to everyone.[21]

Here Nietzsche shows the side of Christ with which he *cannot* agree. Here the signs Christ presents reflect a passive stance to the world, love without regard for station—everyone equal to everyone. These are characteristics of decadent, life-denying thinking that Nietzsche does *not* value. These reactive characteristics in Christ, Nietzsche writes, are a result of a flight from the world of reality:

> *The instinctive hatred of reality*: a consequence of an extreme capacity for suffering and excitement which no longer wants any contact at all because it feels every contact too deeply. *The instinctive exclusion of any antipathy, and hostility, any boundaries or divisions in man's feelings*: the consequence of an extreme capacity for suffering and excitement which experiences any resistance, even any compulsion to resist, as unendurable *displeasure* (that is, as *harmful* as something against which the instinct of self-preservation *warns* us); and finds blessedness (pleasure) only in no longer offering any resistance to anybody, neither to evil nor to him who is evil—love as the only, as the *last* possible way of

life....The fear of pain, even of infinitely minute pain—that can
end in no other way than in a *religion of love*.[22]

Christ fleeing from resistance and displeasure; pleasure in offering no
resistance at all. The glad tidings, yes, but out of fear of pain, even minute
pain. Not, as Nietzsche would have it, life seeking to overcome itself,
struggling to preserve, procreate, and enhance itself.

And what kind of love is this Christian love? Love as self-protection.
Love as refusal of the world in order to love the world. Practice of the glad
tidings in part because their reality is *separate from* the world. The world as
illusion, as mere signs for what is perceived as real—the glad tidings—a sort
of morbid hedonism: spiritual pleasure to avoid real displeasure.

If I have styled Nietzsche as the greatest lover, it is of another type of
love that he speaks. Love out of overfullness, out of joy *in* reality, and
therefore, in pain. Not blessedness in self-protection, but in squandering
one's strength in the struggle *with life*. Not flight from the world, but
redemption *in it*. Nietzsche identifies a love that is a "misunderstanding of
love": "There is a slavish love that submits and gives itself; that idealizes,
and deceives itself." On the other hand, "there is a divine love that despises
and loves, and reshapes and elevates the beloved."[23] "Love translated back
into nature. Not love of a 'higher virgin'!...But love as *fatum*, as fatality,
cynical, innocent, cruel—and precisely in this a piece of nature. That love
which is war in its means."[24]

For Nietzsche Christ is the great symbolist. But so is Dionysus, so is
Nietzsche. Only Christ as symbol manifested the world out of a decadent
nature. Dionysus manifests the same world out of health, the great health:

> Dionysus versus the "Crucified": there you have the antithesis. It
> is *not* a difference in regard to their martyrdom—it is a difference
> in the meaning of it. Life itself, its eternal fruitfulness and
> recurrence, creates torment, destruction, the will to annihilation.
> In the other case, suffering—the "Crucified as the innocent
> one"—counts as an objection to this life, as a formula for its
> condemnation,—One will see that the problem is that of the
> meaning of suffering: whether a Christian meaning or a tragic
> meaning. In the former case, it is supposed to be the path to a
> holy existence; in the latter case being counted as *holy enough* to

justify even a monstrous amount of suffering. The tragic man affirms even the harshest suffering: he is sufficiently strong, rich, and capable of deifying to do so. The Christian denies even the happiest lot on earth: he is sufficiently weak, poor, disinherited to suffer from life in whatever form he meets it. The god on the cross is a curse on life, a signpost to seek redemption from life; Dionysus cut to pieces is a *promise* of life; it will be eternally reborn and return again from destruction.[25]

Thus, Nietzsche's glad tidings are Jesus' glad tidings in so far as they encompass the idea that blessedness is here now and that "there is nothing but the whole."[26] Both live this, but Christ as a *protection against* life; Nietzsche, through the symbol of Dionysus, *as open joying in* life in all of its good and terrible, painful aspects. For strong natures being is holy enough *as it is*. As one seeks the joyful, the good, one should also seek and overcome the painful—*both* are life, reality, holy.

Nietzsche is two: he is Christ and he is Dionysus. But he is also three: he is Caesar as one who wills more power. In his note to Ariadne/Cosima where he claims to be Dionysus and to have hung on the cross, Nietzsche also identifies with Alexander the Great, Caesar, and Napoleon. Nietzsche always claimed admiration for these great conquerors. He is Dionysus versus the Crucified and he is Dionysus and the Crucified. He has thrown out the dross, the weak, life-negating in the evangel, and kept the gold: the life practice of Christ, his *amor fati*, his eternal kingdom, his death as proof of that "kingdom of the heart." These constitute a Dionysian Yes to life, a mystical state of the heart wherein one is all and all is one. "What the signs 'father' and 'son' refer to is obvious—not to everyone, I admit: the word 'son' expresses the *entry* onto the over-all feeling of the transfiguration of all things (blessedness); the word 'father' expresses *this feeling itself*, the feeling of eternity, the feeling of perfection."[27]

Yet the Dionysian Nietzsche is a willer, a willer to more power, not content, not searching for peace, but for war, overcoming. As a conqueror, Nietzsche rides as a spiritual Caesar or Napoleon. He wishes to conquer peoples through spiritual overcoming and he prophesies that it could come to the sword too. One who wills something that has not been willed before —to breed a type of human higher in value, worthier of life, more certain of a future. A Christ, but more 'evil'—that would be Dionysus; combined with the will to this combination—that would be Caesar. Nietzsche: "To overcome everything Christian through something supra-christian, and not merely to put it aside—for the Christian doctrine was the counter doctrine to the Dionysian."²⁸

One of the signs Nietzsche takes for this trinity of reality, spirituality, and willing is Cesare Borgia as pope:

> I envisage a *possibility* of a perfectly supraterrestrial magic and fascination of color: it seems to me that it glistens in all the tremors of subtle beauty, that an art is at work in it, so divine, so devilishly divine that one searches millennia in vain for a second such possibility; I envisage a spectacle so ingenious, so wonderfully paradoxical at the same time, that all the deities on Olympus would have had occasion for immortal laughter: *Cesare Borgia as pope*. Am I understood? Well then, that would have been the victory which alone I crave today: with that, Christianity would have been *abolished*.²⁹

As another sign of this perfection Nietzsche takes the Roman Caesar with the soul of Christ: "Education in those rulers' virtues that master even one's benevolence and pity: the great cultivator's virtues ('forgiving one's enemies' is child's play by comparison), the affect of the creator must be elevated—no longer to work on marble!—The exceptional situation and powerful position of those beings (compared with any prince hitherto): the Roman Caesar with Christ's soul."³⁰ Cesare Borgia as Pope. Caesar as Christ. Jesus, down from the cross, drinking, dancing, and rejoicing in his glad tidings, with blood in his veins. Dionysus the terrible one, the hoary one holding hands gently with Jesus, both plotting with Caesar the triumph of the overhuman.

> What is good? Everything that heightens the feeling of power in man, the will to power, power itself.
> What is bad? Everything that is born of weakness.
> What is happiness? The feeling that power is *growing*, that resistance is overcome.
> Not contentedness but more power; not peace but war; not virtue but fitness.

The weak and the failures shall perish; first principle of *our* love
of man. And they shall even be given every possible assistance.

The problem I thus pose is not what shall succeed mankind in
the sequence of living beings (man is an *end*), but what type of
man shall be *bred*, shall be *willed*, for being higher in value,
worthier of life, more certain of a future
Even in the past this higher type has appeared often—but as a
fortunate accident, as an exception, never as something *willed*.[31]

Here one must be aware that from the perspective of present-day values,
which are still Christian, reactive, self-protective values, that Nietzsche's
glad tidings can also appear to be Nietzsche's terrible tidings. One cannot
do justice to the Dionysian and Caesarian aspects of Nietzsche unless one is
willing to look into this labyrinth. Nietzsche continues after his definition
of love as "reshaping and elevating the beloved" to write: "To gain that
tremendous energy of greatness in order to shape the man of the future
through breeding and, on the other hand, the annihilation of millions of
failures, and not to perish of the suffering one creates."[32] Caesar, Napoleon
battling for empires did not count the dead on their paths to victory. In the
modern world such thinking causes moral condemnation and shudders of
horror, yet our century has been the century of the most massive wars and
slaughters and still, along with the wars of Caesar and Napoleon, for the
wrong reasons, political reasons, and not yet for "great politics." "Great
politics," which is a teaching of a will to strength in each individual, a
triumphant affirmation of the self: "To prepare a *reversal of values* for a
certain strong *kind of man of the highest spirituality and strength of will* and to
this end slowly and cautiously to unfetter a host of instincts now kept in
check and calumniated."[33] Nietzsche is not suggesting a systematic killing of
the weak at the hands of the strong. In the conflict Nietzsche envisions —
where humans fight a spiritual war to overcome two centuries of
decadence, resentment, and life-denying values to turn the spiritual
balance toward life-affirming, triumphant virtues—to the overhuman—the
decadent, the weak would naturally perish. He does suggest in his
discussions of voluntary death as the ultimate act of life affirmation, not
only the culminating voluntary death of the strong, which serves to spur on
the strong, but indicates that pessimists and decadents might *do away with*

themselves because "life itself [would] derive more advantage from this than from any 'life' of renunciation, anemia, and other virtues."[34] Nietzsche's choice of the word *züchten*, which Kaufmann translates as "to breed," also has the meanings of cultivating, growing and training. Rather than the sense of a biological breeding, as if humans were domestic animals and which Kaufmann's translation suggests, Nietzsche's choice of this word is more organic, *a revaluation of values that encourages the cultivation and growth in those who are disposed to it of great health, overflowing strength, and the desire to live in a world that reflects these values as positive and desirable, rather than as criminal.* War, for Nietzsche, is a Dionysian concept. Not the political war of the weak and malcontents to preserve themselves or gain more power, but war and striving arising as the exuberant movement of Dionysian great health—"great politics."

Here we are very far from the Christ who resists nothing, who flees from the real for fear of pain. The irony, of course, is that though Christ and Christian values profess love, peace, and equality some of the fiercest conquerors and wars over the centuries have been fought for these very spiritual beliefs. Nietzsche recognizes that humans have always been warring animals, but wants to channel such instincts toward "great politics," toward willing and creating a stronger life-enhancing type of human for the future.[35] Tracy Strong suggests that Nietzsche's "great politics" culminates in an aesthetic act as he writes to the political houses of Europe trying to prevent the politics of the Reich in favor of "*Geister-krieger,* [spiritual] ideological warfare, 'the like of which has never yet been seen.'"[36]

Dionysus as opposed to Christ represents not a withdrawing from reality, but blessedness in the struggle with and enhancement of reality. In *Ecce Homo* Nietzsche writes: "this type of man that Zarathustra conceives, conceives reality *as it is*, being strong enough to do so; this type is not estranged or removed from reality but is reality itself."[37]

Ariadne proclaims: "With his life and death, Nietzsche puts this question on the line for humankind: two actual crucifixions, Christ on the cross and Nietzsche/Dionysus on the 'cross' of voluntary 'madness.' The choice: either strength in oneself, a creating love, joy in life and death: a triumph! Or weakness and a love that slanders life and seeks to be rid of the self: a decline!"

In *On the Genealogy of Morals* Nietzsche writes:

We modern men are the heirs of the conscience-vivisection and self-torture of millennia: this is what we have practiced longest, it is our distinctive art perhaps, and in any case our subtlety in which we have acquired a refined taste. Man has all too long had an "evil eye" for his natural inclinations, so that they have finally become inseparable from his "bad conscience." An attempt at the reverse would *in itself* be possible—but who is strong enough for it?—that is, to wed the bad conscience to all the *unnatural* inclinations, all those aspirations to the beyond, to that which runs counter to sense, instinct, nature, animal, in short all ideals hitherto, which are one and all hostile to life and the ideals that slander the world. To whom should one turn today with *such* hopes and demands?

The attainment of this goal would require a *different* kind of spirit from that likely to appear in this present age: spirits strengthened by war and victory, for whom conquest, adventure, danger, and even pain have become needs; it would require habituation to the keen air of the heights, to winter journeys, to ice and mountains in every sense; it would require even a kind of sublime wickedness, an ultimate, supremely self-confident mischievousness in knowledge that goes with great health; it would require, in brief and alas, precisely this *great health!*

Is this even possible today?—But some day, in a stronger age than this decaying, self-doubting present, he must yet come to us, the *redeeming* man of great love and contempt, the creative spirit whose compelling strength will not let him rest in any aloofness or any beyond, whose isolation is misunderstood by the people as if it were flight *from* reality—while it is only his absorption, immersion, penetration *into* reality, so that, when he one day emerges again into the light, he may bring home the *redemption* of this reality: its redemption from the curse that the hitherto reigning ideal has laid upon it. This man of the future, who will redeem us not only from the hitherto reigning ideal but also from that which was bound to grow out of it, the great nausea, the will to nothingness, nihilism; this bell-stroke of noon and of the great decision that liberates the will again and restores its goal to the

earth and his hope to man; this Antichrist and antinihilist; this
victor over God and nothingness—*he must come one day.*—[38]

How can this be resolved? The doubleness? This tripleness? This
paradox of inwardness and reality, of *amor fati* and willing, of the glad
tidings, that perfection is here now, and worldly conquest? Michael Platt
has one good answer:

> The premise of *Ecce Homo* is that the peace of *amor fati* and the
> war of publication are not only compatible but, in the case of a
> war to secure the possibility of *amor fati* for others living and yet
> to live, are required by each other. He who says "once more" to
> life loves Eternity and for the sake of the children arising from
> his union with her will go to war against whatever teaching
> hinders his children from one day standing on the peak of
> themselves and rejoicing "once more." To subdue in yourself the
> spirit of revenge without then fighting a public war against it is,
> according to Nietzsche, to be a mere Christ; to fight a public war
> against a sect that spreads this spirit without first having subdued
> it in yourself is to be a mere Caesar. In *Ecce Homo* Nietzsche tried
> to be a Christ who lived on after his redemption to become a
> Caesar ready to fight a war for the earth and perish in it for the
> children of the earth.[39]

Platt carries this to its logical conclusion and it is Ariadne's conclusion, too,
a conclusion that Nietzsche prophesied for himself: "It is as a spiritual
warrior that Nietzsche is a destiny dividing history into a before and after, a
B. N. and A. N."[40]

Nietzsche has killed all the gods in the fourth act so that the way for
the overhuman is prepared. Nietzsche brings together in himself and his
symbolic death: reality (Dionysus: body, instincts, physiology), spirituality
(Christ's glad tidings translated into love of life) and willing (Caesar: love
as war) and he stands as the greatest symbolist in this. Platt goes on in his
article to say that Nietzsche never fought the battle he had prepared for
because he succumbed to madness.

*Ariadne: "No! His 'madness' was his battle and victory! In his own 'death,' in
his acting out of a voluntary play of 'madness,' Nietzsche embodies the highest*

symbol of this triple activity. He wills his death as example toward the end of gaining others to the task of creating the overhuman, through an unheard of hardness against himself, but at the same time, this act was his greatest happiness, his task completed! He is amor fati! *He has become what he is—a great destiny! The glad tidings are that each of us are also* already on the way to the overhuman to the extent that fate as the will to power exhibits itself in us and to the degree that we can deify what we are by struggling against the fetters of moral imperatives, guilt and fear, while glorying in ourselves as nature, instinct, and will to power. *This Caesarian willing of what is, is itself perfection. There is no outside of perfection!"*

"*The world is perfect*"—thus says the instinct of the most spiritual, the Yes-saying instinct; "imperfection, whatever is beneath us, distance, the pathos of distance—even the chandala still belongs to this perfection." The most spiritual men, as the *strongest*, find their happiness where others would find their destruction: in the labyrinth, in hardness against themselves and others, in experiments; their joy is self-conquest; asceticism becomes in them nature, need, and instinct. Difficult tasks are a privilege to them; to play with burdens which crush others, a recreation. Knowledge—a form of asceticism. They are the most venerable kind of man; that does not preclude their being the most cheerful and the kindliest. They rule not because they want to but because they *are*; they are not free to be second.[41]

As long as Nietzsche is remembered pessimism will never again be possible and nihilism overcome. Not because he said so, but because he was the event of their dissolution! Suffering eclipsed by joy and the celebration of overabundance in every moment. Suffering not as something to escape from, rather something seen as an opportunity to more power and fullness. Voluntary death as the joyful victory on the way to eternal life! As Nietzsche transformed himself into this promise at the end he must have been ecstatic! *But for us* he enacted a 'passion' of suffering in order to carry us beyond suffering. One sees that the day of decision that Nietzsche challenges humankind with is one upon which humans must choose a meaning for *suffering*: "to seek redemption from life" or to become what one already is, the tragic but joyfully willed relation to the eternal round of creation out of destruction.

214   The Glad Tidings

Another way of looking at the day of decision conjured up by
Nietzsche brings into play yet a fourth and very important symbolic
persona: the satyr and clown. In *The Madness of Nietzsche* Podach writes:
"In those weeks when Nietzsche was writing *Ecce Homo* and had under-
taken the venture of effecting a European revolution without the legions of
Caesar or the armies of Napoleon, the 'clown' becomes the final mask of
self-control, the counter-poise to the forces that drive him to self-sacrifice.
The 'clown' stands at Caesar's side. [Nietzsche wrote] 'If I seek the highest
Shakespearian formula, this is the one I always find: that he conceived
Caesar as a type.'" Podach continues: "In Shakespeare Nietzsche sees the
supreme example of the fatality of a man who is unable or unwilling to be
what he is: to hold Caesar within the grasp of one's own reality and yet to
do no more than put him on the stage! 'In such a condition,' Nietzsche
wrote, 'one is ripe to "save the world."'"

The question of the meaning of suffering—a world-historical question—hangs in the balance of the question Podach frames: "*Aut Caesar aut
'clown.'*"[42] If the decision of Nietzsche's 'madness' goes *for* him, is celebrated
in joy, he becomes Caesar with Christ's heart, Dionysus reborn: humankind
takes up his challenge! If it goes *against* him, remains fettered in the chains
of resentment morality, he remains the 'clown,' mad, and has lost the game
of chance: humankind moves into nihilism.

Ariadne: "*But all of this also hangs in the balance of me! For as woman, womb,
the birthing one, Dionysus calls to me to consummate the great symbol of our
wedding and the great noon when those who take up his challenge follow
Zarathustra, which means, follow themselves on the way to the overhuman. Oh,
Nietzsche, I come roaring over seas, a dancing tempest, swiftly diamond-
splashing, from the peaks triumphantly pronouncing: 'You are Caesar! But with a
clown's holy, laughing heart!'*"

Notes
    1. Nietzsche, *Nietzsche contra Wagner*, in *Birth of Tragedy and
Nietzsche contra Wagner*, trans. Walter Kaufmann (Toronto: Vintage Books,
1967), p. 191.
    2. See my notes to title.

3. Nietzsche, *Ecce Homo*, p. 327.
4. Nietzsche, *Gay Science*, #153.
5. Nietzsche, *Zarathustra*, p. 191.
6. Nietzsche, *Antichrist*, in *Portable Nietzsche*, p. 608.
7. Ibid., p. 606.
8. Nietzsche, *Will to Power*, #1050.
9. See Nietzsche *Twilight of the Idols*, p. 491.
10. Nietzsche, *Will to Power*, #708.
11. Nietzsche, *Antichrist*, p. 607.
12. See "Reason" in Philosophy and How the "True World" Finally Became a Fable, in *Twilight of the Idols*, pp. 479–85.
13. Nietzsche, *Antichrist*, p. 605.
14. Ibid., p. 609.
15. Otto, *Dionysus Myth and Cult*, p. 137.
16. Nietzsche, *Antichrist*, p. 615.
17. Ibid., p. 614.
18. Ibid., p. 632.
19. Otto, *Dionysus Myth and Cult*, p. 143.
20. Nietzsche, *Zarathustra*, p. 227.
21. Nietzsche, *Antichrist*, pp. 600–601.
22. Ibid., p. 602.
23. Nietzsche, *Will to Power*, #964.
24. Nietzsche, *Case of Wagner*, pp. 158–59.
25. Nietzsche, *Will to Power*, #1052.
26. Nietzsche, *Twilight of the Idols*, pp. 500–501.
27. Nietzsche, *Antichrist*, p. 608.
28. Nietzsche, *Will to Power*, #1051.
29. Nietzsche, *Antichrist*, pp. 653–54.
30. Nietzsche, *Will to Power*, #983; and see Karl Jaspers, *Nietzsche and Christianity*, trans. E. B. Ashton (Henry Regnery Company, 1961), pp. 88–95.
31. Nietzsche, *Antichrist*, pp. 569–70.
32. Nietzsche, *Will to Power*, #964.
33. Ibid., #957.
34. Nietzsche, *Twilight of the Idols*, p. 537.
35. Nietzsche, *Will to Power*, #684.
36. Tracy Strong, "Nietzsche's Political Aesthetics," in *Nietzsche's New Seas*, ed. Michael Allen Gillespie and Tracy B. Strong (Chicago: University of Chicago Press, 1988), p. 169.

37. Nietzsche, *Ecce Homo*, p. 331.

38. Nietzsche, *Genealogy of Morals*, pp. 95–96.

39. Michael Platt, "Behold Nietzsche," *Nietzsche Studien*, #22, 1993, p. 73.

40. Ibid., p. 71.

41. Nietzsche, *Antichrist*, pp. 645–46.

42. Podach, *Madness of Nietzsche*, pp. 131–33.

Interlude: Fear and Trembling

All I gave away all my goods and chattels nothing more remains
for me but you, great hope![1]

It is not his actions which reveal him—actions are always
ambiguous, always unfathomable—; neither is it his 'works.'...it
is the *faith* which is decisive here, which determines the order of
rank here....The noble soul has reverence for itself.[2]

Like Abraham Nietzsche takes his children and the hope of his children
and the knife and he goes to the mountain. He raises the knife, as
Abraham does to slay Isaac, and slays his children and the hope of his
children by taking on the 'appearance of madness.' He removes himself
completely from their fate in the firm belief that his act of sacrifice will
yield them and himself a tenfold life just as Abraham believed he would
reap a higher love in God.

Nietzsche and Abraham are not tragic heros. Neither is a Theseus.
"The tragic hero relinquishes himself in order to express the universal,"
that is, he brings new laws for society. Abraham and Nietzsche are knights
of faith who "relinquish the universal in order to become the single
individual," that is, they go beyond the laws of society to become laws unto
themselves. "Anyone who has learned that to exist as the single individual
is the most terrible of all will not be afraid to say that it is the greatest of
all."[3]

Like Abraham's act Nietzsche's act could only have its effect through
silence. The event must be enacted and yet hidden. For it is not the words
that speak; they merely mask the event of passional physiology, force, and
will to power.

Abraham rose early in the morning. He hurried as if to a celebration, and early in the morning he was at the appointed place on Mount Moriah. He said nothing to Sarah, nothing to Eliezer—who, after all, could understand him, for did not the nature of the temptation extract from him the pledge of silence?[4]

And, like Abraham, if Nietzsche spoke of the event in advance, during its execution or during the long eleven years afterwards, the power of its effect would be broken. Silence takes one out of the realm of heros and into the realm of gods. Silence is a secret and a seduction:

> Despite the rigorousness with which ethics demands disclosure, it cannot be denied that secrecy and silence make a man great simply because they are qualifications of inwardness. When Amor leaves Psyche, he says to her: You will bear a child who will be divine if you remain silent but will be human if you betray the secret. The tragic hero, who is the favorite of ethics, is the purely human; him I can understand, and all his undertakings are out in the open. If I go further, I always run up against the paradox, the divine and the demonic, for silence is both. Silence is the demon's trap, and the more that is silenced, the more terrible the demon, but silence is also divinity's mutual understanding with the single individual.[5]

And, again, who would believe or understand him!

> Abraham remains silent—but he *cannot* speak....Even though I go on talking night and day without interruption, if I cannot make myself understood when I speak, then I am not speaking.... The tragic hero does not know this distress....he has given everyone an opportunity to stand up against him...—and to fight against the whole world is a consolation, to fight against oneself is frightful....The tragic hero does not know the dreadful responsibility of loneliness.[6]

So Nietzsche did not speak; or Nietzsche speaks, but no one understands him: "Have I been understood? Was anyone listening?" If he speaks of the event it must be in a double language, a symbolic language, in a rhapsodic language addressed to the stars and to very small ears.

Abraham made two movements. He made the movement of infinite resignation in giving up Isaac, the thing dearest to him in the whole world, something no one can understand for it was a private overcoming. But then he made the even more singular second movement, the movement of faith in which he said to himself: "But it will not happen, or if it does, the Lord will give me a new Isaac, that is, by virtue of the absurd."[7]

Nietzsche makes these movements, too. He goes into 'madness' leaving his children and the promise of his children, his 'goods and chattels' in the lurch. This noble warrior of new values, this proclaimer of the dead God, this one who almost had us convinced that something more is possible, crouched in the corner of a madhouse, shouting in the night, at the end a silent question-mark. What can the words of a madman ultimately demand? For Ariadne: everything! Nietzsche makes the second movement. The absurd faith that Nietzsche has is that there will be eyes for his drama, ears and a voice for the single silence he is. There must be eyes for the event, ears for the event. One throws oneself into the eternal void and has faith that what has been squandered, relinquished, sacrificed there will be recovered in its fullness. For in its recovery it becomes the eternally resurrected and intensified joy of life. Nietzsche and Abraham are "great by that power whose strength is powerlessness, great by that wisdom whose secret is foolishness, great by that hope whose form is madness, great by the love that is hatred to oneself."[8]

Ariadne: "Isn't this what Dionysus whispered in my ear?"

Nietzsche is like Abraham, but far beyond Abraham. He dies in the form of 'madness'; God does not stop his hand. His children are hurled from the brink, and he does not know that his act of faith has been redeemed. But he believes that it must, but does not know; squanders his life in this belief! In this Nietzsche goes far beyond Abraham. Abraham makes the leap of faith and gets Isaac back again in his life and a greater joy in his faith in God. Nietzsche makes the leap. He does not go to the mountain to sacrifice Isaac, but to sacrifice himself for his children, his works, the overhuman because he must—it is the task assigned to him by the seductive forces of the will to power, by passion. He carries through, he does not reprieve himself at the last moment, but makes the offering. He

must survive on a hope that cannot be realized in his life: "The time for me
hasn't come yet: some are born posthumously."⁹ This is the trick that
posthumous people know:

> "What did you think?" one of them once asked impatiently;
> "would we feel like enduring the estrangement, the cold and
> quiet of the grave around us—this whole subterranean, con-
> cealed, mute, undiscovered solitude that among us is called life
> but might just as well be called death—if we did not know what
> will *become* of us, and that it is only after death that we shall
> enter *our* life and become alive, oh, very much alive, we post-
> humous people!"¹⁰

His highest hope depends on Ariadne. Ariadne will be his hope
realized. Ariadne sees the event, feels the event, pulsates to it, gasps in its
presence, suffers, repulses the terror in it, joys in its presence, weaves the
rope, goes into the labyrinth, and leads him out. And then they both leap
into the labyrinth again. The event is seen, the leap of faith made good!

Kierkegaard, the lover, says to his beloved Abraham:

> Centuries have passed since those days, but you have no need of
> a late lover to snatch your memory from the power of oblivion,
> for every language calls you to mind—and yet you reward your
> lover more gloriously than anyone else. In the life to come you
> make him eternally happy in your bosom; here in this life you
> captivate his eyes and his heart with the wonder of your act....
> You who were the first to feel and to bear witness to that pro-
> digious passion that disdains the terrifying battle with the raging
> elements and the forces of creation in order to contend with
> God, you who were the first to know that supreme passion, the
> holy, pure, and humble expression for the divine madness that
> was admired by the pagans.¹¹

*Ariadne: "Only one century ago, and I your lover do snatch the memory of your
'mad' and silent event from oblivion against all odds. Contemplation of the
wonder of your act rewards me most gloriously! And challenges me to match the
passion of your contending with yourself, for those future ones who would glory in
contending with themselves."*

Nietzsche is like Abraham but far beyond Abraham. Abraham must make his leap once, perhaps twice in his life, and he gains his reward in his life. Nietzsche makes his movements eternally because of the eternal recurrence of the same. He suffers self-sacrifice not once, but over and over. And for the event to take its effect, Ariadne flies to him over and over: this is her eternal joy! The highest risk with chance: eternal suffering or eternal joy? Had Ariadne not flown to him, had the wedding not taken place, only the sacrifice would be eternal. And in that faith that not eternal death but eternal love and life would triumph lay his joy in dying. He knew the joy of his faith in his life, but only the joy of *faith* and not the joy in the confirmation of it. Ariadne must sing her joy and exult for the one who will never *know* but *risked* its confirmation—this greatest of lovers—who was magnificent in his unprecedented act and his belief that the great noon must come and that the marriage would be the seal, the Yes and Amen of the eternal recurrence itself.

Nietzsche is like Abraham but far beyond Abraham. God commands Abraham. Nietzsche commands himself. God stands good for Abraham's deliverance. Only another mortal can stand good for Nietzsche's deliverance as the play of will to power who resounds the event as will to power. Thus, all gods die as superfluous, in the passion of two human hearts—and the overhuman is not lost, but promised in greater possibility!

As Bataille said: "Can the gift a man makes of his madness for his peers be accepted by them without it being returned with interest? And if it is not the derision of he who receives the madness of another like a royal bequest, what could possibly be the response in kind?"[12] Ariadne has been seduced and challenged.

For Ariadne this question can only be answered in one way: "I fly to you enraptured with the intensity of your passion, I leap, squandering all, into your arms, rapturously into death, shouting: You are a god and the earth divine!"

Deleuze saw the wedding of Dionysus and Ariadne:

But Ariadne, abandoned by Theseus, senses the coming of a transmutation which is specific to her: the feminine power emancipated, become beneficent and affirmative, the Anima. "Let the flash of a star glitter in our love! Let your hope be: May I

bear the Overman" (Z I "Of Old and Young Women" p. 92)
Moreover: in relation to Dionysus, Ariadne-Anima is like a
second affirmation. The Dionysian affirmation demands another
affirmation which takes it as the corresponding affirmation of
itself affirmed: "Eternal affirmation of being, eternally I am your
affirmation" (DD "Glory and Eternity"). The eternal return "is
the closest approximation of being and becoming," it affirms the
one of the other (VP II 130/WP 617); a second affirmation is still
necessary in order to bring about this approximation. This is why
the eternal return is itself a wedding ring (Z III "The Seven
Seals"). This is why the Dionysian universe the eternal cycle, is a
wedding ring, a wedding mirror which awaits the soul (anima)
capable of admiring itself there, but also of reflecting it in
admiring itself (VP II 51: another development of the image of
betrothal and the wedding ring). This is why Dionysus wants a
fiancee: "Is it me, me that you want? The whole of me?..." (DD
"Ariadne's Complaint"). (Here again it will be noticed that,
depending on the point at which one is placed, the wedding
changes sense or partners. For, according to the constituted
eternal return, Zarathustra himself appears as the fiancee and
eternity as the woman loved. But according to the constitution
of the eternal return Dionysus is the first affirmation, becoming
and being, more precisely the becoming which is only being as
the object of a second affirmation; Ariadne is this second affirmation, Ariadne is the fiancee, the loving feminine power.)
    As long as Ariadne remained with Theseus the labyrinth
was interpreted the wrong way round, it opened out onto higher
values, the thread was the thread of the negative and *ressentiment*, the moral thread.[13]

Here Deleuze quotes Nietzsche in a note: "We are particularly curious to
explore the labyrinth, we strive to make the acquaintance of Mr. Minotaur
of whom such terrible things are told; what do they matter to us, your path
which *ascends*, your thread which leads *out*, which leads to happiness and to
virtue, which leads towards you, I am afraid of it...can you save us with the
help of this thread? And we, we beg you straight away, hang yourself with
this thread!"[14]

Ariadne: "Dionysus does not rescue me on Naxos. That Theseus left me was my good fortune. When Dionysus wedded me it was not only for me, but more for himself. I, having learned to eschew the hero in man, wanted the divine in man. I killed the hero in Dionysus to keep him divine. The revaluation of all values is not the hero's new law-giving. Nietzsche's leap into 'madness' and silence does not bring universal laws, a common ethical system. Nietzsche's leap demands the single leap of others into the absolute relation with themselves; therein he is no hero, but divinely human. I am not to lead out of the labyrinth, away from the Minotaur. This was my mistake with Theseus, it was Theseus' mistake. Rather, as the wedded one of Dionysus I am to lead all back into the labyrinth, into the heart of the labyrinth, where Dionysus is the Minotaur, where the Minotaur is madness and death, but also love and the eternal recurrence of love and affirmation."

Deleuze continues:

> Dionysus not only asks Ariadne to hear but to affirm affirmation: "You have little ears, you have my ears: put a shrewd word there." The ear is labyrinthine, the ear is the labyrinth of becoming or the maze of affirmation. The labyrinth is what leads us to being, the only being is that of becoming, the only being is that of the labyrinth itself. But Ariadne has Dionysus' ears: affirmation must itself be affirmed so that it can be the affirmation of being. Ariadne puts a *shrewd word* into Dionysus' ear. That is to say: having herself heard the Dionysian affirmation, she makes it the object of a second affirmation heard by Dionysus.[15]

Ariadne: "Dionysus, I love you!"

Nietzsche was like Abraham, but far, far beyond Abraham. Love the hardest, most terrible, and transform it into joy. Go against the 'evidence' — and the either/or of the universal for the absurd experience of joy and singularity in all possibilities!—no evidence is needed—it is not even a category. Abraham joyed in his suffering for God, but Nietzsche joyed in his suffering for the overhuman. To love the suffering Nietzsche in each detail is to elevate the celebratory Nietzsche. Nietzsche does not die tortured and broken on the cross, but dancing and singing in the divine 'madness' of Dionysus. We must love him in 'decline' as much or more than in health for that constitutes the great health. Loving him in health is easy, Christian, but transforming his 'illness' into joy—that is something! Nietzsche is the 'cross' on which we are broken, or resurrected—in either case—a death, an eternal death. Truth made a wager with Nietzsche when she said: offer yourself as suffering and see if they can transmute you into gold![16]

Ariadne: "Zarathustra, I am throwing the golden ball!"[17]

Silence

Words can express the ache of the soul.
Words can render rapture palpable.
Words console the hurting hermit.
And words can seduce the reluctant lover.

Words are the essence of our being.
Words are miracles which bring becoming to light.
The sun rises and sets with words.
Hearts reach out to touch the universe through words.

With words we laugh and cry.
With words we play and skip and run about.
There is joy in the struggle with words.
We want words to do our bidding,
  yet we soon realize that they bid and we obey.

Words are treasures divine.
With words we make heavens and earths.
Words shelter us and words can kill us.
Words turn us into poets, singers, dancers.
Words make us into gods!

As such a word-drunken god I can play at creation and say:
  Dionysus!
  You are my every breath.
  Longing for you is the river longing for the sea.
  Your beauty shakes my heart each time I see you.
  Your existence teaches mine to sing!

But words have silence in their hearts.
It is in this silence,
in this stillness deep in the hearts of words,
that I hear the hushed sound of our souls making eternal love.

Here reverence bows its head soundlessly
                    and I am struck dumb.

Notes

1. Written in the summer of 1888, Nietzsche, KSA, Vol. 13, p. 569.
2. Nietzsche, *Beyond Good and Evil,* #196.
3. Kierkegaard, *Fear and Trembling,* in *Fear and Trembling and Repetition,* ed. and trans. Howard V. Hong and Edna H. Hong (Princeton, N.J.: Princeton University Press, 1983), p. 75.
4. Ibid., p. 21.
5. Ibid., p. 88.
6. Ibid., p. 114.
7. Ibid., p. 115.
8. Ibid., pp. 16–17.
9. Nietzsche, *Ecce Homo,* p. 259.
10. Nietzsche, *Gay Science,* #365.
11. Kierkegaard, *Fear and Trembling,* p. 23.
12. Bataille, "Nietzsche's Madness," see my page 60.
13. Gilles Deleuze, *Nietzsche and Philosophy,* trans. Hugh Tomlinson (New York: Columbia University Press, 1983), pp. 187–88.
14. Ibid., p. 220.
15. Ibid., p. 188.
16. Refers to the end of "On the Poverty of the Richest Man," in *Dithyrambs of Dionysus,* p. 75.
17. "On Free Death," *Zarathustra,* p. 186.

The Dionysus Dithyrambs

The formula for my happiness: a Yes, a No, a straight line, a goal.[1]

Zarathustra: "You do not want to grope along a thread with cowardly hand."[2]

Ariadne: "You are right, Nietzsche, some do not need Ariadne's thread to lead them in and out of the labyrinth. We plunge into the labyrinth ready to test our courage, to work to keep our good spirits even in the midst of the most terrifying truths. You lost yourself in your very own labyrinth to which you gave my name. Now I, Ariadne, lose myself in my labyrinth to which you have given the name Dionysus. Your perfect reader is the one who gets eternally lost in the recesses of the most powerful soul. The Dionysus Dithyrambs, are the celebratory rhapsody of you my Dionysus, the self-condemned one, the fisherman on high mountains who awaits his Ariadnes, those who will take you, Dionysus, as their labyrinth, not once but eternally."

The *Dionysus Dithyrambs* were prepared by Nietzsche for publication in the last months of 1888. They were a continuation of the lyric form of "From on High Mountains," the "Aftersong" to *Beyond Good and Evil* and "To the Mistral" at the end of the second edition of *The Gay Science*. The dithyrambs also come out of high mountains and repeat themes from those poems. While most commentators of the dithyrambs recognize their common theme of death and passing, most also agree that they are hardly songs of praise offered up to Dionysus in a spirit of votive jubilation.[3] I disagree: they *are* songs of praise and jubilation because renunciation and death in the light of the eternal recurrence of the same become a celebration! They are an announcement not only of Nietzsche's act of 'madness,'

227

an act that is also his highest demand of himself, his seventh solitude, but they tell the whole story of his passion and highest hope in the form of a lyrical narrative.

Hollingdale, who translates and prefaces the *Dithyrambs*, tells us that the nine poems that constitute the collection were composed over the six-year period, 1883–88.[4] "Last Will" is the earliest of the dithyrambs. It appears in a notebook of 1883 among notes for Part III of *Zarathustra*. There seems to be clear links between "Last Will" and "Of Voluntary Death," for this first draft of the poem follows immediately upon one of the plans that ends with Zarathustra's voluntary death.[5] "Ariadne's Lament" as "The Magician's Song" and "The Daughters of the Desert" were written in 1884 for Part IV of *Zarathustra*. And "Only a Fool! Only a Poet!" written in 1885 was also included in Part IV of *Zarathustra* and called "The Song of Melancholy." Podach suggests that the five remaining dithyrambs were composed in the period 1884–85 for a planned "Medusa-Hymns."[6] However, Nietzsche saved "Amid Birds of Prey," "The Fire-Signal," "The Sun Sinks," "Fame and Eternity," and "Of the Poverty of the Richest Man" until 1888 and the time of his voluntary death. Nietzsche originally intended "Fame and Eternity" to end *Ecce Homo* and "Of the Poverty of the Richest Man" to go at the end of *Nietzsche contra Wagner*. But he changed his mind and removed them from those works and included them among the *Dionysus Dithyrambs*.

Nietzsche considered many titles for the collection of dithyrambs:

Songs of the Heights. Dedicated to all Men of the Future. By a
    Prophet
Dionysian Songs of a Prophet
The Mirror of Prophecy
The Way to Greatness: Songs of Zarathustra, The Grave of God
Songs of War from the Soul of the Victor: Out of the Seventh
    Solitude
To the Higher Men. Proclamations
Midday and Eternity
The Eternal Recurrence. Zarathustra's Dances and Festivities
The Songs of Zarathustra. Part One: The Path to Greatness
Zarathustra's Songs. Out of Seven Solitudes

The Temptation of Zarathustra or To Those for Whom Pity Has
Become a Sin[7]

These titles definitively show that Nietzsche considered these poems to be
the occasion of much celebration and prophecy. We notice, too, how
closely they repeat and approximate the plans for the death of Zarathustra
(and before that, of Empedocles) and its connection with the death of gods,
the rising of midday, and the heralding of the eternal recurrence with
festivities, the oaths of the higher humans, and prophecies of the future.
These songs are sung from the heights, out of seven solitudes. Up until
December 22, 1888, Nietzsche refers to the dithyrambs as "The Songs of
Zarathustra," but by the first days of January 1889 he writes of them as the
"Dionysus Dithyrambs."[8]

At the same time that Nietzsche was still playing around with
different titles and with which poems to include in the collection of
dithyrambs and which to put in other works, he was also considering which
order to put them in. The following lists in Nietzsche's notes provide some
insight into his thinking on the order of the poems:

1. On the Poverty of the
   Richest Man
2. Amid Birds of Prey
3. Fire-Signal
4. Fame and Eternity
5. Last Will

On the Poverty of the
   Richest Man
Amid Birds of Prey
Last Will
Fire-Signal
Fame and Eternity
The Sun Sinks

1. Fame and Eternity
2. Last Will
3. Amid Birds of Prey
4. The Fire-Signal
5. The Sun Sinks
6. On the Poverty of the
   Richest Man

1. Fame and Eternity
2. Last Will
3. Amid Birds of Prey
4. On the Poverty of the
   Richest Man
5. The Fire-Signal
6. The Sun Sinks
7. On the Poverty of the
   Richest Man[9]

This shows us at least three things: (1) that the overall order can be changed and is not completely set; (2) that certain poems are usually thought of as going together, for example, "Fame and Eternity" and "Last Will," though not in all cases, and perhaps "Fire-Signal" and "The Sun Sinks," though, again, not in all cases, and "On the Poverty of the Richest Man" and "Amid Birds of Prey"; and (3) that "On the Poverty of the Richest Man" is perhaps the most important of the dithyrambs because it is always first or last, heralding the rest of the dithyrambs, or acting as their closure and pledge. Also, the fact that Nietzsche thought of this dithyramb as the conclusion of *Nietzsche contra Wagner* makes it one of the more significant dithyrambs.

The three dithyrambs not included here are "Ariadne's Lament," "The Desert Grows," and "Only a Fool! Only a Poet!" the three dithyrambs from Part IV of *Zarathustra*. On December 9, Nietzsche wrote Peter Gast asking him to retrieve all the copies of Part IV of *Zarathustra* that had been privately printed and distributed to only a few close friends. It was now his idea that its time had not yet come and that it would be more effective to publish it after "a couple of decades of world historical crises—Wars!—to publish it then would be the right time."[10] It is most likely at this point that he decided to include the three *Zarathustra* dithyrambs, "The Song of the Magician," first called "Unloved...Song of Ariadne" but then changed to "Ariadne's Lament," the "Song of Melancholy" becoming "Only a Fool! Only a Poet!" and "Daughters of the Desert" becoming "The Desert Grows: Woe to Him Who Harbours Deserts." In a second clean copy for the printer prepared by Nietzsche including seven of the dithyrambs "Ariadne's Lament" was to have been the last poem, giving it the position of a concluding statement and this is the order in which Podach presents them.[11] However, in this form "On the Poverty of the Richest Man" and "Fame and Eternity" were not included, presumably because of Nietzsche's plans to include them in *Ecce Homo* and *Nietzsche contra Wagner*. Nietzsche's final list of the full order of the dithyrambs and the order Hollingdale uses in his translation is the following:

1. Only a Fool! Only a Poet!
2. The Desert Grows: Woe to Him Who Harbours Deserts...
3. Last Will

4. Amid Birds of Prey
5. The Fire-Signal
6. The Sun Sinks
7. Ariadne's Complaint
8. Fame and Eternity
9. Of the Poverty of the Richest Man[12]

In my narrative of the *Dithyrambs* I will put "Of the Poverty of the Richest Man" after "The Desert Grows" and before "Last Will."

Now, let us begin the narrative of the heights! All of the dithyrambs image Nietzsche's transition to his voluntary living death, his 'madness,' his 'seventh solitude.' This solitude is a place of extreme happiness, it is a waiting for and a baiting of those who must come.

With "Only a Fool! Only a Poet!" Nietzsche sets us up for the No-doing part of his philosophy and task. In *Ecce Homo* Nietzsche writes:

> The task for the years that followed now was indicated as clearly as possible. After the Yes-saying part of my task had been solved, the turn had come for the No-saying, No-*doing* part: the revaluation of our values so far, the great war—conjuring up a day of decision. This included the slow search for those related to me, those who, prompted by strength, would offer me their hands for *destroying*.
>
> From this moment forward all my writings are fish hooks: perhaps I know how to fish as well as anyone?— If nothing was caught, I am not to blame. *There were no fish.*[13]

The Yes-saying part was *Zarathustra*; the No-saying, his works after that beginning with *Beyond Good and Evil*; and his *deed* of 'madness,' the No-doing part.

By now Nietzsche's readers are familiar with his skepticism about language, his skepticism that we can really 'know' anything because of the metaphorical and semiotic nature of language.

> "The wooer of *truth?*—you!" so they jeered—
> "No! only a poet!
> an animal, cunning, preying, creeping,
> that has to lie,

that knowingly, willfully has to lie,
lusting for prey,
gaudily masked,
a mask to itself,
a prey to itself—
that—the wooer of truth?...

Only a fool! Only a poet!
Talking only gaudy nonsense,
gaudy nonsense from a fool's mask
climbing around on deceitful word-bridges,
on mirage rainbows,
between false skies,
hovering, creeping—
only a fool! *only* a poet!...

Here Nietzsche describes the common situation of the human being and
the use of language. One never finds or offers the truth; rather one is forced
to create, in a sort of madness, the poet, the fool, word-bridges, phantasms.
One has to create them and then breathe life into them for they have no
true existence other than their own deceitful seduction and appearance.
"Whatever has *value* in our world now does not have value in itself,
according to its nature—nature is always value-less, but has been *given*
value at some time,...it was we who gave and bestowed it. Only we have
created the world *that concerns man!*"[14] A poet like this is cunning,
creeping, preying, trying to seduce others and himself to the 'truth' of what
he has created, for he can only create lies.[15]

That—the wooer of truth?...
Not still, stiff, smooth, cold,
become an image,
become a god's statue,
not set up before temples,
a god's watchman:
no! enemy to such statues of truth,
more at home in any wilderness than
in temples, full of cat's wantoness,
leaping through every window,

swiftly! into every chance,
sniffing out every jungle,
that you may run,
sinfully healthy and gaudy and fair,
in jungles among gaudy-speckled beasts of prey,
run with lustful lips,
happily jeering, happily hellish, happily blood-thirsty,
preying, creeping, *lying*...

Not the enshrined cool 'truths' of rationalism that weigh evidence and ask for proofs! Tear this belief in 'truth' down, like an eagle goes for all lamb-souls, "stupid with lamb's milk kindliness..."

Thus,
eaglelike, pantherlike,
are the poet's desires,
are *your* desires under a thousand masks,
you fool! you poet!...

You who saw man
as *god* and *sheep*—
to *rend* the god in man
as the sheep in man
and rending *to laugh*—

that, that is your blessedness,
a panther's and eagle's blessedness,
a poet's and a fool's blessedness!"...

Tear down the belief in 'truth,' ideals, the god in man, resentment moralities, in the lamb in man. Nietzsche calls upon panthers and eagles, "those who will lend me their hand even in destroying." These must tear down the old truths and build new 'word-bridges.'

So I myself sank once
from my delusion of truth,
from my daytime longings,
weary of day, sick with light
—sank downwards, down to evening, down to shadows,
scorched and thirsty

with one truth
—do you remember, do you, hot heart,
how you thirsted then?—
that I am banished
from all truth!
Only a fool! *Only* a poet!...

Nietzsche recognizes that his own truths are illusions, that truth simply does not exist, but only poetizing. His whole creating and carrying into one has been a phantasm, the mad phantasies of a fool. But the *only* is to be taken ironically. This is not a despairing dithyramb! To be *only* a poet, *only* a fool, is to live at the height of the will to power, is to escape resentment fixedness and rationality and move into the divine chance of becoming; to provide new scripts for new actors. To begin the *Dionysian Dithyrambs* with this idea is twofold. It reminds us that all that has come before and all to come are only Nietzsche's prevarications, his phantasms and seductions, but in the very admission of this he gives us to know that the activity of creating such poems and the word-bridges they offer are not only the best he has to offer, but they are, along with all other word-bridges, all we have. Because this is all his creating and bringing into one, this dithyramb incites the reader to create her own illusions, phantasms, lies. The sinking down, down to night, the staring long, long into abysses, into ever deeper depths is the labyrinth. For one cannot be a poet or a fool without entering the dangers of the labyrinth. "That I am banished from all truth" means silence. With this Nietzsche destroys and elevates in advance all he goes on to build in the following dithyrambs.

"The Desert Grows: Woe to Him Who Harbours Deserts..." acts as a sort of satyr-play and statement of the culmination of the life-negating Western culture that Nietzsche hopes to destroy and to replace with a Dionysian world. This dithyramb is a warning to and a laugh at the desert of European seriousness: Christianity, rationality, morality, political ideals, all of the plague of modern-day man, the last man, that Nietzsche 'jumps into Aetna' (as Empedocles) to cure. As a counterpoint to Western European culture Nietzsche speaks out of the oriental, the Near Eastern soul, as he did in reviving Zarathustra as the spokesman for the overhuman and eternal recurrence. Nietzsche does not succumb in total to the European desert, for he sits in an oasis.

Here I sit now
in this smallest oasis
like a date,
brown, sweet, oozing golden,
thirsting for a girl's rounded mouth,
but thirsting more for girlish,
ice-cold, snow-white, cutting
teeth: for these do
the hearts of all hot dates lust. Selah.

Again, the image of the woman who must come as the vintager with the knife, the cutting incisors, one to harvest the ripe grapes, and this one to eat the ripe date, brown, golden, waiting.

Like, all too like
that aforesaid southern fruit
do I lie here, by little
flying insects
danced and played around,
and by even smaller
more foolish and more wicked desires and notions—
besieged by you,
you silent girl-kittens
full of misgivings,
Dudu and Suleika
—*sphinxed round*, that I may cram much feeling into two words:

Nietzsche poses himself as the great riddle. As he goes into 'madness,' Nietzsche sits like a Sphinx and poses a question: What happened? Who was that? In "Amid Birds of Prey," as we will see, he contemplates those who are already trying to solve the riddle he is like the little flying insects that dance and play around him above. But for the purposes of this dithyramb, to answer the question of the Sphinx also has to do with guessing questions about legs as it did with Oedipus. The Sphinx's question: "What goes on four legs in the morning, two legs in the afternoon, and three legs in the evening?" Answer: human beings. Here Nietzsche is asking questions about a missing leg. In, *Dionysus*, Otto tells us that the Sphinx, "this man-eating lion-woman reminds us vividly of Dionysus and

not just of him but also of his maenads." Among the references that tell of
the origin of the Sphinx, "there is also the one which says that she was
once a maenad, that is to say, one of the Theban women whom Dionysus
drove mad."[16] These are dancing women like Dudu and Suleika and the
swaying palm tree. Thus, Nietzsche/Dionysus sits in his oasis posing a riddle
that needs to be guessed.

> Drinking in this finest air,
> with nostrils swollen like goblets,
> without future, without memories,
> thus do I sit here, you
> dearest maidens,
> and regard the palm-tree,
> and watch how, like a dancer,
> it bends and bows and sways at the hips
> —if you watch long you follow suit...
> like a dancer who, it would seem,
> has stood too long, dangerously long
> always on *one* little leg?
> —so that she has forgotten, it would seem,
> the *other* leg?

Here, you watch the palm tree dancing and *you* follow suit like a dancer. It
is this dancer, not the swaying palm tree or a dancing maiden that is
missing a leg, it is the European, Western modern-day human, it is we who
are missing the leg.

> At least, in vain
> I sought the missing twin-jewel
> —that is, the other leg—
> in the sacred vicinity
> of her dearest, daintiest
> fluttering, flickering, fan-swirling little skirt.
> Yes, if you would quite believe me,
> you sweet maidens;
> she has *lost* it.

The modern European is not a human; he has not four, two or three legs,
but only one. He cannot even stand up, let alone dance properly. What has

deprived the European of the other leg? The moral roaring, the virtuous howling, Christianity, which is loved best of all by European ardor, Western appetite. And that moral roaring finds its highest manifestation in science, science as another symptom of decadence out of fear. After "The Song of Melancholy" in Part IV of *Zarathustra*, the conscientious man says to the higher men: "But you others what do I see? You are all still sitting there with lusting eyes: you free souls, where is your freedom gone? You are almost like men, it seems to me, who have long watched wicked, dancing, naked girls: your souls are dancing too." But the conscientious man is different, European; he cannot dance:

> I seek more *security*, that is why I came to Zarathustra. For he is the firmest tower and will today, when everything is tottering and all the earth is quaking. But you—when I see the eyes you make, it almost seems to me that you are seeking *more insecurity*: more thrills, more danger, more earthquakes. You desire, I should almost presume—forgive my presumption, you higher men—you desire the most wicked, most dangerous life, of which *I* am most afraid: the life of wild animals, woods, caves, steep mountains, and labyrinthian gorges. And it is not the leaders *out* of danger who appeal to you most, but those who induce you to leave all ways, the seducers.
>
> For the fear of wild animals, that was bred in man longest of all—including the animal he harbors inside himself and fears: Zarathustra calls it 'the inner beast.' Such long old fear, finally refined, spiritualized, spiritual—today, it seems to me, this is called *science*.
>
> But Zarathustra who was just coming back into his cave and had heard and guessed this last speech, threw a handful of roses at the conscientious man and laughed at his "truths." "What?" he cried. "What did I hear just now? Verily, it seems to me that you are a fool, or that I am one myself, and your 'truth' I simply reverse. For *fear*—that is our exception. But courage and adventure and pleasure in the uncertain, in the undared—*courage* seems to me man's whole prehistory. He envied the wildest, most courageous animals and robbed all their virtues: only thus did he become man. *This* courage, finally refined, spiritualized, spiritual, this human courage with eagles' wings and serpents' wisdom—*that*, it seems to me, is today called—"[17]

That is called 'evil'—overhuman—one who dances right over such securities as 'truth,' Christianity, science. After this the wanderer sings the "Daughters of the Desert" but before doing so he says:

> Forgive me an old afterdinner song that I once composed among daughters of the wilderness: oriental; never was I farther away from cloudy, moist, melancholy old Europe. In those days I loved such oriental girls and other blue skies over which no clouds and thoughts hang. You would not believe how nicely they sat there when they were not dancing, deep but without thoughts, like little secrets, like beribboned riddles, like afterdinner nuts—colorful and strange, to be sure, but without clouds; riddles that let themselves be guessed.[18]

Zarathustra and dancing Dudu and Suleika offer the Dionysian path of 'evil' and danger on the way to the overhuman in opposition to the sterile, moral safety of the European. And Nietzsche closes his dithyramb with this verse:

> The desert grows: woe to him who harbours deserts!
> Stone grates on stone, the desert swallows down.
> And death that *chews*, whose life is chewing,
> gazes upon it, monstrous, glowing brown...
>
> *Consumed by lust, O Man, do not forget:*
> *you—are the stone, the desert, you are death...*

Here Nietzsche says to Western humans, do not turn up your noses at oriental, Zarathustrian, Dionysian images of ripe dates and brown dancing girls. Do not turn your eyes from paradise, from inclusion of all sexual, bodily, natural dangers and enticements because of your devouring need for moral roaring. You have chewed off your other dancing leg. You are a desert. You will yet chew yourselves up. Find your Dudu, your Suleika, your Ariadne, recover your lost leg and learn to dance:

> to rediscover the South in one and to spread out above one a bright, glittering, mysterious southern sky; to reconquer southern health and hidden powerfulness of soul; step by step to become more comprehensive, more supranational, more European, more Near Eastern, finally more *Greek*—for the Greek was the first great union and synthesis of everything Near Eastern, and on

that account the *inception* of the European soul, the discovery of
our *"new world"*: whoever lives under such imperatives, who
knows what he may not encounter one day? Perhaps—a *new
day!*[19]

Thus far Nietzsche has spoken of the impossibility of truths and of the
desert of European truths, now in "Of the Poverty of the Richest Man" he
speaks of *his* 'truth':

Ten years have passed—
no drop of water has reached me,
no moist wind, no dew of love
—a *rainless* land...
Now I ask of my wisdom
that it grow not mean in this aridity:
yourself overflow, yourself drop dew,
yourself, be rain to this yellowed wilderness!

Nietzsche is the rain, the dew for the European wilderness; he makes his
own oasis in the wilderness. In summer-fall of 1888 Nietzsche repeats the
refrain of this dithyramb: "It has been ten years already: not a sound
reaches me any longer—a land without rain. One must have a great deal of
humanity left not to die of thirst in the drought."[20] Nietzsche sits on his
mountain; for ten years he has sat there with no answer, no love. He courts
his dark clouds and makes rain of them and pours his own secret dew of
love over the land.

Golden with smiles
let truth approach me today,
made sweet by the sun, made brown by love,
ripe truths alone do I pluck from the vine.

Brown, the vine, ripeness again, the harvest at sweetest maturity. The
vintager is hailed. Here, Nietzsche plucks ripe truths from the vine.

Today I stretched out my hand
to the hairy head of chance,
cunning enough to outwit chance
and lead it along like a child.

Nietzsche is powerful enough to play with chance and win. He wins because his soul, having tasted everything, having entered the labyrinth, always comes back up again. His soul has earned him the name of "the happy man."

> Sick today with tenderness,
> a thawing wind,
> Zarathustra sits waiting, waiting in his mountains—
> in his own juice
> cooked and grown sweet,
> *below* his summit,
> *below* his ice,
> tired and happy,
> a creator on his seventh day.

Again, cooked sweet, steeped in his own juices, waiting. Resting in his seventh solitude, waiting for the culmination of his having created a world. As Zarathustra sits on his mountain waiting in happiness, a realization comes to him in the form of a lovely, wicked girl. She is *his* truth.

> —Soft!
> It is *my* truth!—
> From hesitant eyes,
> from velvet tremblings
> its glance strikes at me,
> lovely, wicked, the glance of a girl...
> She divines the *ground* of my happiness,
> she divines *me*—ha! what is she thinking of?—
> Purple there lurks a dragon
> in the abyss of her glance.

This is Ariadne, Ariadne as Zarathustra's labyrinth, abyss, but it is a lovely abyss. And thus speaks the abyss to Zarathustra, thus speaks Ariadne (Pana, Corinna, Calina, the women connected with the sacrificial death of Empedocles and Zarathustra):

> —Soft! My truth *speaks*!—
> Woe to thee, Zarathustra!

You resemble one
who has swallowed gold:
you will yet have your belly cut open!...

You are too rich,
corrupter of many!
You make too many envious,
you make too many poor...
Even I am cast in shadow by your light—
I grow cold; away, man gifted with riches,
away, Zarathustra, out of your sunlight!...

You must grow *poorer*,
unwise man of wisdom!
if you want to be loved.
Only the suffering are loved,
love is given only to the hungry man:
first give yourself, O Zarathustra!

I am thy truth...

Here, Ariadne, Zarathustra's truth tells him that he must become poor, take on the appearance of a hungry man, a man in need of love before he can expect answering voices, rain to turn the arid land into the verdant garden. How to do this: *give yourself.* This poem was to have been placed at the end of *Nietzsche contra Wagner*. After summing up his antipodal status to Wagner as the foremost symbol of not only German but European culture, this poem announces the truth that he must commit the voluntary death, give himself, become wanting: go 'mad.' In the Epilogue to *Nietzsche contra Wagner* Nietzsche contrasts the

> big country-fair boom-boom with which the "educated" person and city dweller today permits art, books, and music to rape him and provide "spiritual pleasures"—with the aid of spirituous liquors! How the theatrical scream of passion now hurts our ears, how strange to our taste the whole romantic uproar and tumult of the senses have become, which the educated rabble loves, and all its aspirations after the elevated, inflated, and exaggerated!

Wagner and German culture have come to this. Against this Nietzsche writes that "Only great pain is the ultimate liberator of the spirit."

Whether we learn to pit our pride, our scorn, our will power
against it, equaling the American Indian who, however tortured,
evens the score with his torturer by the malice of his tongue; or
whether we withdraw from pain into that Nothing, into mute,
rigid, deaf resignation, self-forgetting, self-extinction: out of such
long and dangerous exercises of self-mastery one emerges as a
different person, with a few more question marks—above all,
with the will to question more persistently, more deeply, severely,
harshly, evilly, and quietly than has ever been questioned on this
earth before. The trust in life is gone; life itself has become a
problem. Yet one should not jump to the conclusion that with all
this a man has necessarily become dusky, a barn owl. Even the
love of life is still possible—only, one loves differently. It is the
love for a woman who raises doubts in us.

Will Ariadne come? She must! Will she come? She will!

What is strangest is this: afterward one has a different taste—a
second taste. Out of such abysses, also out of the abyss of great
suspicion, one returns newborn, having shed one's skin, more
ticklish and sarcastic, with a more delicate taste for joy, with a
more tender tongue for all good things, with gayer senses, with a
second dangerous innocence in joy, more childlike and yet a
hundred times more subtle than one has ever been before.[21]

Here Nietzsche sets up the question of conscience for his time. Do you
want to follow the loud boom-boom or the quiet honesty of one who loves
life even in its hardest questions and doubts, who is willing to give even
himself for life? A superficial and gross entertainment or true joy in the
dangerous innocence of life. Here, Nietzsche comes up against himself, his
mistress truth. If he believes what he has just said, he must give himself up
to that severe, harsh, quiet questioning in pain—he must *give himself!* What
Ariadne is is Nietzsche's divine 'madness,' his loss of himself and the
symbol by which he condemns his age and promises a new future.

In the Middle Eastern Sufi tradition poverty is synonymous with
annihilation and nonexistence. The dervish is he who is poor because he
has nothing of his own. He is totally empty of selfhood. *"First give yourself."*
The true poor Man is in truth the richest of all men, since not existing

himself he subsists through the self: "Like the flame of a candle, he has no shadow....When the candle is wholly annihilated in the fire, you will see no trace of it or its flames."[22] The title of *Ecce Homo* also recalls Nietzsche's poem of that title:

Ecce Homo
Yes, I know from where I came!
Ever hungry like a flame,
I consume myself and glow.
Light grows all that I conceive,
Ashes everything I leave:
Flame I am assuredly.[23]

"Of the Poverty of the Richest Man," is the key dithyramb. It tells us three things. First, Nietzsche will '*give himself*' in a form of want and suffering 'madness,' a form that will allow people to love and pity him. Second, he takes on the active renunciation of all he is and has been to become 'poor,' that is, more intensely spiritual. Again, it is important to emphasize that this renunciation is *not* a giving up of the ego, rather, it is the renunciation of a *creating* love, a love that in 'despising' itself creates an even higher love, a higher spirituality. Third, behind the sign of 'madness,' a sign of suffering and a 'hungry man,' a lush oasis, a flame, a happy man runs crisscross on his Mount of Olives with warm, dancing feet.

In "Last Will" Nietzsche praises his death and it is a death in the service of a goal, the goal of destruction. He wishes to be a dancer in slaughter, the most cheerful fighter, trembling with the joy of victory, rejoicing that he *died* in victory. From "On Free Death" in *Zarathustra*:

I show you the death that consummates—a spur and a promise to the survivors. He that consummates his life dies his death victoriously, surrounded by those who hope and promise. Thus should one learn to die; and there should be no festival where one dying thus does not hallow the oaths of the living. To die thus is best; second to this, however, is to die fighting and to squander a great soul.[24]

The first version of "Last Will" was written in the fall of 1883. One finds it in the notes for *Zarathustra*. In this version it reads:

> Of the One Victory
>
> So, as I once saw him conquering and dying: the friend, who threw godly moments and lightning into my dark youth—
> wanton and profound, storming forward for joy even in the storm of slaughter, forward in bloody pain, where the chosen flags of the enemy neared—
> among the dying the most cheerful, of the victors the most arduous, reflecting, preflecting, standing on his fate—trembling with the joy of victory, laughing, that he conquered in dying—
> commanding, in that he died:—and he commanded that man *destroy and not be sparing*—
> Oh you my will, my in-me, over-me! you my necessity! Give that I also conquer—and save me up for this one victory! Preserve and save me up and guard me from all small victories, you gift of my soul and turning point of all need, you my necessity![25]

This note becomes the following in *Zarathustra*:

> O thou my will! Thou cessation of all need, my *own* necessity! Keep me from all small victories! Thou destination of my soul, which I call destiny! Thou in-me! Over-me! Keep me and save me for a great destiny!
> And thy last greatness, my will, save up for thy last feat that thou mayest be inexorable in thy victory. Alas, who was not vanquished in his victory? Alas, whose eye would not darken in this drunken twilight? Alas, whose foot would not reel in victory and forget how to stand?
> That I may one day be ready and ripe in the great noon: as ready and ripe as glowing bronze, clouds pregnant with lightning, and swelling milk udders—ready for myself and my most hidden will: a bow lusting for its arrow, an arrow lusting for its star—a star ready and ripe in its noon, glowing, pierced, enraptured by annihilating sun arrows—a sun itself and an inexorable solar will, ready to annihilate in victory!
> O will, cessation of all need, my *own* necessity! Save me for a great victory![26]

And finally, and very simply, "Last Will:"

> So to die
> as once I saw him die—
> the friend who like a god cast glances of lightning into my dark
> youth:
> —wanton, profound,
> in the slaughter a dancer—
>
> of fighters the most cheerful,
> of victors the most difficult,
> a destiny standing upon his destiny,
> firm, reflecting, preflecting—:
>
> trembling with joy of victory,
> rejoicing that he *died* in victory:
>
> by dying, commanding
> —and he commanded *destruction*…
>
> So to die
> as once I saw him die:
> victorious, *destroying*…

When one takes these together, there is echoed Zarathustra's promised voluntary death, which becomes the victorious death of Nietzsche/Dionysus. There is no doubt that Nietzsche looks forward to being in control of his death, and in such a way that it becomes his greatest moment, a moment that leads to victory. The victory of noon! The question here is destruction of what? Spiritual destruction of the morally roaring European and actual Caesarian destruction in the world if necessary. Destruction, as we have seen, is basic to Nietzsche's philosophy and task and he wants those who will lend him their hand at destroying. Destruction must precede creation, letting, even helping the last man to perish so that the overhuman may live. But here Nietzsche connects his own death with destroying. In this case the victory takes the form of the will to the destruction of himself. "Cessation of all need, my *own* necessity!" The play of the title, "Last Will," of course, is that it is his last will and testament, that which he leaves to those who survive him, and the idea that this is his *last* instance of willing, and what he wills is that his own 'annihilation' bring about the victory of his glad tidings for humankind. Willing in victory as he ceases to will, as he becomes the necessity of a destiny, the life process, the movement of the eternal return. Willing his seventh solitude, this victory in death.

Ariadne: "Oath-takers, where are you!"

In "Amid Birds of Prey," we find that only a bird of prey can look down into Zarathustra's abyss. Nietzsche has died, gone 'mad,' given himself as his truth demands. He sits as a solitary awaiting those who will turn his death into the victory he knows will come.

> *Solitary*!
> But who would dare
> to visit here,
> to visit *you?*...
> A bird of prey perhaps,
> he might hang,
> with crazy laughter,
> a bird of prey's laughter,
> malicious, in the
> patient stoic's hair...

The bird of prey comes and mocks Zarathustra, the patient stoic. Such birds of prey are mocking, malicious, merciless in their love. Why so steadfast? Why do you hang there? Where are your wings? Self-knower, self-hanger. Why are you the prisoner with the hardest fate, self-excavated, digging into yourself? Such birds of prey want to pick at this corpse until they find answers.

> Lying in wait,
> crouching,
> one who is no longer upright!
> In form like your own grave,
> *deformed* spirit!...

Here, Nietzsche describes his state of waiting, crouching, no longer upright, wearing the mask of 'madness,' in form like his own grave, dead for all practical purposes, deformed. He paints the difference between how proud he lately looked as the great destiny and ruler of the world:

And lately still so proud,
still on the stilts of your pride!
Lately still the godless hermit,
the dweller with the devil,
the high haughty scarlet prince!...

and how he now appears as a corpse "hunted down by himself, he becomes his own booty, he burrows into himself." Here he is "false before himself, uncertain, wearied by every wound, frozen by every frost, choked in his own net." Now in the guise of a 'mad,' crouching corpse he becomes a riddle for birds of prey. Ariadne is such a crazy, hanging bird of prey who looks into such abysses. Nietzsche hangs between two nothings, a rejected past and an unknown future, a question-mark: Will the riddle be guessed? And if so what will the future be?

Now—
contorted
between two nothings,
a question-mark,
a weary riddle—
a riddle for *birds of prey*...
—they will soon "resolve" you,
already they thirst for your "resolution,"
already they flutter about you, their riddle,
about you, hanged man!
O Zarathustra!...
Self-knower!
Self-hangman!...

Nietzsche poses a riddle with his self-hanging, but it is a riddle of the terrible abyss. Only terrible ones, birds of prey, will be able, not to redeem him (*erlösen*), but to unravel (*lösen*) him; to take the thread, to unravel the plot of his self-hanging, self-knowing and lead him out of the cave into the strong glowing noon-day sun. *To truly know the self is to hang the self.* Nietzsche chooses the mantle of 'madness' as his self-annihilation. He will look deformed, contorted, weary, no longer the godless hermit. Most will flee from him, pity and defame the deformed shell he has become, or worse, deify the 'broken' one; only birds of prey who can laugh maliciously and deliciously, and so tenderly, at the spectacle of a 'mad' Nietzsche will see anything further here than collapse, betrayal, negation of the great affirmer. If the birds of prey are to 'resolve' the question-mark that Nietzsche is, the riddle that he poses, they must do it out of the riddles of their own abysses and preying upon abysses.

In "The Sun Sinks" Nietzsche speaks of his own death. Here he has given himself, died victoriously in the destruction of himself and now it comes: "A promise in the air, the great coolness, sudden winds, cool spirits of the afternoon!" An important turn takes place in this dithyramb. The dying in victory and destruction, the crouching and deformed, dying and riddle are transformed into bliss and promise. And now night looks at him with "sidelong seductive eyes?…Stay strong, brave heart! Do not ask why.—" Night represents death and a promise. Nietzsche submits bravely and without question to it.

> Day of my life!
> the sun sinks.
> Already the smooth
> flood stands gilded.
> The cliffs breathe warmth:
> did happiness at midday
> sleep there its midday sleep?—
> From the brown abyss
> light and green it still dazzles up.

Happiness at midday is a reference to Zarathustra's experience of the world as perfection in Part IV of *Zarathustra.*

> What happened to me? Listen! Did time perhaps fly away? Do I not fall? Did I not fall—listen!—into the well of eternity? What is happening to me? Still! I have been stung, alas—in the heart? In the heart! Oh, break, break, heart after such happiness, after such a sting. How? Did not the world become perfect just now? Round and ripe? Oh, the golden round ring—where may it fly? Shall I run after it? Quick! Still!
>
> O heaven over me! You are looking on? You are listening to my strange soul? When will you drink this drop of dew which has fallen upon all earthly things? When will you drink this strange soul? When will you drink my soul back into yourself?[27]

Gilded cheerfulness, come!
sweetest, secretest
foretaste of death!
—Did I run my course too quickly?
Only now, when my foot has grown weary,
does your glance overtake me,
does your *happiness* overtake me.

And in "On Involuntary Bliss" from *Zarathustra* Nietzsche writes:

Away with you, blessed hour: with you bliss came to me against
my will. Willing to suffer my deepest pain, I stand here: you came
at the wrong time.

Away with you, blessed hour: rather seek shelter there—with my
children. Hurry and bless them before evening with *my* happiness. There evening approaches even now: the sun sinks.
Gone—my happiness!

Thus spoke Zarathustra. And he waited for his unhappiness
the entire night, but he waited in vain. The night remained
bright and still, and happiness itself came closer and closer to
him.[28]

Zarathustra wants to perfect himself for his children: "therefore I now
evade my happiness and offer myself to all unhappiness, for my final testing
and knowledge."[29] Zarathustra wants to give his blessed hour to his children
and suffer his deepest pain, but in giving up his happiness he gained a
greater happiness!

Only playing of waves all around.
Whatever was hard
has sunk into blue oblivion—
my boat now lies idle.
Storm and voyaging—all forgotten now!
Desire and hope have drowned,
smooth lie soul and sea.

Seventh solitude!
Never such sweet
security, never such

sunlight warmth.
—Does the ice of my summit still glow?
Silver, light, a fish
my little craft now swims out...

Day has turned into evening and night, life into death. The strivings of day have now turned into oblivion, idleness, forgetfulness. Desire and hope are gone —soul and sea are one! My little craft now swims out. Again in "On Involuntary Bliss" :

> The wind blew through my keyhole and said "Come!" But I lay there chained to the love for my children: desire set this snare for me—the desire for love that I might become my children's prey and lose myself to them. Desire—this means to me to have lost myself. *I have you, my children!* In this experience everything shall be security and nothing desire.[30]

In "Amid Birds of Prey" Nietzsche paints the horror of his crouching, graveside mask of 'madness,' but in "The Sun Sinks" we see that what the birds of prey will find is actually fulfillment, perfection and a great promise.

Here one must talk of the supreme dithyramb, *the* dithyramb of Part IV of *Zarathustra*: "The Drunken Song." Here the day of Nietzsche's life and the night of his death become one in the joy of eternity:

> All joy wants the eternity of all things, wants honey, wants lees, wants drunken midnight, wants tombs, wants tomb-tears' comfort, wants gilded evening glow.
> *What* does joy not want? It is thirstier, more cordial, hungrier, more terrible, more secret than all woe; it wants *itself*, it bites into *itself*, the ring's will strives in it, it wants love, it wants hatred, it is overrich, gives, throws away, begs that one might take it, thanks the taker, it would like to be hated; so rich is joy that it thirsts for woe, for hell, for hatred, for disgrace, for the cripple, for *world*—this world, oh, you know it!
> You higher men, for you it longs, joy, the intractable blessed one—for your woe, your failures. All eternal joy longs for failures. For all joy wants itself, hence it also wants agony. O happiness, O pain! Oh, break, heart! You higher men, do learn this, joy wants eternity. Joy wants the eternity of *all* things, *wants deep, wants deep eternity.*[31]

"The Fire-Signal" has connections to "From High Mountains" in *Beyond Good and Evil* and to "The Venetian Gondola Song." Nietzsche sits in his seventh solitude. On an island, "with a steeply towering sacrificial stone," the sacrificial stone of his voluntary death. Here he becomes a fire-signal "for seamen blown off course, failures, a question-mark for those who possess answers," like those birds of prey who will solve his riddle. This dithyramb also is directly connected to "The Honey Sacrifice" in *Zarathustra* where Zarathustra talks of honey sacrifices and baiting with golden honey in order to catch the strangest human fishes:

> Laugh, laugh, my bright, wholesome sarcasm! From high mountains cast down your glittering mocking laughter! With your glitter bait me the most beautiful human fish! And whatever in all the seas belongs to *me, that* bring up to me: for that I, the most sarcastic of all fishermen, am waiting. Out, out, my fishing rod! Down, down, bait of my happiness! Drip your sweetest dew, honey of my heart! Bite, my fishing rod, into the belly of all black melancholy![32]

Nietzsche's soul has become a flame of the richest poor man and fire-signal for seamen blown off course. The signal lures them to his mountain island, which sits in the belly of all black melancholy, the spectacle of his 'madness,' and then they see his well-baited fishing hooks.

> My soul, my soul itself, is this flame:

> *Six* solitudes he knew already—
> but the sea itself had too little solitude for him,
> the island welcomed him, and on the mountain
> he became a flame,
> and when now he whirls his fishing-line
> it is a *seventh* solitude he seeks to catch.

> Seamen blown off course!...

> to all that knows solitude do I now throw this line:
> give answer to the flame's impatience,
> catch me, the fisherman on high mountains,
> my seventh, *final* solitude!

Here Nietzsche throws his fishing line to catch his seventh solitude. But this final solitude, the answer to the flame and fire-signal, is that the fish he seeks to catch, catch him! What is Nietzsche's seventh solitude?

> *Excelsior.*—"You will never pray again, never adore again, never again rest in endless trust; you do not permit yourself to stop before any ultimate wisdom, ultimate goodness, ultimate power, while unharnessing your thoughts; you have no perpetual guardian and friend for your seven solitudes; you live without a view of mountains with snow on their peaks and fire in their hearts; there is no avenger for you any more nor any final improver; there is no longer any reason in what happens, no love in what will happen to you; no resting place is open any longer to your heart, where it only needs to find and no longer to seek; you resist any ultimate peace; you will the eternal recurrence of war and peace: man of renunciation, all this you wish to renounce? Who will give you the strength for that? Nobody yet has had this strength!"[33]

Nietzsche's seventh solitude is his ultimate overcoming, the point at which he renounces *all* that is his hope and victory. It is his highest overcoming, his infinite resignation, the point at which he risks everything. If Nietzsche's task is to make a new meaning for suffering he must renounce all desire, all happiness, and move into the *No-doing* suffering part of the drama. For to present himself only as the happy victor in the eternal recurrence is no spur and promise for humans on earth who must suffer. However, to offer himself, to give the gift of himself as his mistress truth demands in "On the Poverty of the Richest Man," as the suffering renunciation of his seventh solitude, his highest hardness against himself, to take on, and thus exhibit suffering *as bliss* in light of the eternal recurrence, to demonstrate and act as security in this—this is a spur and promise to the living! The feast and celebration of midday is only found in the quiet solitude of *each* heart. In "On High Mountains" and in "Fire-Signal" Nietzsche sits and waits for those who have found themselves.

In "Ariadne's Lament" Ariadne is the symbol; she stands for the fish, failures, birds of prey, those who are themselves ripe for seven solitudes, those for whom Nietzsche waits. Ariadne is the only one who can desire

Dionysus's love. For his love is not warm and gentle; rather it is a torment, an eternal torment. He wants to crawl into Ariadne's heart in order to steal, listen, and torture to help her question her own soul more deeply. Nietzsche already told us this in "The Night Song:" 'A hunger grows out of my beauty: I should like to hurt those for whom I shine; I should like to rob those to whom I give; thus do I hunger for malice.' Dionysus is the unknown god, the hangman-god, the self-annihilated god. Ariadne asks:

> Shall I, like a dog,
> roll before you?
> Surrendering, raving with rapture,
> wag—love to you?

> In vain!
> Strike again,
> cruellest goad!
> Not dog—I am only your game,
> cruellest huntsman!

> Demand much—thus speaks my pride!
> *Me*—you want all of me?
> me—all of me?...

> Offer me *love*—who still warms me?
> who still loves me?
> offer me, the most solitary,
> whom ice, alas! sevenfold ice
> has taught to long for enemies,
> even for enemies,
> offer, yes yield to me,
> cruellest enemy—
> *yourself!*...

Ariadne, this ascetic, wants the unknown god to give all of himself to her if she is to give all of herself to him. But this is asking too much and he flees. Again, in "The Night Song" Nietzsche had written: 'To withdraw my hand when the other hand already reaches out to it....Thus, do I hunger for malice.' Such a solitary does not give love, but demands more of Ariadne— that she hate herself in order to love herself more deeply—only the solitary soul goes over.

Dionysus Dithyrambs

Lonely one, you are going the way of the lover: yourself you love,
and therefore you despise yourself, as only lovers despise. The
lover would create because he despises. What does he know of
love who did not have to despise precisely what he loved! Go
into your loneliness with your love and with your creation, my
brother; and only much later will justice limp after you. With my
tears go into your loneliness, my brother. I love him who wants
to create over and beyond himself and thus perishes.[34]

Ariadne realizes that she must make the final renunciation: to suffer
without receiving. She calls him back on his terms, realizing that it is better
to have his torment than not to have him at all, and with this she embraces
her own renunciation and self-sufficiency.

No!
come back!
with all your torments!
Oh come back,
my unknown god! my *pain*!
my last happiness!...

Once she shows this movement, Dionysus seals her understanding with the
words: "Must we not first hate ourself if we are to love ourself?" The mystery
of the *Dionysus Dithyrambs* is the annihilation of the self to gain the greater
self, the greater love, the Yes to unconditional suffering in order to love
oneself and the earth. Dionysus is Ariadne's labyrinth. The labyrinth is the
winding and endless path of life, with the Minotaur suffering at the center.
The Dionysian mystery is a paradox: to *will* suffering and in *thus* willing
bringing all of one's willing to the victory of overcoming suffering here in
this life.

All of the *Dionysian Dithyrambs* thus far image Nietzsche's transition
to his living death, his 'seventh solitude,' the negation of the self, the *No-
doing*, which is nevertheless the great Yes to life. In *The Gay Science*
Nietzsche writes:

What is the ultimate noblemindedness? The passion that attacks
those who are noble is peculiar, and they fail to realize this. It
involves the use of a rare and singular standard and almost a
madness: the feeling of heat in things that feel cold to everybody

else; the discovery of values for which no scales have been invented yet; offering sacrifices on altars that are dedicated to an unknown god; a courage without any desire for honors; a self-sufficiency that overflows and gives to men and things.[35]

"Fame and Eternity"!

This coin with which
all the world makes payment,
fame—
I grasp this coin with gloves,
with loathing I trample it *beneath* me.

Remember, this dithyramb was to have been at the end of *Ecce Homo*. Wagner went for fame. Nietzsche wants to separate himself completely from Wagner and the European culture he represents. As he sits in his solitude, he does not seek fame, but something far more: to rule the world. And his assurance of victory comes in a vision to him:

Soft!—
Of great things—I *see* something great!—
one should keep silent
or speak greatly:
speak greatly, my enraptured wisdom!

I look above me—
there seas of light are rolling:
oh night, oh silence, oh deathly silent uproar!...
I see a sign—
from the farthest distance
slowly glittering a constellation sinks towards me...

Ariadne's crown, the constellation Dionysus himself threw into the night sky; the light that rolls toward him is Ariadne and she comes dressed in the eternal recurrence. This echoes one of Nietzsche's last plans for the wedding of Dionysus and Ariadne:

2. On the bridge
3. The wedding—and suddenly, as the sky grows dark
4. Ariadne

With "To the Mistral" in his heart: "Toss it higher, further, gladder, storm up on the heavens' ladder, hang it up—upon a star" and the end of "On Old and New Tablets": "a bow lusting for its arrow, an arrow lusting for its star—a star ready and ripe in its noon," and "Sanctus Januarius," announcing his "highest hope and goal," Nietzsche sings:

Highest star of being!
Eternal tablet of forms!
You come to me?—
What none has beheld,
your speechless beauty—
what? it flees not from my gaze?—

Image of what must be!
Eternal tablet of forms!
—but you know it:
what everyone else hates,
what I alone love:
—that *you* are *eternal*!
that you *must be*!—
my love is ignited only by that which must be.

Image of what must be!
Highest star of being!
—what no longing attains
—no denial defiles
eternal Yes of being,
eternally am I thy Yes:
for I love thee, O eternity!

"The Seven Seals or the Yes and Amen Song" really goes with this last dithyramb. This dithyramb not only reflects the blissful state of the one who has given himself but reaffirms the eternal recurrence of the same and *amor fati*. Ariadne and Eternity are what Nietzsche gains through his work, his self-sacrifice, his love—and now his children approach.

And so we see the narrative of the heights! All words are vanity and yet they are divine and create worlds. Europe, which has lost its dancing leg, will perish unless it rediscovers its southern soul and learns to dance once more. Nietzsche sits too full, too happy, too ripe for the men of his time. His truth tells him to give himself, to make himself poor in the eyes of men, if he wants to be loved; for pity is all they can understand. But behind the sign of 'madness,' Nietzsche's poverty signifies the riches of bliss. He calls upon and praises the voluntary death in victory over the decadent Western world, the victory of those to come. Nietzsche enters the abyss of his own 'mad' voluntary death where he hangs as a question-mark between two millennia. Only birds of prey can see a riddle and promise here. But again, this victorious and terrible death in the renunciation of the seventh solitude is gilded happiness, desireless security. And the bliss of the seventh solitude becomes a fire-signal to other solitaries heralding a mutual hooking and catching upon the seas of the future. "Ariadne's Lament" is a close-up look at this hooking and catching. Ariadne is taught by Dionysus to love her pain, to make it her last happiness, to hate herself as the condition for the greater love of life. Only then will she become the bird of prey and mate for Dionysus. At the end Nietzsche sings rapturously of what must be. Ariadne comes and she comes dressed in what must be, the eternal recurrence of forms of which Nietzsche writes: "eternally am I thy Yes."

And now, in celebration, a dance from a most exalted dancer, a dance from the oriental paradise of love and passion of the spirit. Oh, Rumi sing to us of the "ruins of the heart" of the sage, of the fool, Nietzsche, the one who lies in ruins, but dances with the Heart:

> Love is reckless; not reason.
> Reason seeks a profit.
> Love comes on strong, consuming herself, unabashed.
>
> Yet in the midst of suffering
> Love proceeds like a millstone,
> hard surfaced and straight-forward
>
> Having died to self-interest,
> she risks everything and asks for nothing.
> Love gambles away every gift God bestows.
>
> Without cause God gave us being;
> without cause give it back again.
> Gambling yourself away is beyond any religion.

Religion seeks grace and favor,
but those who gamble these away are God's favorites,
for they neither put God to the test nor knock at the
door of gain and loss.[36]

Ariadne: "Nietzsche the godless, the proclaimer of the dead God! Zarathustra who says God is a prejudice and that he wants humans to create only so far as they can create! Zarathustra who says reject the heavens and be true to the earth! Zarathustra who says, if there were gods how could I not bear to be a god! Nietzsche who examines and turns from all religions to the fortress of the individual human soul: his goal, the perfection of human being and becoming! Oh, this drunken one, this Dionysian wine cup! Dionysus overcoming Dionysus! He has followed the path of the sages and great conquerors: he has crossed over and goes ahead not in the name of God, but in the name of Humankind!"

Epiphany

Oh, paradise, drunken within me!
Oh sun of my heart!
Take, then, this heart of mine,
lead it into gardens dark and fearsome
where rivers run black, brown, down, down...
Take my heart down into your abyss,
deeper, deeper yet, I can find no bottom...
I fall!

A peak catches me!
I see in all directions far and wide,
The sun blinds my eyes!
Out of your deep heights I climb to Zarathustra.
May I embrace him, this deep sufferer?
May I set his soul hard and free?

We tender souls, we sweet fools.
Our dancing feet now take flight and leap—
Come, my beloved, my warrior of seven solitudes,
let us go forth to victory
like an army with doves in our hearts!

We have created the world, what else is here?
We shaped its forms like wicked children at play
who could barely finish building for the
anticipated delight in destroying.
But, oh children, building only comes after destroying,
they are entwined in all eternity.

Oh earth of confusion, whirling in the void,
whirling like winds with cloud skirts outstretched—
whirling until drunk with bliss.
Dionysus, I lost in your labyrinth and you in mine
Twirling, dancing upon the Minotaur's head
we sing glory, glory!
We mad, eternal lovers!

Notes

1. Nietzsche, *Twilight of the Idols*, p. 473.
2. Nietzsche, *Zarathustra*, p. 268.
3. Adrian Del Caro, *Nietzsche via Dionysus: An Analysis of the Dithyrambs*, MA Thesis, University of Minnesota, 1977, pp. 5–6.
4. Nietzsche, *Dithyrambs of Dionysus*, trans. R. J. Hollingdale, Redding Ridge, Conn. Black Swan Books, 1984. All reproductions of sections from the dithyrambs in this chapter reprinted with permission of the publisher.
5. Nietzsche, *KSA*, Vol. 10, p. 594
6. Podach, *Friedrich Nietzsches Werke des Zusammenbruchs* (Heidelberg: Wolfgang Rothe Verlag, 1961), pp. 364–65.
7. Ibid., pp. 365–68 and *Dithyrambs of Dionysus*, pp. 15–16.
8. See the interleaf in *Ecce Homo* and the 'mad' note to Cosima Wagner in my notes to the title of this book.
9. Podach, *Nietzsche's Werke des Zusammenbruchs*, p. 369.
10. Ibid.
11. Ibid., pp. 374–92.
12. Ibid., p. 392.
13. Nietzsche, *Ecce Homo*, p. 310.
14. Nietzsche, *Gay Science*, #301.
15. See Nietzsche, "On Poets," *Zarathustra*.
16. Otto, *Dionysus Cult and Myth*, p. 114.
17. Nietzsche, *Zarathustra*, pp. 414–15.
18. Ibid., pp. 416–17.
19. Nietzsche, *Will to Power*, # 1051.
20. Ibid., #1040.
21. Nietzsche, *Nietzsche contra Wagner*, in *Portable Nietzsche*, pp. 680–82.

22. *The Sufi Path of Love: The Spiritual Teachings of Rumi*, trans. William C. Chittick (Albany: State University of New York Press, 1983), p. 188.

23. Nietzsche, "Jokes, Cunning and Revenge," *Gay Science*, #62.

24. Nietzsche, *Zarathustra*, pp. 183–84.

25. Nietzsche, KSA, Vol. 10, p. 594.

26. Nietzsche, *Zarathustra*, pp. 326–27.

27. Ibid., pp. 389–90.

28. Ibid., p. 275.

29. Ibid., p. 274.

30. Ibid.

31. Ibid., pp. 435–36.

32. Ibid., p. 352.

33. Nietzsche, *Gay Science*, #285. See also #309.

34. Nietzsche, *Zarathustra*, p. 177.

35. Nietzsche, *Gay Science*, #55.

36. Reprinted from *The Ruins of the Heart: Selected Poetry of Jelaluddin Rumi*, Trans. Edmund Helminski, Threshold Books, RD4 Box 600, Putney, VT 05346, p. 18.

Sacred Marriage/Satyr-Marriage

Constantly we have to give birth to our thoughts out of pain, and like mothers endow them with all we have of blood, heart, fire, pleasure, passion, agony, conscience, fate and catastrophe. Life—that means for us constantly transforming all that we are into light and flame—also everything that wounds us; we simply can do no other.[1]

Sacred Marriage: Dance!

On January 4, 1889 Nietzsche writes to Peter Gast:

To my maestro Pietro.
Sing me a new song: the world is transfigured and all the heavens rejoice.

The Crucified[2]

Gast did not receive this note right away, but a few days later. He then sent the following reply, which arrived in Turin on January 9, the very day Nietzsche was already underway with Overbeck to the Basel clinic.

Great things must be happening with you! Your enthusiasm, your health and all that your "pure body, blessed mind" has done or having foreshadowed, must have been aroused out of the most victorious; you are infectious health; the epidemic of health which you once wished, the epidemic of *your* health has arrived. Only in Berlin did the call of the "crucified one" reach me. The weather pulled a terrible face about it; a cold raw oppressive wind invited more to suicide than to dances; I had just said to myself

263

not long ago the words, which I suggested to Wagner once as a
variant of a place in the *Götterdämmergung*:

More often than he
had no one spoken of dances,
Less often than he
had no one danced, etc.

After a few more lines Gast ends his letter: "Full of happiness and joy over
your triumph, full of admiration."[3] Janz writes about this reply: "the parody
on the words from the grandiose monologue of Brünnhilde as she readies
herself for death shows an unparalleled failure to understand Nietzsche.
Köselitz must have known how sensitively Nietzsche would react especially
with regard to the *Götterdämmerung* and one painfully senses how exactly
this dance-parody fits Nietzsche in these last days."[4]

On the contrary, this response would have delighted Nietzsche. The
last months leading up to the "catastrophe" and the staging of the
"catastrophe" itself reflect Nietzsche's orchestration of the most terrifying
and sublime musical conflagration! The increasing tempo, the magnificent
flourishes, the destroying and transforming symphonies of symbolism, the
dissonance ringing out against formerly unknown harmonies, the ever
heightening dynamics leading up to the thunderous, yet dancing finale!
Nietzsche, above Wagner, deserves the title of musical maestro. The silence
that hangs in the air for years, perhaps centuries, after this musical master-
piece is all the more intense in contrast to the crashing transformation at
the end. Gast sees Nietzsche's communication as a transformation of "great
health!"

In his Rubicon letter to Gast of December 31, 1888 Nietzsche writes:
"You will find in *Ecce Homo* an astonishing page about *Tristan*, about my
whole relationship with Wagner. Wagner is altogether the foremost name
in E. H. Wherever I admit no doubts, here too I had the courage to go the
whole way."[5] In *Ecce Homo* Nietzsche writes:

But to this day I am still looking for a work that equals the
dangerous fascination and the gruesome and sweet infinity of
Tristan—and look in all the arts in vain. All the strangenesses of
Leonardo da Vinci emerge from their spell at the first note of

Tristan. This work is emphatically Wagner's *non plus ultra*; with the *Meistersinger* and the *Ring* he recuperated from it. Becoming healthier—is a retrogression, given a nature like Wagner's.

I take it for good fortune of the first order that I lived at the right time and among Germans, of all people, so that I was *ripe* for this work: that is how far the psychologist's inquisitiveness extends in my case. The world is poor for anyone who has never been sick enough for this "voluptuousness of hell": it is permitted, it is almost imperative, to employ a formula of the mystics at this point.[6]

Now what do Brünnhilde's preparatory monologue before death and *Tristan* have to do with each other? Both operas play out the love/death; the death of the hero, Tristan or Siegfried, and the fact that Isolde and Brünnhilde follow them into death willingly so as to be united with the loved one. But this is the same story Nietzsche has been writing in his Empedocles notes and some of the *Zarathustra* notes! It is the story that Ariadne takes as the basic plot of Nietzsche's catastrophic drama of 'madness.' Nietzsche wants to upstage Wagner with an eternal love story, but in the last case *a real one*. When we turn to Brünnhilde's passage that Gast parodies with the metaphor of dance we find:

Never was man
more loyal to friendship;
never was man more true to his promise;
never was known love more faithful.
And yet he was faithless,
broke every promise; he truest of lovers—
none falser than he!

But the passage goes on—Gast's etc.—and Brünnhilde says:

Know you why that was?
He, truest of all men,
betrayed me,
that I in grief might grow wise!

Now I know what must be.

All things, all things,
all I know now;
all to me is revealed!

And what is revealed to Brünnhilde is:

Vanished like air
is the race of gods;
without rulership
I leave the world behind;
my wisdom's holiest hoard
I assign to the world,
Not goods nor gold
for godly state;
not house nor hearth
for lordly pomp;
not empty treaties'
treacherous bonds
for false tradition's
pitiless law:
blessed in joy and sorrow,
only love I bequeath!

Then Brünnhilde rides her horse Grane into the flames of Siegfried's funeral pyre: "Glorious radiance has seized on my heart. I shall embrace him, united with him, in sacred yearing, with him ever one!... Siegfried! Siegfried! See! Brünnhild greets you as wife!"[7] Siegfried had already ridden through the flames surrounding Brünnhilde on the mountain Wotan calls the "bridal fire":

threatening flames shall flare from the rock;
the cavern will fear it,
cringe from its fury;
the weak will flee
from Brünnhilde's rock!
For one alone wins you as bride,
one freer than I, the god![8]

Siegfried rides through the flames for love of Brünnhilde and she rides into the flames to die in love with him. Nietzsche rides into 'madness' and becomes a fire-signal on high mountains through which only a Brünnhilde, an Ariadne, would ride for love:

"Dionysus! Ariadne greets you as wife!"

Gast's reference to this ending of the *Götterdämmerung* is completely apt, for this, too, is Nietzsche's message as he goes into 'madness.' "He truest of all men, betrayed me, that I in grief might grow wise." From "Ariadne's Lament": "Must we not hate ourselves, before we can love ourselves." Or, from "On the Poverty of the Richest One": "You must grow poorer unwise man of wisdom if you want to be loved: *first give yourself.*" Or Zarathustra's advice to his disciples at the end of Part I, which Nietzsche quotes at the end of the preface of *Ecce Homo*: "Now I bid you lose me and find yourselves; and only *when you have all denied me* will I return to you.'" This all sounds so much like "Ariadne's Lament."

The ending of *Tristan*, is as Nietzsche says, "voluptuously hellish" in its romantic exaggeration, but it is the symbolism that concerns us, that concerns Nietzsche. So let us follow the love/death between Tristan and Isolde:

> Tristan: O blessed sunlight!
> Ah blessed day!
> Hail to the joyful
> Sunniest day.
> Turbulent blood,
> Jubilant heart!
> Joy without measure,
> Rapturous pleasure!
> To this bed chained fast
> How can I bear them?
> So up and away,
> Where the hearts are beating!
> Tristan the knight,
> Rejoicing in night,
> Has vanquished death
> Itself today.
>
> (He stands up)
>
> Once bleeding and wounded
> I fought and conquered Morold:

Now bleeding and wounded
Today I capture Isolde!

...

She who can close
My wound forever,
She comes like a queen,
She comes here to heal.
Dissolve O world,
As I hasten to her.

(He staggers to the middle of the stage.)

Of this point in the opera Nietzsche writes in *The Birth of Tragedy*:

We now hear and see only the hero dying, with his despairing cry: "Longing! Longing! In death still longing! for very longing not dying!" And where formerly after such an excess and super-abundance of consuming agonies, the jubilation of the horn cut through our hearts almost like the ultimate agony, the rejoicing Kurwenal now stands between us and this "jubilation in itself," his face turned toward the ship which carries Isolde.[10]

This is the very longing of the ripe grapes for the saving vintager, Ariadne, that Nietzsche writes of in "On the Great Longing" in *Zarathustra*. And then Isolde rushes in, his longing satisfied, Siegfried dies.

Isolde: Tristan! Tristan Beloved!

Tristan: What, hear I the light?
The torch light, ah!
The torch now is out.
To her! To her!
(Isolde hastens in breathlessly. Tristan, nearly fainting, rushes towards her. In the middle of the stage they meet; she receives him in her arms, where he sinks slowly to the ground.)

Isolde: Tristan! Ah!

Tristan: Isolde! (He dies)

Isolde:
'Tis I, 'Tis I,
Sweet dear friend!
Wake and hear once more
When I call!
Isolde calls;
Isolde came.
With Tristan she would die now!
Deaf to my cry?
Grant me one moment
One single moment,
Open your eyes!
The dreary days I waited in yearning
To spend one hour with you close beside me:
You'd cheat Isolde,
Deprived by Tristan
Of even this one single
Ever-fleeting
Final worldly joy?
You're wounded? Where?
Ah, let me heal it.
In joy then we'll share
The night together;
Wounds must not kill you,
Not a wound received in strife:
But let us united
Leave now the light of life!
All broken your glance!
Still your heart.
Have you no fleeting
Breath for me?
Must I in sorrow
Linger here.
I who joyful came to wed you
Boldly over the sea?
Too late!
Hard hearted man!
Treating me so

With cruellest ban?
Ah, no relief
For my anguished grief?
Deaf to my pleading,
Silent, unheeding?
One moment, ah!
Oh, wake once more!
Tristan!—Ah!
Hear!—He wakes!
Beloved—
(She sinks down on the body, unconscious.)

Again, this sounds like "Ariadne's Lament." Isolde cannot stand the anguish
and begins to go mad; her love breathes life into Tristan.

(Isolde, who has heard nothing around her, fixes her eyes with
growing ecstasy on Tristan's body.)
Isolde:
Mildly, gently,
See him smiling,
See his eyes
Softly open.
Ah behold him!
See you not?
Ever brighter,
Brightly shining,
Borne in starlight
High above?
See you not?
How his heart
So proudly swells,
Full and bold
it throbs in his breast?
Gentle breathing
Stirs his lips,
Ah, how calmly
Soft his breath:—
See him, friends!
Feel and see you not?
Can it be that I alone

Hear this wondrous, glorious tone,
Softly stealing,
All revealing,
Mildly glowing,
From him flowing,
Thro' me pouring,
Rising, soaring,
Boldly singing,
Round me ringing?
Brighter growing,
O'er me flowing,
Are they waves
Of tender radiance?
Are they clouds
Of wonderful fragrance?
They are rising
High around me,
Shall I breathe them,
Shall I hear them?
Shall I taste them,
Dive beneath them?
Drown in tide
of melting sweetness?[11]

Nietzsche says in *Ecce Homo* "it is almost imperative to employ a formula of the mystics at this point." In *The Birth of Tragedy* Nietzsche writes: "the [tragic] myth leads the world of phenomena to its limits where it denies itself and seeks to flee back again into the womb of the true and only reality, where it then seems to commence its metaphysical swan song, like Isolde." And then Nietzsche quotes the last lines of the opera:

In the rapture ocean's
billowing roll,
in the fragrance waves'
ringing sound,
in the world breath's
wafting whole—
to drown, to sink—
unconscious—highest joy![12]

(Isolde sighs in ecstacy,...and sinks upon Tristan's body.)

The mystical formula Nietzsche refers to is the "sacred marriage." In his discussion of the end of Wagner's *Götterdämmerung*, Robert Donington writes: "Brynhilde is not expecting to consummate her literal marriage, which she did long ago; but she is expecting to consummate the sacred marriage."[13] It expresses a state of nature prior to human consciousness. Plato refers to the Greek myth: "of man's primordial unity as a spherical hermaphrodite comprising male and female in perpetual embrace until the gods in envy divided the two halves, which have ever since gone in search of one another."[14] Another myth told in its Hellenistic form by Ovid about Hermaphroditus, son of Hermes and Aphrodite, speaks of this unity of male and female:

> He was beloved against his conscious wishes by the nymph of a fountain, in which he nevertheless made so bold as to bathe; whereupon her prayer that they should be united was answered more conclusively than she had bargained for by their emerging transformed into a hermaphrodite. This is not the primordial unity of unconscious nature, but the differentiated unity reached in the human psyche as a result of the long and difficult search for each other by the halves first divided when consciousness began to make us something other than the animals. Notice that it is the feminine element which takes the initiative.[15]

Speaking of Brünnhilde Donington continues:

> She throws a lighted torch onto the pile of logs, which blaze up with a rapidity eloquent of her longing to pass through the flames to the transformed life on the farther side of them. *She has, however, no intention of leaving her human instincts behind her. Life can be transformed without becoming disembodied; the need for austerity may actually grow less.* At all events, she calls to the symbol of instinct, the magic horse Grane: 'Do you know where we are going together? Does the fire's light which is Siegfried's light draw you to it too? Siegfried, Siegfried, see how your holy wife greets you!' She rides into the flames, which spread everywhere until they bring down the hall in ruins.[16]

Of the Hindu tradition of sati, where the wife is expected to follow her husband into the funeral flames, Ananda Coomaraswamy writes:

> In medieval times we have the great stories of Padmavati and other Rajput heroines who chose for themselves a fiery death, when their warriors put on the safron robes of renunciation and themselves went out to an inevitable death: an equal ecstasy must have inspired both. Some say that long ago there was no physical fire, but two lives were so closely bound together (and this idea constantly recurs, with similes such as that of rivers joining) that when one ceased, the inward fire of love consumed the other; and it is on these lines that all mystical interpretations run.[17]

There is a triple notion of flame. The highest level of flame is love, the lowest is actual material fire, and the intermediate level is light. It is not actual fire which consumes Brünnhilde, but the flame of love. So there is a process of transformation of physical flame into light and light into love.

Fire and water, flame and sea. Brünnhilde's fiery sacred marriage and Isolde's watery one are the same. Nietzsche, a flame on an island in the sea, awaits his Ariadne so that the sacred wedding may take place. The Sacred Wedding or *hieros gamos* of Dionysus and Ariadne was one of the very few Attic celebrations of conjugal sex.[18]

Here comes Ariadne, like Brünnhilde, like Isolde, able to long for the sacred wedding, able to place love as the supreme virtue, because of the pain and sorrow of looking at the flame of Nietzsche's 'madness.' Looking at it, transforming it, living through it and with it for years, and becoming flame herself, understanding that it was not sorrow, but joy.

> *One must learn to love.*—This is what happens to us in music: First one has to *learn to hear* a figure and melody at all, to detect and distinguish it, to isolate it and delimit it as a separate life. Then it requires some exertion and good will to *tolerate* it in spite of its strangeness, to be patient with its appearance and expression, and kindhearted about its oddity. Finally there comes a moment when we are *used* to it, when we wait for it, when we sense that we should miss it if it were missing; and now it continues to compel and enchant us relentlessly until we have

become its humble and enraptured lovers who desire nothing better from the world than it and only it.

But that is what happens to us not only in music. That is how we have *learned to love* all things that we now love. In the end we are always rewarded for our good will, our patience, fairmindedness, and gentleness with what is strange; gradually, it sheds its veil and turns out to be a new and indescribable beauty. That is its *thanks* for our hospitality. Even those who love themselves will have learned it in this way; for there is no other way. Love, too, has to be learned.[19]

Now, can we for a moment, agree with Janz that Gast did not understand. Gast understood Nietzsche's announcement of transfiguration and crucifixion as a supreme symbol of health and victory, though he did not know of Nietzsche's impending play of 'madness.' But he understood even more. He knew that Nietzsche must go beyond Wagner. That love must be transformed into dance and that these mysteries should not pull us into gravity and pessimism but give us light feet. Thus Gast's note to Nietzsche says, in light of the "etc." in Brünnhild's monologue: "He spoke of dancing more than anyone, but he himself danced less than anyone. Why? That in grief we might grow wise and know what must be: That we must become dancers!"

> The psychological problem in the type of Zarathustra is how he that says No and *does* No to an unheard-of degree, to everything to which one has so far said Yes, can nevertheless be the opposite of a No-saying spirit; how the spirit who bears the heaviest fate, a fatality of a task, can nevertheless be the lightest and most transcendent—Zarathustra is a dancer—*But this is the concept of Dionysus himself.*[20]

Ariadne: "Ah, my Dionysus. I have learned to love your 'madness' and to turn it into sacred joy. I have removed the mask of 'illness' to see your magnificent health shining forth. I have no further wish than to be consumed in the sacred flames of wedded love as we float out upon the gilded sea in our ship of fools. Wagner is overcome through your love of him! His is only a stage art, his sacred marriages symbolic moments in a decadent age. But oh, Dionysus, you hard, you suffering and joying one, you longer after real futures and eternities, futures and eternities that laugh at ephemeral fame, you gambler with fate, the sacred wedding we consummate here symbolizes victory and a new beginning."

Satyr Marriage: Isoline/Isolin

She promised—she is late—
She would be mine;
But like a dog I wait,
And there's no sign.
She swore again and again:
Was it by rote?
Does she run after all men,
Just like a goat?[21]

In his dedication of the *Dionysus Dithyrambs* to Catulle Mendès, Nietzsche characterizes the poet of *Isoline* as the "first and greatest satyr alive today...and not only today." At the same time Nietzsche pens this dedication, he is correcting proofs of *Nietzsche contra Wagner*. In it he suggests that Wagner's last work, *Parsifal* really should have been a parody and satyr-play:

> I should really wish that the Wagnerian *Parsifal* were intended as a prank—as the epilogue and satyr play, as it were, with which the tragedian Wagner wanted to say farewell in a fitting manner worthy of himself—to us, to himself, and above all *to tragedy*, with an excessive, sublimely wanton parody on the tragic itself, on all the former horrid earthly seriousness and earthly misery, on the *most stupid* form, overcome at long last, of the antinature of the ascetic ideal. After all, *Parsifal* is operetta material par excellence. Is Wagner's *Parsifal* his secretly superior laughter at himself, the triumph of his ultimate artistic freedom, his artistic *non plus ultra*—Wagner able to *laugh* at himself?[22]

On December 26, 1888, at the Renaissance Theater in Paris an operetta by Catulle Mendès (libretto) and André Messager (music), entitled *Isoline* was performed for the first time. It was a great success and Nietzsche had gotten news of it by January 1 when he wrote a draft of the dedication of the *Dionysian Dithyrambs* to Mendès:

[Zwei inedita], [sechs] Acht Inedita, [und] und inaudita, dem Dichter der Isoline [seinem] meinem [unsterblichen] Freund und Satyr mit hoher Auszeichnung [gewidmet] über[r]reicht: mag er mein Geschenk der Menschheit über[r]eichen. Ob, wie, und wann
Nietzsche [Caesar] Dionysus

Turin am 1. Januar 1889

Eight unpublished and unheard [dithyrambs], dedicated with high respect to my immortal friend and satyr, the poet of Isoline: may he offer my gift to mankind. If, how, and when
Nietzsche [Caesar] Dionysus

A second draft reads:

Indem ich der Menschheit eine unbegrenzte [Ehre] Wholthat erweisen will, gebe ich [Ihr] ihr die Dithyramben: ich lege sie in die Hände des Dichters der Isoline, des grössten und ersten Satyr, der heute lebt.
Nietzsche-Dionysus[23]

Nietzsche's final dedication for the *Dionysus Dithyrambs* reads:

In as much as I want to do mankind a boundless favour, I give them my dithyrambs. I place them in the hands of the poet of Isoline, the first and greatest satyr alive today—and not only today...
Dionysus[24]

Several things need to be commented on in these dedications. The signatures in the drafts are interesting: Nietzsche [Caesar] Dionysus, Nietzsche-Dionysus, and finally Dionysus showing that Caesar is an essential part of Nietzsche's thinking about himself and the dithyrambs at this point, and that he is possessive about these dithyrambs because he wants to sign them Nietzsche, but refrains and signs simply Dionysus. The series of signatures in the drafts tells us that Nietzsche is Dionysus. Oddly the name Zarathustra does not come into question even though Nietzsche had thought to call the dithyrambs "Songs of Zarathustra" up until the first of the year. In the first draft the dithyrambs are to be a gift, in the second a boundless favor. Thus, Nietzsche considers them of highest importance.

The first draft calls them unpublished and unheard. They were already at the printers though not yet published and even published they are still very difficult to 'hear.' Nietzsche obviously thinks Mendès well qualified to offer this gift if, how, and when he wishes. Nietzsche indicates the greatest respect and awe for the poet of *Isoline*, not only by calling him great and offering high respect, but by calling him a satyr—for Nietzsche high praise indeed. Nietzsche by this time styles himself a disciple of Dionysus and a satyr, so Mendès is a brother Bacchant and as such worthy to receive the poems of Dionysus. In Nietzsche's first draft above he considered *"[seinem] meinem [unsterbliches] Freund."* If he had chosen *seinem* the dedication would have read: "dedicated with highest respect to the poet of Isoline [from] his immortal friend and saytr." This makes it ambiguous who the satyr is, Nietzsche or Mendès; although the revised dedication speaks only of Mendès as satyr we know that Nietzsche is one too. The signature of Caesar points to a victory and conquest in connection with the *Dithyrambs* and carries the theme of having crossed the Rubicon into 'madness' into the new year. In the first draft we see that Nietzsche only has eight dithyrambs in mind, but must have added the ninth in the next day or two.

This dedication is not only a reference to Catulle Mendès and his operetta *Isoline*, but it can also be read as a play on words: Isoline=Isolation, Ital. *Isolato*, pp. of *Isolare*, Latin *insula*, island. Nietzsche takes his bark and floats out to sea to his island of the seventh solitude. The Blessed Isles. Isolationist—a person who believes in or advocates isolation; person who wants his country to take no part in international alliances. Isolde—from Tristan and Isolde—love story. Mendès' operetta takes place on the Island of Cytheria, the island of love. Nietzsche is *also* the poet of Isoline. In this sense he gives the dithyrambs to himself, just as he writes *Ecce Homo* to himself. Hollingdale quotes Nietzsche from *The Birth of Tragedy*:

> "It is an unimpeachable tradition that Greek tragedy in its oldest form depicted only the sufferings of Dionysus," he says, but goes on to assert that "Dionysus never ceased to be the tragic hero.... all the famous figures of the Greek stage...are only masks of that original hero Dionysus." ...Later, and possibly better known formulations of what he means by a "dithyramb" are in their essence no more than a repetition of this original assertion that

the dithyramb is the language in which Dionysus speaks for and of himself.[25]

Nietzsche, along with Mendès, is 'the first and greatest satyr alive today' as he begins his satyr-play, takes on the appearance of 'madness.' And not only 'of today' because the play of 'madness' will be repeated eternally.

In the last months before his 'breakdown' Nietzsche was greatly occupied with an appreciation of operetta. In a letter to Peter Gast, November 18, Nietzsche writes:

A completely other question moves me very deeply—the Operetta-Question, which your letter touched on. We have not seen each other since this question became clear to me—oh so clear! As long as you misunderstand the concept of "Operetta" with any condescension, or any vulgarity of taste, you are— please excuse the strong expression!—only a German....Ask yourself again, how Monsieur Audran defines operetta: "The paradise of all delicate and refined things," the most sublime sweetness included. I recently heard "Mascotte"—three hours and not one measure of Viennese (*Wienerei=Schweinerei*). Read any feuilleton about a new Paris operetta: there are among them in France at this time true geniuses of witty self-possession, malicious goodness, of archaisms, exoticisms, and of completely naive things. One requires 10 pieces of the first order, so that an operetta, under an enormous pressure of rivalry, remains at the top. It offers a true science of finesses of taste and of effects. I promise you, Vienna is a pigsty....If I could show you one veritable Paris Soubrette, which creates—,in one single role, for example, Mad. Judic or Milly Meyer, the scales would fall from your eyes and from the operetta. Operettas have no scales: the scales are pure German....—And here comes a kind of reception (*eine Art Recept*). For our bodies and souls, dear friend, a little poisoning with the woman Paris (*Parisin*) simply a "redemp- tion"—we would be us, we would be ourselves and cease to be silly asses (*Horndeutsch*)....Forgive me, but I can write *German* for the first time only from the moment on when I can think of my readers as parisian. The *Case of Wagner* is operetta-music.[26]

In another letter to Gast of November 25 Nietzsche writes:

You may also find in my fundamentally cheerful and malicious *Actualität* perhaps more inspiration to the *Operetta* than anything else: I make so many dumb poses with myself and have such private attacks of *Hanswurst*, that I grin not less than half an hour on the open street, I know no other word....For the last four days I have lost the possibility of bringing a serious expression to my face—I think, in such a situation, one is ripe to become *World-redeemer*?[27]

Also, *Nietzsche contra Wagner*, divided into ten sections, takes on the shape of operetta. But in addition to this play with operetta in his works, which is calculated to counter the seriousness and heaviness of Wagnerian opera and European writing style, Nietzsche is setting up his *real* operetta of 'madness' in which he will play world-redeemer.

The question of redemption and ruling the world is played out in *The Case of Wagner* in the following way:

> The first German Wagner Association, that of Munich, placed a wreath on [Wagner's] grave, with an inscription that immediately became famous. It read: "Redemption for the redeemer!" Everybody admired the lofty inspiration that had dictated this inscription; also the taste that distinguished Wagner's admirers. But many (strangely enough!) made the same small correction: "Redemption *from* the redeemer!"—One heaved a sigh of relief.—[28]

In a postscript to a letter to Gast of August 11, 1888, Nietzsche writes: "The leitmotiv of my bad joke 'Wagner as redeemer' is based naturally on the inscription in the wreath of the Munich Wagner Society, 'redemption of the redeemer' (or redeemed the redeemer), the last line of *Parsifal*."[29] Dieter Borchmeyer writes of this ending line, "Redeemed the Redeemer can in no sense be interpreted to mean that the new redeemer Parsifal has superseded the old one, in the way that each new Grail king replaces the previous one. If Parsifal participates in the redemptive acts of God, it is in the manner of a Christian saint, rescuing the Saviour, who is immanent within the grail, from the guilt tainted hands of Amfortas."[30] Nietzsche as Antichrist does not want to redeem the redeemer as Parsifal does in Wagner's opera, nor does he want to redeem Wagner; rather he wants to erase Christianity and Wagnerian opera (German culture) and become the "redeemer" of the world himself (*Welt-erlöser*), this meant in great irony and in earnest. In "The Priests" in *Zarathustra*, Nietzsche plays with the concept of Christ as redeemer and Wagner as redeemer. The redeemer as Nietzsche understands a redeemer is one who redeems to be overcome in the creation of future redeemers.

> A sultry heart and a cold head: where these two meet there arises the roaring wind, the "Redeemer." There have been greater ones, verily, and more highborn than those whom the people call redeemer, those roaring winds which carry away. And you, my brothers, must be redeemed from still greater ones than all the redeemers if you would find the way to freedom.[31]

Nietzsche connects the writing of feuilletons with operetta. Nietzsche's references to feuilletons and what he calls "bad jokes" come together in his last letter to Jacob Burckhardt: "Since I am condemned to *entertain the next eternity with bad jokes*, I have a writing business here which really leaves nothing to be desired—very nice and not in the least strenuous. The post office is five paces away, I post my letters there myself, to *play the part of the great feuilletonist of the grande monde.*"[32] The whole letter to Burckhardt is a series of short feuilletons. Feuilletons in French newspapers are sections of short fiction and critical notices, having a sense of dilettantism or frivolity about them. Nietzsche in complete irony is *the feuilletonist of the great world*— all of his 'mad' notes are feuilletons, sent all over Europe to friends and heads of states as well as the Vatican. They are "bad jokes" that fulfill the needs of his new profession as the "buffoon of the new eternities." To Ferdinand Avenarius, December 10, 1888:

> In these years during which a terrible task, the Revaluation of all Values, lies on me, and I literally have to carry the fate of mankind, it belongs to my proofs of strength and to the extent of my strength to be *Hanswurst*, satyr or, if you can imagine it, "Feuilletonist"—able to be, as I already was in the *Case of Wagner*. That the deepest spirit must also be the most frivolous, that is almost the formula for my philosophy: it could be that I have already completely cheered myself up in an improbable way over and above all other "Great Ones."[33]

Now, clearly Nietzsche connects all of this jesting and bad jokes, the writing of feuilletons, and operettas with the *Dionysus Dithyrambs* and what they mean. Why does Nietzsche call Mendès a satyr? And why in his 'mad' notes does he also call Seydlitz and Deussen satyrs as well? Podach offers the last letter Nietzsche wrote to Reinhard Von Seydlitz on January 2 or 3: "Friend Seydlitz shall be, together with Monsieur Catulle Mendès, one of my greatest satyrs and festival animals. Dionysus."[34] To Paul Deussen he writes: "After you have irrevocably risen to the position that I have really created the world, it appears that friend Paul will also be provided for in the world plan: he shall be, together with Monsieur Catulle Mendès, one of my greatest satyrs and festival animals. Dionysus"[35]

Why does Nietzsche connect Seydlitz and Mendès at this point? One connection is that Nietzsche, Mendés, and Seydlitz all had trouble with Bayreuth and the 1876 *Festspiel*. Nietzsche had known Mendès and probably spoken to him many times. Cosima's diary put them together specifically a couple of times in 1870. Mendès and his wife were good friends of the Wagners for many years. However, Mendès had a serious political and cultural falling out with Wagner just before the 1876 *Festspiel* over a piece Wagner had written called "A Capitulation: Comedy in the Antique Manner," the point of the piece being that what it ultimately mocks is not the Parisian capitulation to the German army, but the German surrender to Parisian opera and operetta. Mendès attended the Bayreuth Festival but did not set foot inside the gate of Wahnfried.[36] At the same time, Seydlitz, who had just finished reading manuscripts of the second part of *Human All Too Human*, from which Nietzsche included four sections in *Nietzsche contra Wagner* in 1888, wrote to Nietzsche: "I have decided...not to go to Bayreuth. I woke up to this last idea with the sense of having narrowly escaped a danger....I cannot abide absolutism."[37] So in their own ways and for their own reasons, Mendès, Seydlitz, and Nietzsche boycotted the 1876 *Festspiel*. Perhaps it is this that makes of them satyrs and not Christians or nationalists. Why Deussen becomes a satyr is not clear. Perhaps he, too, declined to attend the *Festspiel?*

Nietzsche's dedication to Mendès, the poet of *Isoline*, of the *Dionysian Dithyrambs* is so surprising that one must get hold of the operetta, *Isoline*, to see if it helps clarify the matter. If one gets hold of the operetta, *Isoline: A*

Fairytale in Three Acts and Ten Scenes, *which is available in an 1888 piano and voice edition*, what does one find? Perhaps the satyr-operetta that Nietzsche would like Wagner to have written in place of *Parsifal*, the opera of chastity and Christianity. In the same section of *Nietzsche contra Wagner* quoted above, "Wagner as the Apostle of Chastity," Nietzsche criticizes Wagner for his celebration of chastity and Christianity in *Parsifal*: "The preaching of chastity remains an incitement to anti-nature: I despise everyone who does not experience *Parsifal* as an attempted assassination of basic ethics."

> There is no necessary opposition between sensuality and chastity; every good marriage, every love affair, that comes from the heart is beyond this opposition. But in a case in which this opposition really exists, fortunately it need by no means be a tragic opposition. This would seem to hold at least for all the better turned out, more cheerful mortals, who are far from counting their labile balance between angel and *petite bete* as necessarily among the objections to existence: the finest, the brightest, like Hafiz, Goethe, have even considered this one attraction more. Such contradictions actually seduce to existence. On the other hand, it is only too easy to understand that, should those whom misfortune has changed into the animals of Circe ever be brought to the point of adoring chastity, they will see only their own opposite in it and will *adore* it—oh, with what tragic grunting and fervor one can imagine. And at the end of his life Richard Wagner undeniably wanted to set this embarrassing and perfectly superfluous opposition to music and produce it on the stage.[38]

When we turn to *Isoline* we find an erotic love story between Isoline and Isolin, where the eventual consummation of sexual love becomes the ultimate mystery. It makes one ask: What if Parsifal had succumbed to Kundry's advances? It is also somewhat of a parody of Shakespeare's *Midsummer Night's Dream*, with Oberon and Titania playing leading roles. *Isoline* is a playful, mocking operetta with language both pretty and obscene in its metaphors and light, rollicking humorous music. Let us follow a shortened version of the the story.

Isoline, whose mother, Queen Amalasonthe, has kept her in a tower to protect her from love, has a dream in which Eros calls all young lovers to set sail for the fabled island of love, Cytheria. In the dream Isoline sees Isolin and Isolin sees her and they fall in love: "adorable love unites us in a prodigious mystery." Eros: "In love one dies, but one is reborn." Isoline awakens and laments her Isolin who had only been a dream.

Then, in the plot of the operetta, Isolin really comes to Isoline's tower drawn by her voice: "because your soul is the sister of my loving soul." They decide to run off together. Isolin: "Let's fly from stars to stars." The tower walls fall and Oberon carries them up into the sky. Queen Amalasonthe sees them and vows never to let them marry.

Meanwhile a chorus of "desolate" women complain that they are not beautiful, that they are the desolate and unhappy ones. Soon they persuade Isoline that she, too, is ugly and desolate and she begins to doubt that she is worthy to love Isolin. Isolin asks: "Why is your heart changing Isoline? It is so cruel. It was so sweet. But even though everything changes my love for an angel of flame on a pure altar is immortal." He prepares to kill himself with a dagger. When Isoline grabs the dagger to prevent him, she sees her reflection in it and sees that she is beautiful. Isoline: "Ah, ah, I'm happy." She bursts out laughing. "Little tear, good mirror, how clear you are, how clearly one can see through you. I'm pretty and I'm laughing and I forget. I forget the old women who lied to me. The ear that is an islet an opening too small. Ah." Isolin and Isoline decide to marry. The desolate ones are also transformed by love. Eros urges Isolin and Isoline to hurry to the chapel of gold and he says: "I triumph." However, Titania enters and says: "Not yet."

Titania and Queen Amalasonthe, with all her soldiers, challenge Isolin to a battle rather than let him marry Isoline. All are singing, battle, battle. Isolin replies: "Yes, queen, battle. Isoline is a good stake."

In the next scene Oberon comes upon Titania asleep. He laments about how they used to love "and dance on the lake in the pale moon of the brown night." She awakens and he gets her to agree to make love again. But before they do they talk of Isoline and Isolin and take fighting sides again.

As Isolin goes to fight the queen's army Titania lays a trap for him. Nocturnal fairies dance with him and attempt to seduce him at night in a forest clearing. He dances and the attempt to seduce him takes place but fails as he breaks away.

In the battle Isolin wins and Queen Amalasonthe surrenders. Oberon: "Triumph!" Titania says: "Alas!" Queen Amalasonthe cannot reconcile herself to the marriage.

The ninth scene is entitled: The Nuptial Choir, Duet and Finale Chorus: "They are united the loved ones. The day of hymen is theirs for them." Isoline and Isolin are alone together. They sing the following duet while being watched secretly by others.

Isolin: From your breast which is bared the perfume tells me you are a flower and the gold of your eyes reveals a star. And these treasures, your eyes, your hands, your arms are mine. I want them. I'm taking them, come, come.

Isoline: Music of love is sung again.

Isolin: It is the door of ineffable enchantment. I love you, I love you and I carry you madly.

Isoline: I adore your arms which carry me to madness.

(Violante and Nicette who have been peeping on the lovers): They are going to pass the happy door alas. It is the fatal moment. He loves her and he is carrying her to madness.

Isoline: I love you, I love you and I carry you.

Isolin: I love you, I love you and I carry you to madness. But the kiss that I have waited for so long. Oh lip adored. The kiss which my breathless desires were hoping for. The kiss which is shared on the sacred hour by the conjugal lover equal to the God's drunkest of love in the high imperium. Let me collect it finally. Lip, adored lip.

Isoline: You want it.

Isolin: Yes I want it. Dear mouth, divine chalice.

They make love.

Isoline: What is happening to me? Isoline!

Isolin: What is happening to me? Isolin!

Roselio, Queen Amalasonthe: Isoline, Isolin, Isoline, Isolin. Double miracle. She is boy but he is girl. She is boy, but he is girl.

Isoline: I am different, even more ardently day burns. It is of male pride that I have a full heart.

Isolin: I love differently as well, a more tender heart is burning. A softer excitement that I have a full heart. It is the portal of the door of the ineffable. I love you, I love you, I carry you to madness.

Violante, Nicette, Roselio, Queen: They are going to cross over the happy portal, charming miracle, charming miracle. He embraces her, carries her to madness.

Isoline: I adore your arms which carry me, your arms which carry me to madness.

Isolin: I love you, I love you, I carry you madly.

In the last scene and finale, they all go to the Island of Cytheria where Titania yields to Oberon: "Like before my fond heart melts in langorous delight and our beings joined in one will be in vaporous nights, in vaporous nights, like music and perfum."[39]

In direct contrast to the long sombre *Parsifal*, which praises chastity and Christian virtues, *Isoline* is a comic operetta, pagan in its celebration of sexual soul love and its victory over resentment and prudery. The divine chalice of *Parsifal* becomes Isoline's sexuality. According to Wagner Kundry is like the serpent of paradise. "Just as Eve is promised that 'Ye shall be as gods,'…we find Kundry telling Parsifal: 'The full embrace of my loving will surely raise you to godhead.' Parsifal kisses Kundry to be infected with sin and suffering, so that he may become wise (reject the sins of the flesh) and so that they may both be redeemed in Christ."[40] In *Isoline* redemption comes in the consummation of a passionate, magic, sexual love. Rather than eternal separation of sexual love in chastity, Isoline and Isolin become eternal hermaphrodite. *Isoline* can be read as a delightful parody of *Parsifal*.

I have given only an indication of the whole of this sexual, lewd, satyr-play on innocent love and sexual appetite. But more than a satyric praise of the intoxications of love and madness and the reversal of *Parsifal*, there are many details in this operetta that repeat motifs in Nietzsche's drama of 'madness': the brown night, the prominence of gold, raise the golden anchor, the chapel of gold, flame of a pure altar, the small island of the ear, setting sailing over the sea, the carrying into madness of the lovers (Dionysus and Ariadne), celebration of love, intoxication, the mystery of sexuality that literally turns Isoline and Isolin into a hermaphrodite (the sacred marriage), the ultimate mystery of sexual love in this operetta, love and death as eternal rebirth, the idea of sister souls, flying to the stars, laughter and forgetting of resentment and life negating values in favor of nature and celebration. All of these colors, thoughts, and images are found in the *Dithyrambs* themselves.

When one reads this operetta there is no doubt that Nietzsche read it as well. It is most likely that Nietzsche himself purchased the operetta in the piano and song version available in 1888. Nietzsche had to have known it in some detail to call Mendès a satyr, for its contents validate such an appellation and his dedication.

"And now", says Ariadne, "My phantasm takes hold of all of this. The Dionysian Dithyrambs are the portal of 'madness,' Dionysian madness. I love Dionysus and I want him to carry me to 'madness.' The brown night, the sea, the altar flame on high mountains, his sister soul called to mine. He whispered in the island of my small ear, not the resentment of old women, but the secret of the solitary. For he is Isolin and I am Isoline. Across the rocking waves, up to the highest stars we fly to the Island of Cytheria in the arms of Eros, locked for eternity in each other's frame. The steel of the knife, death, has reflected our beauty back onto us and we laugh and sing. The bell is sounding, the old midnight bell which joins midnight to noon, joy and woe beckon us to set sail. In A Midsummer's Night Dream Hippolyta was right, you know, Nietzsche knows it. I, Ariadne, know it. All of this phantasm that apprehends more than cool reason ever comprehends, this airy nothing that gives forms a local habitation is not only the illusion of the madman, the lover and the poet, rather it is their minds transfigured so together, which more witnesseth than fancy's images, and grows to something of great constancy, but howsoever, strange and admirable. The 'sacred

marriage' is wedded with erotic sexuality and laughter! Dionysus and Ariadne: we are transfigured in the mystery of a sacred wedding as we dance on earth to the flutes of Pan as the primal couple: satyr and maenad."

Notes

1. Nietzsche, *Gay Science*, Preface, #3.
2. Middleton, *Selected Letters*, p. 345.
3. NB, III, 5, pp. 419–20.
4. Curt Paul Janz, *Friedrich Nietzsche Biographie: Die Jahre des Siechtums/Quellen*, Band 3 (München: Carl Hanser Verlag, 1979), p. 78.
5. Middleton, *Selected Letters*, p. 344.
6. Nietzsche, *Ecce Homo*, p. 250.
7. Richard Wagner, *Twilight of the Gods*, Opera Guide Series, ed.: Nicholas John (New York: Riverrun Press, 1985), pp. 122–24.
8. Richard Wagner, *The Valkyrie*, Opera Guide Series, ed.: Nicholas John (New York: Riverrun Press, 1983), pp. 107–8.
9. Nietzsche, *Ecce Homo*, p. 220.
10. Nietzsche, *Birth of Tragedy*, pp. 127–28.
11. Richard Wagner, *Tristan and Isolde*, Opera Guide Series, ed.: Nicholas John (New York: Riverrun Press, 1981), pp. 87–92.
12. Nietzsche, *Birth of Tragedy*, p. 131.
13. Robert Donington, *Wagner's 'Ring' and Its Symbols* (New York: St. Martin's Press, 1974), p. 269.
14. Ibid., p. 270.
15. Ibid., pp. 270–71.
16. Ibid., p. 272; emphasis added.
17. Ananda Coomaraswamy, "Sati: A Vindication of the Hindu Woman," a paper read before the Sociological Society, November 12, 1912.
18. Eva C. Keuls, *The Reign of the Phallus: Sexual Politics in Ancient Athens* (New York: Harper and Row, 1985), pp. 171–75.
19. Nietzsche, *Gay Science*, #334.
20. Nietzsche, *Ecce Homo*, p. 306.
21. Nietzsche, "Song of a Theocritical Goatherd" in Songs of Prince Vogelfrei, *Gay Science*, p. 361.
22. Nietzsche, *Nietzsche contra Wagner*, pp. 674–75.
23. Podach, *Nietzsches Werke des Zusammenbruchs*, pp. 373 and 412.
24. Nietzsche, *Dithyrambs of Dionysus*, pp. 20–21.

25. Ibid., p. 16.
26. NB, III, 5, pp. 478–79.
27. Ibid., p. 489.
28. Nietzsche, *Case of Wagner*, p. 182.
29. NB, III, 5, p. 390.
30. Dieter Borchmeyer, "Recapitulation of a Lifetime," in Richard Wagner, *Parsifal*, pp. 19–20.
31. Nietzsche, *Zarathustra*, p. 205.
32. Middleton, *Selected Letters*, p. 347.
33. NB, III, 5, pp. 516–17.
34. Podach, *Nietzsches Werke des Zusammenbruch*, p. 412.
35. NB, III, 5, p. 574.
36. Curt von Westernhagen, *Wagner, A Biography*, Vol. II, trans. Mary Whittall (Cambridge: Cambridge University Press, 1978), pp. 428 and 432.
37. Ronald Hayman, *Nietzsche, A Critical Life*, p. 212.
38. Nietzsche, *Nietzsche contra Wagner*, pp. 673–75.
39. *Isoline*, Conte des Fées entrois Actes et 10 Tableaux, Poëm des Catulle Mendès, Musique de André Messager, Partition Piano et Chant, réduite par l'Auteur, Paris: Enoch frères & Costallat, 1888. Translated by Kimball Lockhardt for this work.
40. Dieter Borchmeyer, "Recapitulation of a Lifetime," pp. 18–20.

Incipit Parodia:
Of Satyrs, Asses, and Festivals

"*Incipit tragoedia*" we read at the end of this awesomely aweless book. Beware! Something downright wicked and malicious is announced here: *incipit parodia*, no doubt.[1]

The satyr was the archetype of man, the embodiment of his highest and most intense emotions, the ecstatic reveler enraptured by the proximity of his god, the sympathetic companion in whom the suffering of the god is repeated, one who proclaims wisdom from the very heart of nature, a symbol of the sexual omnipotence of nature which the Greeks used to contemplate with reverent wonder.[2]

I estimate the value of men, races, according to the necessity by which they cannot conceive the god apart from the satyr.[3]

Nietzsche finished Part IV of *Zarathustra* in the winter of 1885. He had forty copies privately printed, and distributed only seven copies to friends. But in December 1888 he changed his mind and in a letter of December 9 to Gast he enlisted Gast's help in trying to recover all copies. He felt that it was not the right time to send it out and that it would be much more effective after a period of catastrophes and wars. If this was Nietzsche's plan, then *Zarathustra* Part IV was to be made public many years after the *Dionysus Dithyrambs*. From that perspective the *Dithyrambs* become a prelude to Part IV. And from this perspective, Part IV is not just a story, but a prophecy of the future, which Nietzsche wanted to have published after the conditions for that future had taken place. Part IV is a script of what Nietzsche hopes from the future human, the higher humans. The higher humans, the solitaries, the fish that he hopes to snare as he sits in the solitude of his 'madness.' Thus, the *Dionysus Dithyrambs* herald the coming of the higher humans after the honey sacrifice of the voluntary death and after wars and crises. Part IV of *Zarathustra* shows how the coming of the higher humans should be played out.

Nietzsche gives us two stories or scripts and two real dramas, both as satyr-plays. The first story, the *Dionysian Dithyrambs*, is a *story* of Nietzsche's *actual* performance of a dancing, singing, satyrical 'madness' and ecstacy. This is how he characterizes it when he writes to Cosima as *Hanswurst*. Nietzsche tells the *story* of sitting on the mountain, crouching and ecstatic as he waits for fish, then *actually* sits in the sanitorium at Basle and Jena, then in his mother's and sister's houses. The second story is Part IV of *Zarathustra*, which tells the *story* of the higher humans who come up to the mountain and of their comic celebrations with Zarathustra, a story that is to guide the *actual* drama and satyr-play of the *real* higher humans who will come to Nietzsche.

In *Beyond Good and Evil* Nietzsche writes:

> We are the first age that has truly studied "costumes"—I mean those of moralities, articles of faith, taste in the arts, and religions—prepared like no previous age for a carnival in the grand style, for the laughter and high spirits of the most spiritual revelry, for the transcendental heights of the highest nonsense and of Aristophanean mockery of the world. Perhaps this is still where we shall discover the realm of our *invention*, that realm in which we, too, can still be original, say as parodists of world-history and carnival clowns of God—perhaps, even if nothing else today has any future, our *laughter* may yet have a future.[4]

And in *Ecce Homo* Nietzsche writes: "I am a disciple of the philosopher Dionysus; I should prefer to be even a satyr to being a saint." And he writes: "I do not want to be a holy man; sooner even a buffoon.—Perhaps I am a buffoon."[5] Nietzsche's actual performance as buffoon and satyr in 'madness' plays out the festivities and great antics of Zarathustra with the higher men in Part IV of *Zarathustra*.

"Yes!" says Ariadne, "I was there when Zarathustra celebrated with the higher men. I was behind the bushes with Nietzsche and my beloved Dionysus. We tittered and laughed and cried and danced for sheer delight and joy as we watched the proceedings. We almost gave ourselves away!"

At one point Zarathustra said to the higher men: "it seems to me that you are poor company; you who utter cries of distress upset each other's hearts as you sit here together. First someone must come—someone to make you laugh again, a good gay clown, a dancer and wind and wildcat, some old fool."[6]

"Yes!" Ariadne thought, "and what a joyful old satyr-play we then beheld! What Dionysus, Nietzsche, and I saw there on the mountain in Zarathustra's cave was comedy, malicious, divine comedy!"

> If the authentic comic action is a sacrifice and a feast, debate and passion, it is by the same token a Saturnalia, an orgy, an assertion of the unruliness of the flesh and its vitality. Comedy is essentially a Carrying Away of Death, a triumph over mortality by some absurd faith in rebirth, restoration, and salvation....The archaic seasonal revel brought together the incompatibles of death and life. No logic can explain this magic victory of Spring over Winter, Sin, and the Devil. But the comedian can perform the rites of Dionysus and his frenzied gestures initiate us into the secrets of the savage and mystic power of life.[7]

Zarathustra taught the higher men dancing and laughing:

> You higher men, the worst about you is that all of you have not learned to dance as one must dance—dancing away over yourselves! What does it matter that you are failures? How much is still possible! So *learn* to laugh away over yourselves! Lift up your hearts, you good dancers, high, higher! And do not forget good laughter. This crown of him who laughs, this rose-wreath crown, to you, my brothers, I throw this crown. Laughter I pronounced holy: you higher men, *learn* to laugh![8]

In *Beyond Good and Evil*, Nietzsche writes about an order of rank among philosophers depending on their laughter—all the way up to those capable of golden laughter. "And suppose that gods too, philosophize, which has been suggested to me by many an inference—I should not doubt that they also know how to laugh the while in a superhuman and new way—and at the expense of all serious things. Gods enjoy mockery: it seems they cannot suppress laughter even during holy rites."⁹ Zarathustra is "the laughing prophet" who makes laughter holy. And it is not surprising, for his namesake Zoroaster was said to have come laughing from the womb as a sign of his gift of prophecy.¹⁰

Ariadne: "Dionysus loves good mockery and when his buffoon Zarathustra created this most comic of rituals for the higher men he left the bushes and entered the festivities in Zarathustra's cave though no one knew it except I. He was not content to watch but had to jump in and take part. He disguised himself as the old magician who taunted and tickled Zarathustra with his magician's song and tempted the higher men with the melancholy song, but oh, how he laughed to himself as he sang. Zarathustra must have felt the divine play there, for he was indeed wise and wicked too when he took his stick and beat the disguised god with green lightning bolts in his eyes."

In his analysis of Part IV of *Zarathustra*, Gary Shapiro writes:

> The thrashing of the magician in Part IV "with all his force" and "with furious laughter" is a carnivalesque ritual in which the apparent king is dethroned and then beaten. Such thrashing... "is as ambivalent as abuse changed into praise. The one who is thrashed or slaughtered is decorated. The beating itself has a gay character; it is introduced and concluded with laughter."¹¹

Ariadne: "And I saw much more the night the higher men celebrated with Zarathustra. There was the great communal dinner, 'The Last Supper,' at which Zarathustra taught not goodness but 'evil,' not neighbor love but the egoism of one's own work and will, that the world is a gamble and a jest, and above all, the arts of dancing and laughing. This is how the higher men are to celebrate the feast and festival of noon after the sacrifice of the voluntary 'madness' is turned to joy. And they celebrated a great festival in honor of the ass, of which Zarathustra said to the higher men:

> *Verily, you have all blossomed; it seems to me such flowers as you are require new festivals, a little brave nonsense, some divine service and*

ass festival, some old gay fool of a Zarathustra, a roaring wind that blows your souls bright....And when you celebrate it again, this ass festival, do it for your own sakes, and also do it for my sake. And in remembrance of me.[12]

And in remembrance of the satyr 'madman' Nietzsche who taught us to laugh! Zarathustra not only thrashed Dionysus but parodied both Christ and himself at the same time as Nietzsche did with his signatures of The Crucified and Dionysus! Zarathustra took leave of the higher men by praising them and imparting to them his new gospel, his glad tidings in the 'Drunken Song' as Nietzsche did when he parted from us! During the general frenzy at midnight, the cave was full of noise and laughter, the party was in full swing:

> *The old soothsayer was dancing with joy; and even if, as some of the chroniclers think, he was full of sweet wine, he was certainly still fuller of the sweetness of life and he had renounced all weariness. There are even some who relate that the ass danced too, and that it had not been for nothing that the ugliest man had given him wine to drink before. Now it may have been so or otherwise; and if the ass really did not dance that night, yet greater and stranger wonders occurred than the dancing of an ass would have been. In short as the proverb of Zarathustra says: 'What does it matter?'*[13]

Zarathustra divulged the mystery of 'The Drunken Song,' the mystery: that midnight too is noon, pain too is joy, a sage too is a fool and that all of this is the eternal round of life. Yet even this deepest of life's mysteries was preceded with 'What does it matter?' And this itself may be the deepest mystery of all. 'The Drunken Song' celebrates not only Zarathustra's intoxication and that of the higher men but the drunkenness of the world itself. 'The Drunken Song' is the wisdom of the philosopher Dionysus, who the whole time Zarathustra was singing it, hopped for glee from one cloven foot to another and finally brayed out Yea-uh!"

In *The Will to Power* Nietzsche writes: "Festivals include: pride, exuberance, wantonness; mockery of everything serious and philistine, a divine affirmation of oneself out of animal plenitude and perfection——...The festival is paganism par excellence."[14] What the higher men learned in feasting with Zarathustra, in performing the ass festival, in learning to dance and sing, is to say Yes to everything like the ass does *even if* it does not matter. And after this festival the ugliest man, the one with the least to live for, said: "one day, one festival with Zarathustra, taught me to love the earth."[15] The conscientious man said to Zarathustra: "You yourself—verily, overabundance and wisdom could easily turn you too into an ass."[16] And it was, indeed, overabundance and wisdom that turned Zarathustra and Nietzsche into buffoons. In Overbeck's letter to Gast of January 15, 1889, describing his going to get Nietzsche in Turin he writes: "mainly it was utterances about the profession which he had allotted to himself, to be the clown of the new eternities, and he, the master of expression, was incapable of rendering the ecstasies of his gaiety except in the most trivial expressions or by frenzied dancing and capering."[17]

Ariadne: "Not trivial expressions, but the highest expressions!"

So the lesson for the higher humans is that they despised themselves and the world and sought Zarathustra. But Zarathustra leaves them to seek themselves, to become Ariadne's in transforming the No-saying and No-doing parts of their souls into a holy Yes if they wish to join the great noon and turning point in history. These higher men of the future have been initiated into the art of destroying and creating with laughter. And this is fitting because for Nietzsche and Zarathustra laughter follows upon the hardest tasks. No tender shepherds or higher humans for them. The parable of the shepherd:

> A young shepherd I saw writhing, gagging, in spasms, his face distorted, and a heavy black snake hung out of his mouth. Had I ever seen so much nausea and pale dread on one face? He seemed to have been asleep when the snake crawled into his throat, and there bit itself fast. My hand tore at the snake and tore in vain; it did not tear the snake out of his throat. Then it cried out of me: "Bite! Bite its head off! Bite!"....The shepherd bit as my cry counseled him; he bit with a good bite. Far away he spewed the head of the snake—and he jumped up. No longer shepherd, no longer human—one changed, radiant, *laughing*! Never yet on earth has a human being laughed as he laughed![18]

The snake is the nausea that attaches to the idea that the last man, too, must eternally recur and that the shepherd is on his way to the overhuman in having overcome that nausea. This is what the higher men, now equipped with laughter, dance, and festivals, must do in the process of finding themselves. They must spew from themselves the nausea, terror, and suffering of themselves and of life, even more, the suffering of humankind, and accept *all* in joy and affirmation. We must bite off the head of nausea, terror, and suffering that Nietzsche offers to us in the spectacle of his 'madness' and laugh a *new* superhuman creatively 'evil' laughter. Part IV initiates us into the prankish 'madness' of those who would, like Zarathustra, overcome pity for the sake of the overhuman.

Don't we see that Nietzsche could never end on a tragic note? For the end of tragedy is always death, while the end of comedy is a wedding, fertility, spring, rebirth out of death, eternal return. In Greek tragedy the comic satyr-play always had the last word. Not *incipit tragoedia*, which is only the way of the hero, Theseus, but *incipit parodia*, the way of divine humans. Paradoxically the realities of destruction, death, and suffering do not lead to tragedy for a "tragic age" as Nietzsche prophesied it, but to comedy. Nietzsche: "I know no higher symbolism than this Greek symbolism of the Dionysian festivals. Here the most profound instinct of life, that directed toward the future of life, the eternity of life, is experienced religiously—and the way to life, procreation, as the holy way."[19]

Thus, does Nietzsche/Dionysus speak to his fish, his birds of prey. To laugh at Yes and to laugh at No, even doing no, perishing, and to create festivals to this highest of powers.

Ariadne: "So you, who come to Nietzsche's mountains, you had better be instructed by Zarathustra in the wonders of laughter, for only as laughing, divine satyrs, revelers out of health, exuberance, maliciousness, wickedness, and joy will he recognize you, his children. And as you come thus, in the spirit of comedy, will you populate the next eternities."

Notes

1. Nietzsche, *Gay Science*, Preface to Second Edition, p. 33. See also *Beyond Good and Evil*, #25.
2. Nietzsche, *Birth of Tragedy*, p. 61.
3. Nietzsche, *Ecce Homo*, p. 245.

4. Nietzsche, *Beyond Good and Evil*, #223.

5. Nietzsche, *Ecce Homo*, pp. 217 and 326.

6. Nietzsche, *Zarathustra*, p. 391.

7. Wylie Sypher, "The Ancient Rites of Comedy," in *Comedy*, ed. Wylie Sypher (Baltimore: Johns Hopkins University Press), 1956, pp. 220–21.

8. Nietzsche, *Zarathustra*, pp. 407–8.

9. Nietzsche, *Beyond Good and Evil*, #294.

10. See Gary Shapiro, *Nietzschean Narratives* (Bloomington: Indiana University Press, 1989), pp. 109–10.

11. Ibid., pp. 105–6.

12. Nietzsche, *Zarathustra*, pp. 428–29.

13. Ibid., p. 430.

14. Nietzsche, *Will to Power*, #916.

15. Nietzsche, *Zarathustra*, p. 429.

16. Ibid., p. 427.

17. Middleton, *Selected Letters*, p. 353.

18. Nietzsche, *Zarathustra*, pp. 271-272.

19. Nietzsche, *Twilight of the Idols*, p. 562.

For, I Love You, O Eternity!

> Oh, how should I not lust after eternity and after the nuptial ring of rings, the ring of recurrence? Never yet have I found the woman from whom I wanted children, unless it be this woman whom I love: for I love you, O eternity. *For I love you, O eternity!*[1]

More than Ariadne Nietzsche loves eternity, the eternal recurrence of the same, for it is eternity that gives us the fabulous playground of all things. This moment has occurred and will occur an infinity of times, and this all happens at this moment. Past and future and present collapse into one. Time is not a medium through which matter passes. Rather this moment, this matter, are and are becoming eternally in this moment.

Another way to say it. If each moment is eternal—the eternal recurrence of the same moment—then each moment in becoming never began and will never end. And if each and every moment is eternal then all moments are here now —they are with me. The whole of becoming in this moment now. The whole of existence at a stroke. The eternal tablet of forms here now. There is nothing but this moment, but this moment is everything—all moments. Difference is freed through the eternal sameness of each moment. Each moment is a different moment only by virtue of human consciousness that conceives of linear time. However, there is no time beyond human consciousness; only the ever-present copresence of the whole. The next moment, the whole of existence once again, is a dice throw of chance, but this chance is a return, because all moments and things are eternally existing. "Everything becomes and recurs eternally:"[2]

all things themselves are dancing: they come and offer their hands and laugh and flee—and come back. Everything goes, everything comes back; eternally rolls the wheel of being. Everything dies, everything blossoms again; eternally runs the year of being. Everything breaks, everything is joined anew; eternally the same house of being is built. Everything parts, everything greets every other thing again; eternally the ring of being remains faithful to itself. In every Now, being begins, round every Here rolls the sphere There. The center is everywhere. Bent is the path of eternity.[3]

In this moment, then, I am heir to and part of all moments, all things, all people, all events; the whole is with me now. However, my human intelligence is not capable of *knowing* or *experiencing* this, but only of conceiving of it. I can think, Nietzsche is here now, his warmth touches me, his eyes look at mine. He is with you now, his warmth touches you, his eyes look at yours. You and he are here now. And a tree on a mountain top in ancient Greece is yours and mine too and a tortured baby crying somewhere in the world. We sit in this eternal moment of moments and create, then recreate the eternalness of this moment, the moment when we are with Nietzsche, looking into his eyes and everything else too: all joy and all horror!

Ariadne, the orgiastic soul of woman sings:

I look into your green, honey eyes.
They are a sea cradling, cradling
My life, my spirit,
my all is rocked in the cradle of your terrible depths.
Your labyrinthian eyes invite me, draw me, please me.
I search them out again and again.

It is the golden thread of life
which has you looking into my trembling eyes.
In my eager eyes there is a sea rocking, rocking,
Upholding you, your spirit, your all.
My veiled eyes invite you, draw you, please you.
You search them out again and again.

Thus, turning our radiant and profane eyes, and hearts,
toward one another again and again,
we are eternally transfigured.
We will, and it becomes our creation for eternity.
Our existence is a commanding of woe
and a drowning in the joy of the all!

Nietzsche is not dead and gone; he is here now with all his joys and sorrows. I have never been born and never die; I am here now. We are together in each moment in the eternal recurrence of that same moment. We are all things, we are all joy and all woe. What will we do with this supreme realization of power? Cross over? Go down? Yes, but we *are* already that!

> Now I bid you lose me and find yourselves; and only when you have all denied me will I return to you. Verily, my brothers, with different eyes shall I then seek my lost ones; with a different love shall I then love you. And once again you shall become my friends and the children of a single hope—and then shall I be with you the third time, that I may celebrate the great noon with you.[4]

This 'idea' is divine! In the great noon, which is here now, Rumi is here, and Zarathustra, Hitler is here, the last man is here and the overhuman too! "Eternal tablet of forms! Image of What must be! Eternally am I thy Yes: for I love thee, O eternity!" This is the wedding of Dionysus and Ariadne.

> If we affirm one single moment, we thus affirm not only ourselves but all existence. For nothing is self-sufficient, neither in us ourselves nor in things; and if our soul has trembled with happiness and sounded like a harp string just once, all eternity was needed to produce this one event—and in this simple moment of affirmation all eternity was called good, redeemed, justified, and affirmed.[5]

Nietzsche writes of the means by which we might endure this thought of eternal recurrence of the same:

> No longer joy in certainty but uncertainty; no longer "cause and effect" but the continually creative; no longer will to preservation but to power; no longer the humble expression "everything is *merely* subjective," but "it is also *our* work!—Let us be proud of it!"[6]

To *endure* the idea of the recurrence one needs: freedom from
morality; new means against the fact of *pain* (pain conceived as a
tool, as the father of pleasure; there is no cumulative consciousness of displeasure); the enjoyment of all kinds of uncertainty,
experimentalism, as a counterweight to this extreme fatalism;
abolition of the concept of necessity; abolition of the "will";
abolition of "knowledge-in-itself." Greatest elevation of the
consciousness of strength in man as he creates the overman.[7]

No longer joy in certainty but uncertainty means that the next moment,
no matter how dangerous, is set like a jewel in the coexistence of all
moments. If it is a suffering moment think of the joy that is also occurring
to you at the same time! No cumulative displeasure, rather pain as the
father of pleasure in each moment. There is no cause and effect because all
is copresent. And in the next moment all is copresent once again,
rearranged according to chance. Each moment is continually creative
because it never begins nor ends. Preservation is a category only in linear
time, in the eternal recurrence of the same you are eternally existing,
suffering, joying, perishing. Power, the ever more intimate realization that
the world is *your* eternal creation. *All* things meet in you and go with you:
willing being. And you are *all* things, you go with them: cessation of all
need, becoming. Highest moment of individuation and creation *in* the
highest moment of dissolution. No longer "everything is *merely* subjective,"
which posits a world separated from us, objective. Rather, "it is also *our*
work!;" each of *our* moments *is* all of existence.

Freedom from morality: How could one judge the ever-present,
copresent existence of all? *Amor fati.* One creates in and of the all with all
of its elements as tools of power. There can be no necessity here, only
freedom, no will, no knowledge-in-itself; these are categories for men, but
for overhumans they are laughable fetters upon the vast freedom of a far-
ranging creation, their creation that plays with the infinite elements of past
and future eternity available to them in every moment. Zarathustra: "I led
you away from these fables when I taught you, 'The will is a creator.' All 'it
was' is a fragment, a riddle, a dreadful accident—until the creative will says
to it, 'But thus I willed it.' Until the creative will says to it, 'But thus I will
it; thus shall I will it.'"[8]

It was for this that Nietzsche took on the voluntary 'madness,' the renunciation of the seventh solitude to show us in his eternal moment how to create and endure the eternal recurrence. To teach us that the more we delve into pain, our pain, human pain, eternal pain, the more power in creative joy and bliss we will affirm. He is with us in pain. He exults with us in joy. We dance in power with him right now! Catastrophe, seduction, phantasm, creating, that means playing with the power of the eternal recurrence of the same. Zarathustra:

> If ever one breath came to me of the creative breath and of that heavenly need that constrains even accidents to dance star-dances; if I ever laughed the laughter of creative lightning which is followed obediently but grumblingly by the long thunder of the deed; if I ever played dice with gods at the gods' table, the earth, till the earth quaked and burst and snorted up floods of fire—for the earth is a table for gods and trembles with creative new words and gods' throws: Oh, how should I not lust after eternity and after the nuptial ring of rings, the ring of recurrence?⁹

Notes

1. Nietzsche, "The Seven Seals," *Zarathustra*, p. 340.
2. Nietzsche, *Will to Power*, #1058.
3. Nietzsche, *Zarathustra*, pp. 329–30.
4. Ibid., p. 190.
5. Nietzsche, *Will to Power*, #1032.
6. Ibid., #1059.
7. Ibid., #1060.
8. Nietzsche, *Zarathustra*, p. 253.
9. Ibid., p. 341.

Wedding of Dionysus and Ariadne: Dance, Sing, Rejoice!

Venezia (or Wedding Vows of the South)

Oh, my fisherman husband
sitting on the shore of Naxos
in your wondrous golden boat,
I heard your melody resounding through the distance.

The world is no longer dumb...
Listen with the ear of your love as

I, in that distance
sitting on my shore
in my wondrous golden boat,
Send my soul and song to penetrate the evening darkness.

Now Love and Eternity take up our songs
and smite the watery distance between us!
We are now mountain and wave, rainbow and dancing star,
promise and womb of what has been and must be...

"On Naxos wine gushed forth from a spring. This miracle, which is mentioned by Propertius in his hymn to the god, supposedly took place for the first time at the marriage of Dionysus and Ariadne."[1] And it was said that Dionysus led Ariadne to a mountain peak on the Island of Naxos, whereupon he, himself, and then she disappeared.[2]

Nietzsche enacted his divine drama of 'madness' at the time of the winter solstice, which he baptized as "Sanctus Januarius" and which was

303

the recurring time of some of his greatest exaltations and sufferings. The moving of the old year to the new, from winter to spring, from death to life is symbolized in the blood of St. Januarius, which becomes liquid again once each year. Nietzsche announces his drama of voluntary death in January 1882 and enacts it in January 1889. The yearly festival of the epiphany in most Christian churches is held on January 6 and commemorates the revealing to the Gentiles of Jesus as the Christ. Otto tells us that the winter epiphany of the god Dionysus was celebrated on the Island of Andros on the Nones of January, which is January 5. Therefore, "it is precisely in winter, when the sun gets ready to start on its new course, that Dionysus makes his most tumultuous entry."[3] It is no coincidence that Nietzsche/Dionysus plays out his Dionysian 'madness' and comedy of spring and eternal renewal at the beginning of January and that Zarathustra leaves his cave "glowing and strong as a morning sun that comes out of dark mountains" as he heads toward his great noon!

You bold searchers and researchers, do you now scorn the Thesean thread for the divine temptations of the labyrinth? Nietzsche's 'madness' was millennial. Those who dance, sing, and celebrate the wedding of Dionysus and Ariadne as their own wedding, those Ariadnes share with Nietzsche a most sublime vision:

> Anyone who knows how to experience the whole of man's history *as his own history* will feel in a highly generalized way all the grief of a sick person who is robbed of health, of the graybeard who reflects upon the dream of his youth, of the lover who is robbed of his beloved, of the martyr who sees his ideal collapse, of the hero at nightfall after an undecided battle which has brought him wounds and the loss of a friend. But to be able to carry this enormous accretion of griefs and to be the hero who at the outbreak of a second battle still greets his dawn and fortune as one whose horizon stretches ahead thousands of years and reaches back into the past and who is heir to all things noble and all the spirit of the past—the responsible heir of an aristocratic line; the likes of him was never seen before nor even dreamt before. To take all this upon one's self—the oldest of things and the newest, the losses, the hopes, the conquests, the victories of humanity—to contain all this finally in one soul and compress

all into one emotion, this must yield a happiness never before known by man—the happiness of a god full of power and love, full of tears and ringing laughter, a happiness which like the sun at evening lavishly and continually gives of its inexhaustible richness and pours into the sea, and like the sun feels most luxuriant when even the poorest fisherman rows as if with golden oars. Let this divine emotion be called—humanness![4]

Those who cannot dance, sing, and rejoice at this wedding, well... Which are you my brothers and sisters? Which...?

(Nietzsche, Dionysus, Ariadne, and Claudia are heard laughing behind the curtain beginning to fall over this divine play called *To Nietzsche: I Love You. Ariadne.*)

Dionysus presents himself to us in two forms: as the god who vanishes and reappears, and as the god who dies and is born again. The second conception has evolved into the well-known doctrine of numerous rebirths of the god. Basically, however, both conceptions (his vanishing, which is paired with his reappearance, and his death, which is followed by his rebirth) are rooted in the same idea. Both tell of the god with the two faces, the spirit of presence and absence, of the Now and the Then, who is most grippingly symbolized in the mask. With him appears the unfathomable mystery of life and death cemented together into a single entity, and the mystery of the act of creation affected with madness and overshadowed by death. This is why he bears with him not only all the energy and exuberant joy of a life which is at the height of its activity but also his entire destiny. From his all-too-early birth, from his origin in his mother who perished in flames, sorrow and pain pursue him. His victories become defeats, and from radiant heights a god plunges down into the horrors of destruction. But it is just because of this that the earth also brings forth its most precious fruits through him and for him. Out of the vine, "the wild mother," there erupts for his sake the drink whose magic extends all that is confined and lets a blissful smile blossom forth out of pain. *And in the arms of her eternal lover rests Ariadne.*[5]

Thus, the arrow finds its mark, the Gordian knot of the drama is cut through, the catastrophe turned into a phantasmatic seduction and longing for a *new* epiphany—not of any God, but of the overhuman!

(Again, explosions of laughter, both golden and evil, from behind the curtain now drawn.)

Notes

1. Otto, *Dionysus Myth and Cult*, p. 98.
2. Ibid., p. 181.
3. Ibid., p. 200.
4. Nietzsche, *Gay Science*, #337.
5. Otto, *Dionysus Myth and Cult*, pp. 200–201; emphasis added.

Laugh, You Higher Ones!

The thousandth year is breaking you higher ones!
It is yours!

Has the great lover's seduction left you cold—
or are you broken open, impatient with desire?
Your desire you must yourselves satisfy!
Do not wait for the impossible,
      though certainly it will come!
For it is here.
Your beloved will come!
For he is here.
Dance, sing, rejoice!

Have you met the challenge?
Will you take the oath—to yourselves?
Will you throw yourselves into eternity blessing chance?
There are no fetters but those in your own heart.
What is your secret? Take wing!
What danger can there be? — Death?
But what joy!—Death!
Merely the gateway to madness and eternity!
Dance, sing, rejoice!

Rumi:

Whatever mate you desire, go!
Become obliterated in your beloved!
Assume the same shape and attributes!

The lovers, who are each other's spirit die in their
mutual love.

Those who sought that vision today die happy and laughing
in vision's midst.

Nietzsche/Dionysus: I, together with Ariadne,
have only to be the golden balance
of all things.

*Ariadne: I, together with Nietzsche/Dionysus,
have only to be the golden balance of all things.*